ORIGINAL SIX

Best of the

Brian McFarlane

FENN

Fenn Publishing Company Ltd.
Bolton Canada

BEST OF THE ORIGINAL SIX
A Fenn Publishing Book / First Published in 2004

Fenn Publishing Company Ltd.
Bolton, Ontario, Canada

Library and Archives Canada Cataloguing in Publication

McFarlane, Brian, 1931-
    Best of the original six / Brian McFarlane.

ISBN 1-55168-263-X (bound)
ISBN 1-55168-306-7 (pbk)

    1. National Hockey League-History. 2. Hockey teams-United
States-History. 3.Hockey teams-Canada-History. I. Title.

GV847.8.N3M4195 2004   796.962'64'09045   C2004-903141-4

Printed and bound in Canada

CONTENTS

Bruins

Contents

Red Wings

Rangers

Blackhawks

INTRODUCTION

by
Ted Lindsay

It's been 40 years since I played my last game in the NHL. All of my 17 years in the league were spent in the Original Six era. Every day I meet fans who witnessed games between those teams — Toronto, Montreal, Detroit, Chicago, Boston and New York — and most of them still insist that those rivalries were the fiercest, most thrilling they ever saw.

Those of us who played in that era will agree that today's players are bigger, faster and stronger. They are better equipped and better coached. And they have sticks that shoot bullets. And yet, we are quick to argue that none of today's stars is tougher or more talented than big Gordie Howe or Milt Schmidt, more dynamic than my arch rival Rocket Richard, more rugged than Tim Horton, more spectacular than the era's goalies — Plante, Sawchuk, Bower and Hall to mention a few.

And today's NHL, with the constant movement of players from team to team, can't boast of line combinations that performed dazzling feats year after year. The Original Six produced Montreal's Punch Line (Richard, Lach and Blake), the Production Line I played on in Detroit (with Howe and Abel), Chicago's Million Dollar Line (Hull, Hay and Balfour) and Boston's Kraut Line (Schmidt, Bauer and Dumart).

In my era, teams faced each other 14 times a season and rivalries were often acrimonious. There was no fraternization, no players' association (although I tried to start one and was banished from Detroit), no cosying up with rival players at golf tournaments or hockey schools.

Original Six teams were often forced to travel between cities on the same train, and even though the teams occupied separate Pullmans, how we'd bristle when we passed opposing players headed for the dining car. Just the sight of Rocket Richard ambling down the aisle was enough to bring a scowl to my face and spoil my appetite for a week. It's a wonder we didn't go at each other with knives and forks, plucked from a dining car table.

In those days, we'd talk about pride and loyalty to our team and to our city, and our passion for the game. Few players thought the grass was greener elsewhere. My teammate Alex Delvecchio was a Red Wing for 24 years. Milt Schmidt and his Kraut Line mates were loyal Bruins for as long as they played. Beliveau and the Richards — Maurice and Henri — wore the Habs logo with great pride throughout their careers. It was unthinkable that they would play anywhere but in Montreal. Kids in English Canada idolized Apps, Kennedy, Armstrong, Bower and Keon because they wore the Maple Leaf year after year.

Some memories of those good old days of Original Six hockey will never fade. The stories of that era are well worth chronicling and you'll find many gems in the pages ahead. I guarantee it.

Ted Lindsay
Honoured Member,
HOCKEY HALL OF FAME

Habs

How the Canadiens Got Their Name

In researching the Montreal Canadiens' famous name, I went back through the records to 1908 and a meeting held, not in Montreal, but in Renfrew, Ontario, a small town in the Ottawa Valley. It seems that a Renfrew club, a power in the Upper Ottawa Valley league — a circuit once described as "a fence corner league" — wanted a crack at the Stanley Cup, which was then a challenge cup. At this meeting, it was decided to import star players, offering jobs and other enticements, until a Cup challenge could not be ignored.

In 1909, Renfrew iced a professional team playing in the Federal Hockey League against clubs from Cornwall, Smiths Falls and Ottawa. Goalie Bert Lindsay (the father of Ted Lindsay), an import who ran a successful poolhall in town, helped Renfrew win the Federal League championship.

A year later, there was talk that the Federal League's competitor, the Eastern Canada Hockey Association, was winding down and a new league was to take its place. Organizers were tabbing it "the greatest league ever formed," and Renfrew wanted in. Three teams from Montreal, the Wanderers, Shamrocks and the all-Francophone Nationals, were reported to be charter members of the new circuit, the Canadian Hockey Association. Representatives from Quebec and the Ottawa Senators (the 1909 Stanley Cup champions) were invited to join.

Renfrew's bold hockey ambitions led team executive Ambrose O'Brien, then 24, to Montreal's Windsor Hotel, where he urged the CHA to consider his application. "Let's make it a six-team circuit," he pleaded. "I'll gladly pay the $30 initiation fee you're charging new teams." O'Brien won the support of the Wanderers and

Shamrocks, but the Ottawa executives scoffed at his application and persuaded their colleagues to reject the Renfrew bid.

O'Brien left the meeting room dejected, but he was not nearly as devastated as Jimmy Gardner, the manager of the Wanderers. His team, thought to be a shoo-in, had just been denied a franchise in the new league. The reason? The other owners had decided the Wanderers' home arena, the Jubilee Rink, was too small.

Gardner stomped around the hotel lobby, cursing the men who had sabotaged his club's plans. Finally, he sat in a chair next to the equally disconsolate O'Brien.

"Ambrose, let's show those arrogant pups a thing or two," he said. "I've got the Wanderers, you've got a good team in Renfrew and I know you own a couple of teams in Haileybury and Cobalt. Let's start a new league of our own. But we'll need a second team here in Montreal. Why not organize a team of French-speaking players, like Le National? We'll call it *Les Canadiens*. Who knows? In time, such a team could become more popular than any of the other Montreal clubs." And with those words, he laid the foundation for what would become the world's winningest hockey team.

Some historians say that the idea for a team called the Canadiens originated, not with Gardner or O'Brien, but with James Strachan, founder of the Wanderers. But O'Brien, who put up the money to finance the hockey franchise, insisted until his death that it was Gardner's idea and Gardner who proposed the name.

In his book *O'Brien*, Canadian sportswriter Scott Young poses the following question: If the owners of the Wanderers were so sure that a French-Canadian team would be a hit, why did they present it so grandly, and free of charge, to a 24-year-old from Renfrew? There is a lurking possibility, suggests Young, that it was one of those frequent instances where the progenitors of a great idea prefer to let someone else risk the money to find out if it is really viable after all.

At any rate, the name *Les Canadiens* appears to have first surfaced during the conversation between Gardner and O'Brien in the lobby of the Windsor Hotel on November 25, 1909.

A week later, on December 2, the new league was formed in Montreal. It was called the National Hockey Association. The next day, on December 3, after papers were drawn up, the new Montreal club became a reality. Financed by wealthy Irish-Canadians from Renfrew, and by T.C. Hare of Cobalt, the *Club de Hockey Canadien* promptly hired Jack Laviolette as manager and first employee. The team was about to take its first tentative strides into the world of pro hockey. Despite the Jubilee rink's limited seating capacity of only 2,700, *Les Canadiens* booked it for all home games.

To help manage the club's affairs, Ambrose O'Brien hired Joe Cattarinich, who, like Laviolette, was a player of note. Cattarinich signed Newsy Lalonde and Didier Pitre, both flashy goal scorers, to the Canadiens' sparse roster. The public was told that the franchise for the new team was to be transferred to a syndicate of Montreal sportsmen or investors as soon as such a group could be put together.

The season opened on January 5, 1910. *Les Canadiens* got off to a fast start, defeating Cobalt 7–6 in overtime in the league's first-ever game. During their first season, the team wore blue jerseys with a narrow white band across shoulders and chest, upon which a large white *C* was superimposed. Their pants were white and their stockings red.

Meanwhile, the CHA floundered from the beginning; most games attracted only a few hundred fans. In mid January, after a mere two weeks of league play, CHA moguls swallowed their pride and pleaded with the NHA for admission, suggesting total amalgamation as their salvation. But Ambrose O'Brien and Jimmy Gardner remembered how they had been slighted a mere two months before. The NHA operators agreed to admit only two franchises to their fold: Ottawa and the Montreal Shamrocks. When these clubs abandoned the CHA, the league folded.

O'Brien generously offered the defunct *Le National* the chance to take over his Canadiens and was amazed when the answer was no. It ranks as one of the greatest missed opportunities in the history of sport.

After the merger, the seven-team league started afresh with each team playing a 12-game schedule. The Canadiens, alas, won only two games. A Montreal team did, however, enjoy a glorious campaign that winter: Jimmy Gardner's Wanderers captured the league title with 11 wins and only one defeat, and they went on to claim the Stanley Cup. They also skated off with a glistening new trophy, the O'Brien Cup, made of silver from the O'Brien mines in Cobalt, Ontario, and valued at $6,000, making it far more expensive than the $50 bowl Lord Stanley had donated to hockey before the turn of the century.

In 1910, a Montreal sportsman and promoter named George Kennedy approached O'Brien with a bit of a problem. Kennedy was the proprietor of an outfit called the *Club Athlétique Canadien*, and he felt the NHA team was infringing on his rights to the name. The French-speaking Kennedy, who was born Georges Kendall, was mollified when he was offered the hockey franchise. He quickly accepted and under his ownership, the Canadiens' emblem became a green maple leaf, originally superimposed with a gothic *C*, but later embroidered with the initials "CAC." Imagine, a maple leaf on a Montreal sweater! By 1915, the uniforms had come to take on the appearance of the modern-day red sweater, and in 1917 a horseshoe-shaped *C* surrounding a smaller *H* was designed — an emblem that has remained constant, and constantly popular, for almost 90 years.

There is a misconception that the letter *H* stands for "Habs" or "Habitants" — meaning farmers or rural residents — stemming from the fact that most Canadiens were French-Canadians from the countryside. But the *H* really stands for "hockey."

Illness Ends Series in Seattle

In the spring of 1919, the Stanley Cup was shipped to Seattle, Washington, where it was to be awarded to the winners of the series between the Metropolitans, the champs of the Pacific Coast Hockey Association, and the Montreal Canadiens, winners of the NHL title. The series turned out to be one of the most unusual in the history of hockey. It was a hard-fought, hard-luck series, one that ended in tragedy.

The Canadiens and Metropolitans were evenly matched. After five games, each team had won two games, while another had ended in a draw. Montreal's Newsy Lalonde was the scoring star in game two, potting all four Habs goals. The fourth game ended in a rare scoreless tie despite an hour and 40 minutes of overtime. Some reporters called it the greatest game ever played on the Pacific coast. In that game, a few of the players appeared to be labouring, and with good reason: the dreaded Spanish flu epidemic that had swept across North America that year had struck the combatants. Several players, more of them on the Canadiens than the host Metropolitans, were so afflicted that they could barely skate.

In game five, the Canadiens eked out a 4–3 victory to knot things up at two wins apiece. By now the ill-starred series had produced more flu victims as well as a number of serious injuries. In mid-game, Montreal's "Bad Joe" Hall staggered off the ice and was rushed to a nearby hospital. He was followed by teammate Jack McDonald. After the game, five Canadiens required medical attention, and team owner George Kennedy also complained of feeling poorly.

But Kennedy desperately wanted the Stanley Cup. When officials decided to suspend the series and call it a tie, Kennedy resisted. "Let me borrow some lads from the Victoria club," he pleaded. "I'll put them in Montreal uniforms and we'll finish this thing yet." But the Seattle executives vetoed his proposal and instructed workers to start removing the ice from the arena.

In a display of sportsmanship, the Seattle club declined to claim Lord Stanley's trophy, although technically they could have commandeered it on the grounds that Montreal did not have enough players available for the deciding game. After much discussion, the Stanley Cup trustees decided that Toronto, winners of the Cup in 1918, would be allowed to retain the trophy for another year.

With their season over, a solemn band of Canadiens, some bruised and battered, others pale and haggard from the effects of the flu, boarded their train for the long return journey to Montreal. Left behind in hospital was 38-year-old Joe Hall, whose condition was described as serious. A few hours after his mates departed, Hall suffered a fateful setback. He was found to be suffering from pneumonia, and within days he was dead.

"Bad Joe" Hall was never as nasty as his nickname might suggest. Born in England, he played hockey in Canada and the United States at the top level for more than 15 years, having started out in Winnipeg and Brandon, Manitoba. He was a tenacious checker, hence the nickname. Frank Patrick, president of the PCHA, said of Hall, "The game of hockey suffered a huge loss with his passing. Off the ice he was one of the jolliest, best-hearted, most popular men who ever played the game." Hall left a wife and three children.

Forum Built for Maroons, but Habs Played There First

When construction of the original Montreal Forum neared completion in the fall of 1924, the Montreal Canadiens were not its first tenants — the Montreal Maroons were. The Maroons, owned by the Canadian Arena Company, had been granted an NHL franchise through the generosity of Canadiens' owner Leo Dandurand, who had a grand vision of a unique hockey rivalry between the Maroons and his Canadiens, one that would last for decades.

The Habs, locked into a contract to use the Mount Royal Arena, watched enviously as the huge edifice took shape. The original Forum, designed by architect John S. Archibald, cost $1.5 million, contained an artificial ice plant and held seats for 9,300 fans.

The Habs' home opener was scheduled for November 29, 1924, against Toronto, but mild weather in Montreal turned the Mount Royal Arena, which had natural ice, into a swimming pool. Dandurand acted swiftly, making arrangements to move the opening game to the new Forum, which could guarantee solid ice. Despite a heated protest from officials of the Mount Royal Arena, Dandurand transferred players and equipment to the new building. As a result, it was the Habs and not the Maroons who played the inaugural game in the new ice palace. More than 8,000 fans witnessed the match, which the Canadiens won 7–1 over the

Toronto St. Pats. The Forum was the first NHL arena designed expressly for hockey and it would serve Montreal fans well for the next 72 seasons.

The Canadiens moved into the Forum permanently in 1926. Today's hockey fans have not seen anything like the heated rivalry that existed between the Habs and the Maroons. Heated? It was explosive. When the English-backed Maroons met the French-supported Canadiens, the on-ice battles were often overshadowed by skirmishes in the stands. Emotions became so feverish that a missed goal or "undeserved" penalty would trigger a rash of pushes and punches, with police and ushers rushing in to keep the rival factions of fans apart. The damage was usually minimal — a torn jacket, a hat yanked off and thrown away, the occasional black eye and enough 1920s-style "trash talk" (in both official languages) to shock fans 10 rows away.

It was the genius of Dandurand that created both the rivalry and the friction. He sanctioned a second NHL franchise for the city. It cost the Maroons' Jimmy Strachan a mere $15,000 for the privilege of sharing the Canadiens' territorial rights to Montreal. Dandurand once said, "I assumed that an English team competing against the mostly French Canadiens would turn into the biggest rivalry in the NHL — and it did."

The Maroons were the first of the two Forum tenants to taste Stanley Cup success. They captured the trophy in 1926 by defeating the Victoria Cougars in the finals on the Forum's ice. It marked the last time a team representing a league other than the NHL was a Cup challenger. In 34 years, no fewer than 14 leagues had been represented in Cup playoffs.

The following year, the Canadiens and Maroons met in a memorable two-game playoff series, which the Canadiens won two goals to one after 12 minutes of overtime. Howie Morenz scored the series-winning goal, and each game attracted an estimated crowd of 11,000. Ottawa then eliminated the Habs, and the Senators went on to capture the Stanley Cup.

In 1928 the Canadiens finished first in the Canadian Division standings but were upset by the Maroons in the two-game playoff, three goals to two. Somehow, an estimated 13,000 fans packed the Forum for each encounter.

That was the season the Maroons were edged three games to two in the finals against the Rangers. In game two, Rangers goalie Lorne Chabot was struck over the eye by a Nels Stewart shot. Forty-four-year-old Lester Patrick, the New York coach, replaced him. The Rangers won the game in overtime and went on to win the series and the Cup. When the Roaring '20s gave way to the Great Depression, the Maroons and Canadiens both encountered financial problems, while the Forum was mortgaged to its rafters and there was talk of turning it into a streetcar barn.

When the Maroons withdrew from the NHL in 1938 (Leafs owner Conn Smythe vetoed a plan to move the team to St. Louis, where the Ottawa Senators had already moved, and failed, four years prior), the Canadiens had the Forum all to themselves. Over time they created hundreds of memorable moments within its walls. Twelve of Montreal's 24 Stanley Cup triumphs were celebrated on its ice surface, plus two more by the Maroons.

On March 24, 1936, the Maroons and the Red Wings started a playoff game at the Forum and finished it in the early morning hours of March 25, in the sixth overtime period — the longest NHL game ever played.

On a March day the following year, the building became a cathedral when a multitude of fans, fighting back tears, filed solemnly past the bier of superstar Howie Morenz, whose sudden passing shocked millions.

The building withstood a barrage of rocks and bottles hurled at it by rioting fans on the night of March 17, 1955, following the suspension of Rocket Richard and the termination of a game with Detroit.

There were league and team records established by such Habs legends as Rocket Richard, Jacques Plante, Jean Beliveau, Steve Shutt, Guy Lafleur and others. On New Year's Eve, 1975, a superb exhibition game between the Canadiens and the Soviet Central Red Army team — a 3–3 tie — was labelled by veteran observers as "one of the best hockey games ever played." The Habs outshot the touring Soviets 38–13 and controlled most of the play, but some fabulous saves by Vladislav Tretiak, who outshone Montreal's Ken Dryden, saved the visitors from certain defeat.

By then, the Forum looked nothing like the original arena. In 1946, when Frank Selke was lured to Montreal from Toronto, he dedicated himself to renovating the Forum. He ordered new plumbing installed. "The place stinks," he complained, "especially the restrooms." And the drab brown paint that seemed to cover every surface was quickly covered over with much brighter colours.

In 1968, further renovations and additions costing $10 million brought seating capacity up to 16,500. This became the arena we knew and loved until its doors closed on March 11, 1996. On that night, a flaming torch was passed from hand to hand, between former captains Butch Bouchard, Maurice Richard, Jean Beliveau, Henri Richard, Yvan Cournoyer, Serge Savard, Bob Gainey and Guy Carbonneau, before it was finally handed to the incumbent, Pierre Turgeon. The ovation for Maurice Richard was so long that it left the Hall of Famer with tears in his eyes and overcome with emotion.

Montrealers Pay Tribute to the Magnificent Morenz

"To the hockey palace his fame helped to build and where he knew his greatest triumphs, the body of Howie Morenz was taken today for public funeral services."

So began one newspaper account of the unique funeral of a gallant hockey star: Howie Morenz. The place was the Montreal Forum, and the date was March 11, 1937.

"Howie will lie over the centre-ice circle, guarded by his teammates and the men he first broke into professional hockey with 15 years ago. In that circle, Morenz countless times had faced off the puck and cannonaded down the rink with the speed and skill that made him one of the game's greatest."

At the Forum, jammed to capacity with his devoted fans, Morenz's flower-banked bier was passed by an endless line of fans and friends. Many wiped tears from their eyes as they came to pay their respects to a magnificent athlete. Arrayed along the walls were floral tributes that had poured in from near and far. There were even floral arrangements in the shape of his uniform number, 7, a numeral that would never again grace the back of any Montreal Canadien. There were two floral hockey sticks, one from the "boys in the balcony" at Boston Garden, fans who had jeered, and grudgingly cheered, him. The other was from Joe Choquette, who lovingly made the hockey sticks Morenz used.

Asked to comment, Cecil Hart, the Canadiens manager, sobbed: "It's just terrible. I can't talk about it. I have known and loved him since I first signed him to a Canadiens contract in 1922."

"No one can ever take his place with us," said Aurel Joliat, his tiny linemate.

"He was the greatest of all time," lamented coach Dick Irvin, "and the world of hockey will seem bereft without him."

Toronto Maple Leafs owner Conn Smythe said, "The news is so shocking I can hardly credit it. I guess the old machine, one of the grandest hearts ever fabricated in a hockey frame, just broke up. Hockey men everywhere will miss him. To the Canadiens, it comes as a paralyzing blow."

Earlier in the 1936–37 season, on January 28, the Canadiens played Chicago. Montreal's 6–5 victory was overshadowed by an alarming incident in the first period. Morenz darted after the puck and was bodychecked by six-foot, three-inch Chicago defenceman Earl Seibert. Howie's skate blade got caught in a crack in the boards; while it was embedded there, his leg twisted around and snapped with a crack that could be heard throughout the arena. He fell to the ice, writhing in pain. In an instant, his season and his career were over.

He spent more than a month in hospital before dying, on March 8, of complications related to the injury. In the *Toronto Star*, Andy Lytle wrote, "It was his heart that gave out, the experts said sorrowfully. To those who knew the strong vein of sentimentality that surged in the make-up of this remarkable athlete, it was as if the fiber of the man slowly disintegrated as he faced the uncertainties of a hockeyless future."

Seibert, a gentle giant and 10-time All-Star, who would, like Morenz, be inducted into the Hockey Hall of Fame, shouldered the blame for the tragedy. "I was the guy who killed him," he said. "I didn't mean to hurt him, but I gave him the bodycheck. I pinned him to the boards when his skate got caught and he fell."

He was not penalized on the play, but neither he nor the Habs faithful could accept that he was blameless. "My father never got over that incident with Morenz," his son Oliver said after Seibert's death in 1990. "For years afterward, the fans in Montreal booed him at the Forum."

So highly regarded was Morenz that a rival coach once ordered his players not to hit him during a game. In New York one night, Morenz skated out to face the Rangers. "Don't hit Morenz tonight," Lester Patrick admonished his players. "The little guy is nursing a leg so sore he shouldn't be playing. He only dressed because he knows the New York fans are anxious to see him perform. So get in his way, but go easy on him and his gimpy leg."

In the southwestern Ontario towns of Stratford and Mitchell, where he grew up, Howie Morenz had been known as a shy little fellow who almost gave up the game he loved before he ever got started.

Morenz and his family moved down the road from Mitchell to Stratford when Howie was in high school. Asked to try out for a local team, Morenz showed up with only his skates and a stick, for he had no other equipment — not even gloves. In the scrimmage that followed, the heavier, well-padded players on the ice belted him around and he left the tryout in tears. He showed his bruised and bleeding hands to the coach and told him he wasn't coming back. Then he threw his skates over his shoulder and walked out into the night.

He stayed away from the game until the Stratford side ran into some old rivals from nearby Kitchener and suffered a bad beating. The coach realized he needed an offensive star and recalled that young Morenz had shown some promise in the brief tryout he'd been given. He called on Howie and pledged to find him some hand-me-down equipment if he would give hockey another try. Morenz agreed. In the return match with Kitchener, he was the outstanding player on the ice.

Soon he was playing for Stratford's senior amateur team, and his potential was such that Ernest Sauve, a referee, tipped off the Montreal Canadiens. "You better grab this kid," he said. "He's a great-looking prospect."

11

But young Morenz had no burning desire to play professionally. He enjoyed small-town life in Stratford. It took a visit from Cecil Hart, who would later become coach of the Canadiens, to convince the reluctant star to commit his hockey future to Montreal. The fact that Hart dropped $850 in Morenz's lap helped to settle the matter.

He became an instant fan favourite in Montreal — the fastest man on ice, who earned the nicknames the Mitchell Meteor, the Stratford Streak and the Canadien Comet. His highest-scoring season was 1929–30, when he collected 40 goals. On three occasions he captured the Hart Trophy as the NHL's most valuable player, twice he led the league in scoring, and he played on three Stanley Cup–winning teams. Over the course of his 14-year career, many of them on a line with Aurel Joliat and Johnny Gagnon, he was one of the most dynamic figures in the game, scoring 270 regular-season goals.

The Habs angered their fans in 1934, when they traded Morenz to Chicago. After he had spent a season as a Blackhawk and split another year between Chicago and New York, the Habs heeded the wishes of their fans and reacquired Morenz for what turned out to be his final campaign.

Aurel Joliat: 130 Pounds of Might and Muscle

"Old-time hockey players like me were the dumbest bunch of athletes in the world," Aurel Joliat once said. "We never got paid what we deserved, and most of us didn't have sense enough to save what money we got."

Joliat, then 85, was reminiscing about the pioneer days of the National Hockey League and his career with the Canadiens. Born in Ottawa, he joined the Habs in 1922 (traded for a fading Newsy Lalonde) and played left wing on a line with Howie Morenz and Billy Boucher. He stayed around until 1938, when he retired as the highest scoring left winger in history, with 270 goals.

"Retired? Hell!" he would often snort. "They fired me when the Montreal Maroons folded and some of their players moved over to the Canadiens. I'm still damn mad about that."

"And don't say I played with Morenz," he added with a wink. "Although I tried to. Morenz was so fast, I had to scoot well ahead of him on a rush or I was always lagging behind him, trying to catch up. Nobody ever played with Morenz."

Was Aurel a tough hockey player? He proved that as a teenager when he fell off a roof, tumbled 35 feet to the ground and landed on his back. He played 13 seasons in the NHL with two displaced vertebrae, which caused him great pain and forced him to wear an elaborate truss at all times. Then there were stomach ulcers that he mostly ignored. He was tough enough to become a star kicker with his hometown Ottawa Rough Riders, until a broken leg caused him to think seriously about concentrating full time on hockey.

"Well, I guess I was tough enough," he once said. "You had to be to survive. But I wasn't the toughest; that mule-headed sonofabitch Eddie Shore was the meanest, toughest player I ever met. I was rushin' up the ice at the Forum one night when my lights went out. Shore hit me with a check that almost killed me. I was, what, 130 pounds at the time, and he musta been 190. He dislocated my shoulder, and they carried me off in a lot of pain.

"Then I look around, and Shore is leading a fancy rush. Forget the sore shoulder! I leaped over the boards and intercepted the big bugger — hit him with a flyin' tackle. Hit him so hard he was out cold on the ice. He had it comin', I'd say."

Joliat led the NHL with 29 goals in 1925, played on three Stanley Cup–winning teams, and was named MVP in 1934. In 1985, sixty years after he played in the opening game at the Montreal Forum, he was invited back as an honourary member of the Canadiens' "Dream Team." At the age of 83, he delighted the fans with a vigorous display of skating and stickhandling. He even took a couple of pratfalls, one of them caused by the red carpet laid on the ice. "The ghost of Eddie Shore must have put that damn rug in front of me," he muttered.

The late Bill Galloway, a hockey historian and one of Joliat's best friends, recalled a time when Joliat, then in his 70s, was invited to Boston for a reunion of living hockey legends. Among the celebrities was Punch Broadbent, another tough customer who had been a thorn in Joliat's side throughout their playing days.

In the pressroom prior to the dinner, the two old-timers got embroiled in an argument over an incident that had occurred in a game played back in the '20s. Soon they were nose to nose and their voices, raised in anger, silenced the other conversations in the room. Then punches were thrown, and a dandy fight developed. Finally, scratched and bleeding, the two old adversaries were pulled apart by half a dozen bystanders. They were marched off to their rooms and told to cool off and behave themselves. But the fight wasn't over: moments later, Joliat barged into Broadbent's room, flew at him with clenched fists, and round two was under way. Once again the peacemakers came running.

NHL President Clarence Campbell was called, and he persuaded the two legends of the game to call a truce. By then they were so battered and bruised that Campbell barred them from a group photo of the assembled celebrities and told them to forget about attending the dinner that night. "Order room service and we'll pay for it," he barked as he departed.

The next morning, Joliat was seen roaming the hotel lobby. "I'm looking for my old pal Broadbent," he told acquaintances. "I'd like to buy him breakfast — or better still, a few beers if we can find a bar that's open."

Not long after the Boston shenanigans, Joliat told the Ottawa sports columnist Earl McRae that he'd like to make a comeback in the NHL. "If a team made me the right offer, I'd come back," he said straight-faced. "I'd show 'em."

"How long do you think you'd last out there?" McRae asked.

"About five minutes."

"Only five minutes a game?"

"Game, hell — five minutes a *shift!*"

Five for the Rocket

On March 23, 1944, in a semifinal playoff game against the Toronto Maple Leafs, Maurice Richard went on a scoring rampage.

The Leafs had finished third in the NHL standings that spring, 33 points behind the Habs, who lost only five games all season. Montreal was expected to win the Cup with ease, so the team was infuriated when the Leafs stunned the Canadiens 3–1 in the series opener.

In the first period of game two at the Forum, Toronto's Bob Davidson checked the Rocket closely and successfully. The Leafs continued to stymie the Habs until midway through the second period, when Richard got a lucky break. Richard was able to shake loose of his check after a Montreal fan at rinkside reached over the boards and grabbed Davidson's stick, wrestling it away from him. The Leaf rushed over to referee Bill Chadwick to appeal for help; but Chadwick was too busy watching Richard rush in on goal, where he scored the all-important first goal against his boyhood pal, Paul Bibeault. Meanwhile, the fan had tossed Davidson's stick back on the ice, making sure it flew over his head. Davidson retrieved it too late to prevent the Rocket's goal.

Chadwick had the fan thrown out of the arena, but the damage had been done. Davidson was so rattled that he let Richard get loose again moments later, and suddenly it was 2–0 for Montreal. The Leafs got one goal back, but then Davidson lost the puck at the Toronto blue line and turned in frustration in time to see Richard notch his third goal of the period.

Richard added a pair of goals in the third to complete his five-goal demolition of the Leafs. Montreal won the game 5–1 and went on the capture the series, four games to one. In the finals, they steamrolled their way past Chicago in four straight to win the Cup. But would any of that have happened without the help of the interfering fan?

A number of other players have scored five goals in a playoff game: Newsy Lalonde (for the Canadiens in 1919), Darryl Sittler (for Toronto in 1976), Philadelphia's Reggie Leach (also in '76) and Mario Lemieux (with the Pittsburgh Penguins in 1985). Only once has a player scored more goals in a playoff contest involving an NHL team. During the 1917 finals, Bernie Morris of the Seattle Metropolitans had a six-goal outburst against the Canadiens.

Veteran sportswriter Elmer Ferguson, who was asked to pick the three stars of the game that night in 1944, jolted the Forum crowd when his third-star selection was announced.

"Tonight's third star," bellowed the public-address announcer, "Maurice Ree-chaaard!"

The fans murmured in protest. How could Ferguson pick Richard as only the *third* star when he had scored all five of his team's goals? There couldn't possibly have been two players on the ice who had outshone him.

"Tonight's second star," the announcer continued, "Maurice Ree-chaaard!"

Now the fans understood what Fergie was up to. They began to applaud wildly.

"And tonight's number one star: Maurice Ree-chaaard!"

Thousands of eardrums were all but punctured by the roar that rocked the Forum's rafters.

Blake Shines in '44 Cup Triumph

Hector "Toe" Blake brought much glory to the Canadiens as a player and coach. One of his personal highs as a playoff performer took place in the spring of 1944, when he sparked Montreal to a 5–4 overtime victory over Chicago in the fourth and final game of the Stanley Cup finals. The Habs trailed by three goals in the final period of game four when Blake went to work, setting up plays that led to three straight Montreal goals and a tie score. Then, after nine minutes of overtime, he slapped in the game winner as 12,880 fans roared their appreciation. Blake's five-point night gave him a new playoff scoring record, with 18 points, and the win climaxed Montreal's most successful season ever. Aside from winning eight straight playoff games over Toronto and Chicago, they set a new regular-season scoring mark of 234 goals and a regular-season point record of 83.

The Rocket Set the Standard

When Rocket Richard potted 50 goals in 50 games during the 1944–45 NHL season, Montreal fans marvelled at the feat. They had never seen a player with such a scoring touch, nor had they witnessed such a productive line as the trio of Richard, Elmer Lach and Hector "Toe" Blake. They were aptly named the "Punch Line." The line averaged 4.4 points per game, a record that has never been matched, and they finished one, two, three in the individual scoring race. Lach collected 80 points, Richard 73 and Blake 67. The Habs finished in first place with 80 points and lost only eight games all season.

But it was Richard's desperate attempt to garner 50 goals in a like number of games that captured the headlines. And he did it, as he did most things on the ice, in spectacular style, delivering his bombshell in the third period of the final game, just as the final seconds were being swept off the clock at the Boston Garden. His 50th was the fourth goal in Montreal's 4–2 victory over the Bruins, the final goal in Montreal's season.

Decades later, Richard would draw a blank when asked to recall the milestone marker. "I just don't remember how it was scored," the 76-year-old Rocket confessed.

However, the victim of his history-making goal, former Boston goalie Harvey Bennett, remembered it well. "Elmer Lach gave him a hell of a lot of help on the play," Bennett told *The Hockey News*. "In fact, Elmer knocked me on my ass, and when I was down and out, *bang*, Richard whipped it in the net."

The historic goal was scored on March 18, at 17:45 of the third period, 135 seconds from the end of the season.

"I didn't know until later he was going for 50 goals," said Bennett. "That's why he was always in front of me in that game. And that's why Montreal took about 24 shots on me in the final period. Geez, Richard must have taken a dozen himself."

Richard added another six goals in six playoff games, for a total of 56 goals in 56 games. But his finest season individually ended on a sour note when the Leafs, who had trailed the Habs by 28 points with a mediocre record of 24–22–4, upset Montreal in the semifinals, four games to two.

When the Habs collided with the third-place Leafs, McCool shut them out 1–0 right in the Forum. Ted Kennedy, another youngster headed for stardom, scored the only goal of the game. McCool was outstanding again in game two, which went to Toronto, 3–2. Back at Maple Leaf Gardens, Bob Davidson checked Richard to a standstill, holding him scoreless for the third successive game. The Canadiens fought their way back in the series with a 4–1 victory, but Gus Bodnar's overtime goal won game four for Toronto, 4–3. The Canadiens stormed back in game five, in which Richard scored four goals, giving the Leafs a solid 10–3 trouncing. But if the Habs thought beating McCool in game six would be as easy, they were wrong. The youngster allowed two goals, but his teammates scored three, and the highest-scoring team in hockey, the one with the best overall record, was eliminated.

McCool went on to chalk up three consecutive shutouts against Detroit in the finals, leading his Leafs to the Stanley Cup championship in a series that lasted the full seven games.

Riot at the Forum

Shortly after 9 p.m. on March 17, 1955, during a game between the Canadiens and the Detroit Red Wings, an unknown spectator lobbed a tear-gas bomb into the lower-level seats of the Montreal Forum. Most of the 16,000 fans watching the game that night were focused on one man in a rinkside seat: NHL President Clarence Campbell. Most were barely aware that Detroit had coasted to a 4–1 lead when the bomb went off.

Campbell, accompanied by his secretary Phyllis King (later his wife), arrived at the Forum almost 15 minutes after the opening whistle. When he strolled to his seat, the crowd stood and booed his every step. Then came the projectiles: programs, peanuts, toe rubbers, coins, even an egg. As the objects rained down on him, Campbell sat stoically and tried to ignore them. He even smiled once or twice.

He had been warned to stay away. During the past 24 hours his office had been deluged with phone calls. One caller had shouted, "When I catch up to him, I will kill him!" A woman had warned, "Don't show up at the next hockey game or you'll be murdered." A man called to say he would plant a bomb in Campbell's office and blow him to smithereens.

There were extra police on duty at the Forum that night, but few if any appeared willing to protect Campbell from the howling mob.

Everyone in Canada knew why Campbell had suddenly become the most detested man in the province of Quebec. On the previous day, the league president had suspended Maurice "Rocket" Richard, the idol of all of French Canada, for attacking a Boston player and a game official during a match at Boston Garden four days earlier. The suspension — not for a game or two, but for the rest of the season *and the entire playoffs* — had shocked Montrealers and triggered an outburst of hysteria and unbelievable animosity toward the stern-faced Campbell.

No matter that the fiery Richard, never one to shy away from confrontation on the ice, had been in Campbell's court several times before. No matter that he'd paid more fines (totalling $2,500) than any player in league history; for him to miss the playoffs was unthinkable, a calamity. In the minds of Montrealers, Richard *was* the playoffs.

A suspension also meant he would lose the NHL scoring title to teammate Bernard Geoffrion. At age 33, it might be Richard's last opportunity to win the Art Ross Trophy. Campbell was a cad, Montrealers said. His decision was preposterous and so unfair. His cruelty was unforgivable. Surely it was another example of an Anglo punishing a French-Canadian. "If the Rocket's last name was Richardson, he'd have received a slap on the wrist," wrote one reporter.

In far-off Detroit, Ted Lindsay, who had often tangled with the Rocket, dumped fuel on the fire. "He should have been suspended for life," snarled Terrible Ted. Others, none of them Richard fans and none living in Quebec, supported Campbell's decision to ban the Rocket.

At the Forum, in the closing moments of the first period, a young man shoved his way past an usher and attacked the NHL chief. He lashed out twice with his fists before the ushers could intervene. When the period ended, another wild-eyed fan rushed in and squashed two tomatoes on Campbell's chest.

Hugh MacLennan, the well-known Canadian writer, was sitting a few rows in front of Campbell. He would later say, "To understand the feelings of the crowd that night is to understand a good bit of the social conditions of Quebec of the 1950s. I remember knowing with very frightening and distinct certainty that with the mood of the mob, anything could happen."

When the tear-gas bomb went off about eight or ten yards away from where Campbell was sitting, sending a cloud of smoke in the air, everyone reacted. Fans bolted from their seats and headed for the exits. Most covered their faces with gloves and scarves. Campbell leaped up and fought his way through the crowd to the Forum clinic, where he huddled with fire department officials. After a brief, animated discussion, a decision was made to clear the building. And Campbell made another decision — to forfeit the game to Detroit.

Jacques Belanger, the public address announcer, ordered the spectators to stay calm and move quickly to the exits. He reminded them to keep their ticket stubs. Meanwhile, the organist kept busy, but few could hear him over the roar of the crowd. Fortunately, there was no real panic; otherwise hundreds might have been trampled in the stampede.

Outside the Forum, a crowd of several thousand gathered. Many were hoodlums and demonstrators without tickets to the match. They began throwing objects that scarred the brickwork of the building and shattered windows. Some smashed the windows of nearby streetcars and pulled their cables off the overhead wires, stalling traffic in all directions. People with blood flowing down their faces were loaded into police cars, which pushed their way through the throng.

The angry mob moved along St. Catherine Street. Cars were overturned, a newspaper stand was set afire, and bricks and bottles were tossed through shop windows. Looters snatched up valuable merchandise. Dozens of fans, wild for revenge against Campbell, were arrested and hauled away. Many of them were teenagers. Fewer than 250 policemen faced a howling mob of more than 10,000, and order was not restored until after 3 a.m.

"Can you imagine fans rioting over a suspension in any other city?" Dick Irvin Jr. asked recently. "Would they riot in the streets if a star athlete in baseball or basketball was suspended? Of course not. But the Rocket's suspension — that was something else."

Before the Red Wings left the city, manager Jack Adams delivered a parting shot: "You newspapermen have turned Richard into an idol, a man whose suspension can turn fans into shrieking idiots. Now hear this: Richard is no hero. He let his team down, he let hockey down, and he let the public down."

The following day, Richard, who had watched the uproar from his rinkside seat, pleaded with his fans to stay calm. He seldom discussed the event in retirement, except to say, "It was Mr. Campbell who incited the fans. If he had not gone to the game that night..."

Richard lost the scoring crown to Geoffrion that spring, by a single point. Many fans unfairly blamed Geoffrion for not passing up scoring opportunities in the handful of games that remained so that Richard could be the winner.

The ugly incident, often called *l'affaire Richard*, was blamed for the elimination of the Habs from the 1955 playoffs. With their star player sidelined, with Beliveau battling an illness and with their emotions still in turmoil, the Habs were beaten by the Detroit Red Wings in the finals. Detroit won game seven at the Olympia, where they had not been defeated since December 19.

The Habs, to their credit, stayed on the ice to congratulate the new champions. The previous year, they had snubbed the winners and had been criticized in the press for their poor sportsmanship.

Old-time Montreal fans still deal in "ifs." If Richard had stayed out of trouble, *if* his punishment had been less severe, *if* the decision hadn't affected the entire team, the Habs might have won the Stanley Cup instead of the Wings.

And *if* they had? The record book shows that Montreal, the following season, began a string of five consecutive Cup victories.

It should have been six in a row, argue the old-timers. Such a tragedy. And it was all the fault of that man Campbell.

Past Misdeeds of the Rocket

When NHL President Clarence Campbell suspended Rocket Richard in March 1955, he might have argued that he had long erred on the side of leniency when called upon to judge the frequent on-and-off-the-ice escapades of the temperamental right winger.

Shortly after the incident, hockey writer Gord Walker reached into the newspaper clipping files and listed some of the turbulent episodes in which Richard was, more often than not, the central figure.

April 10, 1947. In a Stanley Cup playoff game at Montreal, Richard slashes Toronto's Vic Lynn, who is knocked unconscious and needs six stitches to close a cut over his left eye. Later, during the same period, Richard slashes Bill Ezinicki's head for eight stitches. The Rocket draws a major penalty for the first offense and a match penalty for the second. He is fined $250.

March 13, 1951. Richard is fined $500 for molesting referee Hugh McLean in the lobby of a New York hotel. On the night before the attack, Richard had been given a game misconduct penalty for fighting in the penalty box with Leo Reise. Then he struck linesman Eddie Mepham with his stick. New York and Boston writers protest the leniency of the decision, pointing out that Ted Lindsay and Bill Ezinicki had been fined $300 and suspended for three games each for a stick-swinging bout earlier in the season.

October 31, 1951. During a game in Toronto, Richard swings his stick at a rinkside spectator. After the game, he swings his stick at another patron. No disciplinary action is taken.

November 1, 1951. Richard whirls his stick over his head to deter Fern Flaman of Boston as both players race for the puck. The two players start to fight, and during the bout, Richard is seen kicking Flaman in the chest with his skate. Then he punches Bill Juzda to the ice. Richard draws two majors and a misconduct. An automatic fine of $50 accompanies the latter penalty. No league action is taken.

October 21, 1952. Richard is fined $10 plus costs for assaulting a policeman at Valleyfield, Quebec, where the

Canadiens played an exhibition game. He was in street clothes, nursing a groin injury, when he took exception to verbal abuse from the fans. He got into a fight and punched a policeman during the scuffle.

January 21, 1953. Detroit's Jack Adams warns Richard to "Behave — or else." Adams claims Richard crosschecked Wings defenceman Marcel Pronovost, knocking out two teeth. The next night, he broke Glen Skov's nose with a board check. Richard said Adams was "full of bull" and that "I just got mad and took a run at everybody."

March 9, 1953. General John Reed Kilpatrick, president of Madison Square Garden, protests "a mere five-minute penalty" to Richard after the Rocket whacks Ranger Ed Kullman over the head with his stick, slicing open his scalp for eight stitches.

December 13, 1954. Richard apologizes to league president Campbell for articles ghost-written under his byline in a French-language newspaper. In the articles, Richard refers to Campbell as a "dictator" and says "he smiles and openly shows pleasure when an opposing club scores against us." He suggests the league president was guilty of racial discrimination and added, "If Mr. Campbell wants to throw me out of the league for daring to criticize him, let him do it." After accepting the Rocket's apology, Campbell orders Richard to post a $1,000 bond as a show of good faith.

December 29, 1954. Richard charges Leafs rookie Bob Bailey and butt-ends him in the face, knocking out two teeth. He repeatedly tries to retrieve his stick to renew his attack on Bailey after the fight between them is stopped. He flicks his glove in the face of linesman George Hayes and refuses to leave the ice when ordered to by the referee. He is fined $250.

Clarence Campbell once said, "Fines never bothered Richard. For every $250 I fined him, Quebec businessmen would send him

$1,000. Richard could do no wrong in Quebec. I was always the villain."

Unlike most Habs fans, the Rocket never saw the Canadiens perform when he was growing up. There was never any money in the Richard household for such a treat and nobody ever offered to take him to a game. So the first NHL game he saw was one he played in.

On December 27, 1944 — now married to Lucille, the sister of a man who coached him in minor hockey — he moved into new digs on Papineau Street. He worked all night and grabbed a couple of hours' sleep, missing the morning skate, before reporting to the Forum. Complaining that he was "almost too tired to suit up," he went out and scored a team-record eight points (five goals and three assists) against Detroit in a 9–1 rout.

Former NHL referee Red Storey has often said, "There'll never be another Rocket, even if they're playing hockey a thousand years from now. I've played every game, refereed a few thousand and seen a lot of dedicated men. I never saw one like the Rocket, never saw one born to score goals like he was born to do."

Dick Irvin: Great Player, Great Coach

In 1913, Dick Irvin scored all nine goals in a senior hockey game as his Winnipeg Monarchs defeated a strong Toronto team, 9–1. His remarkable scoring outburst earned Irvin a place in Ripley's popular "Believe It or Not" syndicated newspaper feature. A year later, his inspired play for the Monarchs brought Winnipeg the Canadian senior championship and the Allan Cup.

Irvin moved west, playing and starring in Regina and Portland. In 1926 the Portland Rosebuds (owners of the most unusual nickname for a team before the Mighty Ducks of Anaheim came along) were sold intact to Chicago interests and became the Blackhawks. Irvin played brilliantly for Chicago, finishing second in the NHL scoring race in 1926–27, a point behind Bill Cook of the Rangers and four points ahead of Howie Morenz. Early in his second season as a Blackhawk, the husky Red Dutton slammed

Irvin to the ice. He suffered a fractured skull and was told that his playing days were over.

When Chicago won only seven games in each of the next two seasons, and finished 30 points behind Boston in the American Division in 1929–30, Irvin was called upon to coach the band of non-achievers. He turned out to be a natural behind the bench; the Hawks improved remarkably and won 24 games in 1930–31. One of Irvin's innovations was to throw three fresh forward lines, playing short shifts, at the opposition. That season the Hawks won playoff series from Toronto and Rangers before bowing to Montreal in the Stanley Cup finals.

When the Hawks inexplicably dropped him as coach after coming so close to a title, Toronto's Conn Smythe snapped him up. His Leafs had stumbled through the opening games of the 1931–32 season, but Irvin turned things around, leading them to a Stanley Cup triumph — a fitting way to wrap up their inaugural season in their new home, Maple Leaf Gardens.

After nine seasons with the Leafs, Irvin moved on to Montreal, where the Canadiens fortunes were plumbing new depths. It wasn't long before he molded a winning combination, guiding the Habs to Cup wins in 1944, 1946 and 1953. Records fell in bunches: on February 6, 1943, Elmer Lach recorded six assists in an 8–3 win over Boston; on November 21, the Habs rocked the Bruins 13–4, tallying 35 scoring points in the game; and on December 28, 1944, Rocket Richard collected eight points in a 9–1 win over Detroit.

Irvin's 1943–44 team lost only five games out of 50 and established a team-record winning percentage of .830. His club went 13 games into the season before tasting defeat and later won 13 consecutive games at home. Incredibly, they completed the schedule without losing any of their 25 home encounters. The following season, 1944–45, was almost as good: they lost just twice on Forum ice.

In 1946, Irvin's Canadiens defeated Boston in the Stanley Cup finals, four games to one. Elmer Lach led all playoff scorers with 17 points in nine games. In the 1953 finals, Irvin called on goalie Jacques Plante to replace Gerry McNeil in the Montreal net. Plante responded with a glittering 1.75 goals-against average in four games as the Habs once again ousted the Bruins by a margin of four games to one.

Irvin finished his amazing coaching career back in Chicago in 1955–56, taking over a club that had finished in the NHL basement for seven of the previous nine years. Before he could begin one of his patented rebuilding jobs, he was forced to deal with a personal challenge, a lengthy battle with cancer, one he was unable to win. He died in Montreal in May of 1957.

Irvin missed the playoffs only twice in 27 seasons and passed along his gift for language, his love of the game and his fascination for hockey statistics to his son Dick, the longtime *Hockey Night in Canada* broadcaster.

During his final season as a coach, Irvin told a *Sports Illustrated* reporter that he knew exactly how many NHL goals he'd seen: 8,705. "My players have scored 4,721 goals and been scored on 3,984 times," he claimed. He followed up by telling the astonished scribe that his hockey travels had carried him over a million miles, most of it by train. At the time, he reigned as hockey's winningest coach. Today he ranks third in coaching wins behind Scotty Bowman and Al Arbour.

One of the highlights of Irvin's annual training camp in Montreal was the scrimmage he supervised on the final day. He would order a full-length intra-squad game, pitting the rookies against the veterans. He'd visit the veterans' dressing room and bark at them, "Fellows, there's an eager bunch of youngsters in the next room dying to take your jobs away. Are you going to let them push you aside?" Then he'd lecture the rookies: "Listen, I've only got room on my club for two or three of you and today's the day I decide who sticks. A lot depends on who can go out there and knock the Rocket or big Bouchard flat on his arse."

Those sessions were often more entertaining than the regular-season match-ups. When Montrealers heard what sounded like cannon balls echoing off Mount Royal, they'd nod wisely and tell bystanders, worried perhaps that another war had broken out, "No, it's just Dick Irvin's last-day-of-training-camp game."

Asked about such do-or-die confrontations, Irvin would simply smile and say, "It may sound mean, it may sound brutal,

26

but it seemed to work. Some kids earned their ticket to the NHL by busting their arse in that final day of camp."

Doug Harvey: Marching to a Different Drummer

When he died of cirrhosis of the liver on a cold December day in 1989, hockey men were quick to react to the passing of Doug Harvey. "When I joined Montreal," said Jean Beliveau, "he was the best defenceman I'd ever seen."

"I feel very sad," said Maurice Richard. "We had a lot of fun together. Doug was great, always willing to help."

"Harvey was the best defenceman of our day," added former Leafs captain George Armstrong. "Playing against him was like playing against Wayne Gretzky or Bobby Orr. Those kind of players always find a way to beat you."

Howie Meeker, another ex-Leaf who played against Harvey for several seasons, recalled the defenceman's ability to control a game. "The tough son of a gun always came out of nowhere to become the biggest thorn in our side. He was like Bobby Orr, only a shade slower. He was a Mack truck for Montreal, always controlling the pace of the game. You knew what he was doing, you could see him do it, but you couldn't do much about it."

Doug Harvey had an unselfish nature and a flair for the dramatic. Late in the 1947–48 season, teammate Elmer Lach needed one point to win the NHL scoring title. Harvey made a grand rush up the ice late in the final game, drew the attention of the opposing goalie, and flipped the puck across to Lach who slapped it in.

When he broke in with Montreal in 1947, fans would have scoffed had they been told this lackadaisical rookie would lead the Canadiens to six Stanley Cups — or capture seven Norris Trophies as the NHL's top defenceman. Or play 20 NHL seasons and be named a First Team All-Star 10 times.

They didn't see his talent at first, only his lack of it. They booed him when they first saw him play. He looked so nonchalant, so hesitant, and even careless with the puck in the Montreal zone. Initially, his style drove coach Dick Irvin to distraction. And yet, despite his imperfections, he never seemed to cough up the puck or make a major mistake. And he controlled the tempo of the game like no other player in history. In time, everyone relaxed. They began to appreciate his novel approach, and the plaudits began to pour in. He shrugged them off. Despite all the team and personal accomplishments that followed, triumphs that gave Montreal fans so much joy and happiness, Harvey himself was seldom happy. He was a troubled man.

He was known as a drinker who cursed and raged against the hockey establishment. "I didn't drink," he would protest, "unless I was real thirsty." He was an angry man who snarled at the mention of such hockey pioneers as Frank Selke and Conn Smythe. For many years Smythe managed to keep Busher Jackson, a noted alcoholic, out of the Hockey Hall of Fame. "What the bleep did Smythe know about beating them in the alley?" he asked. "His son [Stafford] was even worse."

When the Hall of Fame selection committee ignored Harvey in 1972, the year they waived the waiting period to usher in Gordie Howe and Jean Beliveau ahead of schedule, he blamed Selke. "They don't want me in there because I've been known to hoist a few," he said. "At least I don't sneak around the corner to drink, like some guys. And they've never forgiven Ted Lindsay and myself for helping form the NHL Players' Association. We were blackballed when we did that."

The Hall of Fame welcomed Harvey the following year but, still angry, he ignored the honour. "I'll be out fishing that day," he said, and kept his word, failing to show for the once-in-a-lifetime ceremony.

In the mid 1980s, the Canadiens finally got around to retiring Harvey's famous jersey number 2. Camil DesRoches, a public relations fixture at the Forum for decades, arranged a dinner for Doug, his family and 35 of his friends. "It was a joyous occasion," recalled DesRoches. "The following night, Doug's sweater was retired before the Hartford game. The ceremony was on national TV."

Marching to his own drummer did not sit well with some of the Habs executives. When the Canadiens required a captain to replace Butch Bouchard in 1956, the players were quietly urged to vote for Maurice Richard and ignore Harvey, despite his obvious leadership qualities.

After helping Montreal win five consecutive Cups (1956–60), he was traded to New York in 1961, even though he was a First Team All-Star and the holder of the Norris Trophy.

"I would have been traded earlier," he once said. "But we kept winning all those Cups. Selke knew if he traded me then the fans would have rioted."

With the Rangers, as player/coach, Harvey led the team into the playoffs for the first time since 1958, but he gave up the coaching job after one season. "I liked the playing part best," he said. "You know, being with the boys, tossing back a few after the game. Having fun. I never really liked coaching that much."

He played briefly with the Red Wings in 1966–67 and joined the St. Louis Blues for the playoffs in 1968. His final season was in 1968–69, when he gave the Blues the best a 45-year-old could offer.

Harvey was a versatile chap. He was an outstanding ballplayer with the Class C Ottawa Nationals, good enough that the Boston Braves of the National League sought his services. He was also a brilliant football player who just missed playing on a Grey Cup champion in 1944 — the year he quit football to join the Royal Canadian Navy. It was said that he could punt a football 65 yards. In the navy, he turned to boxing and won the Canadian Navy heavyweight championship.

Five in a Row is Fantastic

The 1959–60 season was another banner year for the Montreal Canadiens. The regular schedule ended with Montreal in first place with 40 wins and 92 points — 13 points more than second-place Toronto. The other two clubs, third-place Chicago and fourth-place Detroit, had to fight their way into the postseason and played sub-.500 hockey, managing only 69 and 67 points respectively.

Now the Habs set out to capture an unprecedented fifth consecutive Stanley Cup. The roster was basically the same as the one that had started the dynasty in 1955–56. Still with the club were future Hall of Famers Jacques Plante, Doug Harvey, Tom Johnson, Maurice and Henri Richard, Boom Boom Geoffrion, Dickie Moore and Jean Beliveau. But many of these heroes were getting on in years. Injuries were beginning to take their toll. Other teams were getting stronger. The Habs would face Chicago in the first round, and there were fears that two rising stars, Bobby Hull and Stan Mikita, combined with Glenn Hall's masterful goaltending, would derail the Canadiens.

But the Habs handled the Hawks easily, sweeping the series in four straight games and outscoring their opponents 14–6.

Toe Blake's men braced themselves for the finals against Toronto. New coach Punch Imlach was trying to build a dynasty of his own with the Leafs, a team that was gaining strength and confidence as the season wound down.

Imlach showed up for the first game at the Forum with several four-leaf clovers pinned to his clothes. But the foliage brought him no luck once the puck was dropped. The Habs banged in three goals before the 12-minute mark and coasted to a 4–2 victory.

In game two, Moore and Beliveau scored in the first six minutes of play. The Leafs got one back in the third period, but they couldn't stick the puck past Plante for the equalizer. Montreal 2, Toronto 1. Game three in Toronto resulted in an easy 5–2 win for Montreal, highlighted by the goaltending wizardry of Jacques Plante as well as Rocket Richard's first goal of the 1960 playoffs. It would prove to be the final goal of the Rocket's illustrious career. It was his 82nd playoff goal, then the most in NHL history. In time, Wayne Gretzky, Jari Kurri, Mark Messier, Glenn Anderson, Mike Bossy and Brett Hull, most of whom would play in many more playoff games than Richard, would surpass his record.

After 18 seasons, Richard must have had retirement in mind when he skated in to retrieve the history-making puck. Five months later he would attend Montreal's fall training camp, score four or five goals in one of the early scrimmages, then walk into Frank Selke's office to announce that he would play no more.

In game four, another fast start by Montreal left the Leafs frustrated and discouraged. Beliveau and Harvey scored 18 seconds apart within the first ten minutes and Jacques Plante recorded the shutout in a 4–0 triumph. The Habs had done what no other NHL club had managed to do: win five straight Stanley Cups. While the Habs drank from the Cup, fans predicted their winning streak would stretch into six, seven, even 10 in a row. There was no inkling that the early '60s would belong to the Blackhawks and Leafs.

A modest victory celebration followed the final game, played in Toronto. Perhaps Doug Harvey said it for all the players when he told reporters, "When you win eight straight games in the play-offs and you win five Cups in a row, there's not a whole lot to get excited about."

By winning in the minimum number of games, the Canadiens equaled a record set by the Detroit Red Wings in the 1952 playoffs.

It was during these years that goaltender Jacques Plante became the premier netminder in hockey — and the most contro-versial. He revolutionized the game and changed the art of netminding for the better. He is best remembered for becoming the first goaltender in modern-day hockey to don a face mask (on November 1, 1959, against coach Toe Blake's wishes), and the first to wear one over an extended period. But an even greater gift to the game was his insistence that goalies could contribute more — by roaming from their nets, by passing the puck to teammates, by trapping loose pucks behind the goal, by shouting instructions to teammates. He may have driven Blake and the fans wild, but he captured seven Vezina Trophies and six Stanley Cups. He must have been doing something right.

Boom Boom Goes for the Record

Boom Boom Geoffrion's NHL career almost came to an end during a routine practice session at the Montreal Forum. It happened on January 28, 1958. Geoffrion collided with a teammate and fell immediately to the ice, doubled over in pain. Before he lapsed into unconsciousness, he told his mates, "Somebody get me a priest."

The problem was a ruptured intestine. Geoffrion was rushed to a nearby hospital, where he underwent emergency surgery.

There were reports that his pulse had stopped for at least 15 seconds. He was a very sick individual.

During his recovery, Geoffrion's wife, Marlene (the daughter of Howie Morenz), pleaded with her husband to give up the game. "My father died from hockey," she told him. "I don't want to lose you, too."

Boom Boom said he would think about it. But as he regained his strength, he knew it was far too early to quit. He was, after all, a key performer on what many were calling "the greatest hockey team ever assembled," a club that had won two straight Stanley Cups and was almost halfway to a record five in a row.

What's more, Geoffrion had a couple of personal goals he wanted to achieve before hanging up his skates. First, he had a burning desire to surpass the number of career goals his illustrious father-in-law had scored: 270. And he wanted a crack at Rocket Richard's record of 50 goals, a mark established back in 1944–45.

His fans had always predicted huge things in hockey for Geoffrion, but he always seemed to fall short of their expectations. There was still much for him to achieve.

Injuries had been a major problem. Aside from the ruptured intestine, they included two shoulder separations, three broken ribs, a fractured wrist, four broken noses, a broken ankle and a broken toe. In his only injury-free season — 1954–55, the year he was booed for winning the Art Ross Trophy when he edged suspended teammate Rocket Richard — he finished with 38 goals and 75 points. He would set no records in 1957–58, since the intestinal operation kept him out of the lineup for 28 games.

When the 1960–61 season opened, Geoffrion was in good health and cautiously optimistic about his prospects for the next six months. By then, at age 29, he had scored 254 goals, leaving him 16 short of Morenz. By early December, he had potted 15.

On December 7, 1960, the Habs were in Toronto for a game with the Leafs. When Boom Boom called home that day, his son Danny, who was celebrating his sixth birthday, made him promise to score two goals "so that you'll have more than Mama's daddy had."

That night, at 9:13 of the first period, Jean Beliveau fed Boom Boom a pass and he slammed the puck past goalie Johnny Bower for his 270th goal. He had tied Morenz!

Beliveau led another rush a few minutes later and pushed the puck ahead to Geoffrion, who slapped one from inside the Leaf blue line. The red light flashed, signalling goal number 271. At that moment Geoffrion became the fifth-highest scorer in NHL history, behind Rocket Richard, Gordie Howe, Ted Lindsay and Nels Stewart.

Now Geoffrion began to focus on a 50-goal season. But most of the offensive fireworks that season were being generated by a Toronto left winger, a lanky 23-year-old named Frank Mahovlich who by mid January was leading Geoffrion 37–27.

That's when another injury — a strained knee — sent Geoffrion to the sidelines for several days and cost him six games. With 15 games left to play, Mahovlich had 43 goals, Geoffrion 32.

Would the Big M surpass the Rocket? That was the question everyone was asking Geoffrion. Nobody even considered him a threat.

Perhaps the slight angered Boom Boom. Perhaps he knew it would be his last chance to see his name in the record book along-side his boyhood idol and teammate, the mighty Rocket. But something inspired him to play even better. In the next two games he scored five times. Then he scored three more goals. When he hit 40 goals (Mahovlich had 45), your author was a late-night sports reporter on CFCF-TV in Montreal. I made a bold prediction one night — who knows why? — and called for Geoffrion to score 10 goals in the next 10 games to tie the Rocket. I can't recall what I predicted for Mahovlich, or if I even mentioned him. Perhaps I assumed the Big M would tie the mark, too, or even break it.

Anyway, Geoffrion made me look like a true psychic as he embarked on a memorable scoring spree. He scored three goals in one game and two in another. He tied Mahovlich, and then passed him. With three games left to play, it was Geoffrion 49, Mahovlich 47.

The next game for Geoffrion was at the Forum against Mahovlich and the Leafs. It was March 16, 1961.

I sent a cameraman to the Forum and ordered him to follow Geoffrion's every move from the moment he stepped on the ice. I shuddered to think that Boom Boom would score and we wouldn't have the highlights for our late broadcast.

The Leafs' Bert Olmstead shadowed Geoffrion that night and stuck to him like a wet shirt, bottling him up through two periods of play. With 10 minutes left in the game and the Canadiens leading 4–2, Geoffrion had a marvellous chance. He pulled goalie Cesare Maniago out of position, shot — and hit the post!

High in the crowd, rubbing shoulders with the fans, the conscientious cameraman captured the action on film. But when Boom Boom hit the post, a fan jumped up in front of his camera and, waving his arms in excitement, struck the cameraman on the hand.

The cameraman howled in pain and stopped filming for a few seconds. He cursed the fan, shook his injured hand in the air, blew on it, and prepared to resume filming.

You guessed it. At that precise moment, Geoffrion scored!

Beliveau had won a face-off and whipped the puck to Gilles Tremblay, who swiftly relayed it to Geoffrion. Instinctively he fired the rubber past Maniago and the Forum rocked. Red Fisher said it was "like Christmas and New Year's Eve and everybody's birthday. The fans rose to their feet with a tremendous roar. A piercing whistle sang across the Forum and from the seats came the rubbers, the programs and the hats..." On the ice, Geoffrion was locked in the arms of Beliveau, and in seconds the two were buried under a sea of red, white and blue jerseys.

Back at the TV station, I whooped for joy. Geoffrion had tied the record and my bold prediction had come true. In a few minutes, the cameraman would arrive with the precious film of the historic moment in hand.

I greeted him when he burst through the door.

"Have you got the film?"

"Sure do. Got it right here."

"Great! Let's get it edited and on the air."

"There's just one problem."

"What's that?"

"I missed the damn goal. You see, this idiot in front of me jumped up and hit my hand. That's when Boom Boom scored. Sorry about that." His face brightened. "But I've got lots of footage of guys congratulating Geoffrion. And a good shot of him *almost* scoring, only he hit the post. We could use that sequence and viewers might think it was his 50th."

I had a sudden urge to throttle the man. How could he shoot hundreds of feet of costly film and miss Geoffrion's historic marker?

But he did. He had.

If you had seen our coverage that night, you would have been impressed. Several shots of Geoffrion skating and shooting. A great shot of him hitting the goal post. And shots of people congratulating him and falling on top of him. As for the goal itself, you probably thought you blinked and missed it. That's what we hoped, anyway.

Rousseau's Strange Penalty Shot

It happened in 1960–61, during Bobby Rousseau's first year with Montreal. The Canadiens were playing the Boston Bruins at the Forum and Rousseau was awarded a penalty shot against Bruce Gamble, the Bruins netminder.

Traditionally, players taking a free shot move in close and either shoot for a corner or try to deke the goalie. Not Rousseau. He tried something totally unexpected. He cradled the puck at centre ice, gathered speed and suddenly unleashed a slap shot from 45 feet out — just inside the blue line. Gamble, taken by surprise, moved too late and the red light blinked on.

Rousseau, despite being an excellent team player and a fine skater with a powerful shot, seldom received the attention he deserved. Perhaps it's because he avoided physical contact whenever possible. Or because he wore a helmet before they became commonplace.

"When I first broke in I didn't worry about getting hit," he once told me. "Then I discovered the hard checks I took slowed me down. Two or three stiff checks and I'd be drained by the end of the game. So I figured I'd simply avoid some of the big body checkers."

His frantic leaps to stay intact were not appreciated by many of the Forum faithful. They saw his style as lacking in courage. And they faulted his decision to wear a helmet.

"Look at it this way," Rousseau said at the time. "In pro football, all the players wear helmets. They don't have pucks and sticks flying around their heads. In hockey, a skate can slice you open and a skull can be fractured against the boards. Hockey players don't fall on nice, soft grass. They crash to the ice. Seems to me all hockey players should be wearing helmets."

One of 12 children of a factory supervisor in St. Hyacinthe, Quebec, Rousseau credits a best-selling book for his scoring success in the NHL — 245 goals in 15 seasons with Montreal, Minnesota and the New York Rangers.

"I picked up *The Power of Positive Thinking* during my third season in the league," he recalled. "And the book did wonders for me, helping me to have a great deal of confidence in my ability on the ice."

He must have been reading a chapter from the book before a game with Detroit one night at the Forum. It was February 1, 1964. He scored five goals in the game. Only one Canadien had scored more: Newsy Lalonde potted six in a 14–7 rout of Toronto back in 1920.

Fergie Feared Maiming an Opponent

John Ferguson played eight seasons with Montreal, from 1963–64 to 1970–71, during which he scored 145 goals in 500 games.

"Fergie, you could have played longer than you did," I told him once. "When you retired you talked about all the great business opportunities that were open to you. But didn't you quit when you did mainly because you were afraid you were going to hurt someone on the ice?"

He gave me a long look, and then said, "You've got that right. I was beginning to worry about doing some serious damage to someone."

Perhaps he was thinking of some of the young turks who had challenged him, only to wind up on the seat of their hockey pants, nursing a swollen jaw or a bloody lip. Or perhaps it was Eric Nesterenko who crossed his mind. Remember Eric, a tall winger with Chicago? In the Stanley Cup finals in 1965, Fergie and Nesterenko collided in a corner. They snarled at each other. Then

Fergie's fist went *pop!* and the Chicago player folded to the ice. A couple of seasons later, they tangled again in the third period of a game. This time Fergie delivered three punches — *pop, pop, pop!* — and Nesterenko collapsed again. Fifteen minutes after the game, the doctors were still attending to him where he lay on a table in the Blackhawks dressing room.

The late Paul Rimstead once asked Fergie if Toe Blake ever sent him on the ice with instructions to fight a rival player. Fergie hesitated, and then replied, "Never in front of the team. He'd take me aside and say, 'Listen, you'd better straighten that guy out.'

"I always knew what he meant."

It was an incident in a Western Hockey League game that helped start Ferguson on the road to the heavyweight championship of the NHL. He was just a kid then, a stick boy for the Vancouver Canucks. During a rough game one night, the league's most feared player, hardrock defenceman Larry Zeidel, fought the Canucks' Phil Maloney in front of the Vancouver bench. Fergie looked on, wide-eyed, as Zeidel pummelled his smaller opponent. The stick boy was enraged when none of Maloney's teammates came to his rescue.

"From that moment, I hated the Canucks," Fergie would say later. "I vowed that that would never happen with any team I might get to play for."

Years later, Ferguson made it to the American Hockey League, with Cleveland. One night he encountered Zeidel, by now a veteran of hundreds of hockey scraps. They dropped the gloves and squared off. Zeidel never knew what hit him as Fergie's punches left him bruised and bloody.

"Yeah, I felt good about that battle," Fergie said. "I gave him a few shots to make up for his treatment of Maloney."

One of Fergie's own teammates almost took a drubbing from him one night. When a pair of Habs began to get the worst of a punch-up in New York, Fergie leaped up on the bench and was about to go to their aid. A teammate grabbed him by the arm and said, "Fergie, why bother?"

Fergie shook loose and jumped into the fight. After serving a penalty, he came back to the Montreal bench still seething — not at the Rangers but at the Canadien who had told him not to bother. The player will never know how close he came to being punched out by one of his own teammates.

Fergie's ambition in hockey was not only to enjoy a lengthy career in the NHL but also to forge a reputation as the meanest, rottenest player ever to perform in the league. There are many scarred old-timers who played against him who are willing to step forward and testify that he fulfilled those ambitions admirably.

Hating an opponent was not a seasonal thing with Fergie. He carried ill-feelings with him throughout the year. "When you were as mean as I was," he says, "you can't turn it on and off like a faucet. That's why I never rubbed elbows with players from other teams at banquets, summer schools or on the golf course."

Despite his sometimes-violent nature, John Ferguson was first and foremost a player. He performed hard and well and with the kind of emotion fans appreciate. Most Montrealers emphatically rank him as one of the most entertaining and popular players in the Habs' long history.

Dangerous Dickie Moore

It would be impossible to recall the Toe Blake era in Montreal without mentioning their star left winger Dickie Moore, who, despite bad knees and bad shoulders, was a true Montreal superstar for most of his dozen years with the Habs. He played on six league champions and an equal number of Cup winners. He joined the Habs midway through the 1951–52 season and averaged a point a game in 33 games. At that clip, he would have surpassed teammate Bernie Geoffrion in points, had he played the full season as Geoffrion did. And Geoffrion won the Calder Trophy as top rookie that season.

In 1957–58, Moore won the NHL scoring title over teammate Henri Richard (84 to 80) and won it again the following season, this time edging out Jean Beliveau (96 points to 91) and breaking Gordie Howe's record for points in a season.

In 1963, Moore retired to nurse his aching joints, but he made two comebacks, with Toronto in 1964–65 — the Toronto trainer said Moore's knees were the worst he had ever seen — and with St. Louis in 1967–68. When St. Louis made it all the way to the Stanley Cup finals in 1968, Moore played like a 20-year-old, notching seven goals and seven assists in the postseason. He limped away from the game — for good, this time — after the Blues lost to the Habs in four straight.

After his playing days, he became a successful businessman, starting up a company that rents out construction equipment. He was also a frequent guest on our *Hockey Night in Canada* telecasts out of the Forum. Moore was inducted into the Hockey Hall of Fame in 1974.

Dick Irvin Recalls the Unknown Goaltender

My friendship with Dick Irvin goes back a long way. Old-timers around Montreal may recall that we worked together on CFCF-TV when it first went on the air in Montreal in the early 1960s. A few years ago, Dick wrote a fine book, *The Habs*, in which he describes the most emotional and dramatic event he has covered in more than a quarter-century of broadcasting Montreal games.

Dick says, "It was a playoff series that had everything, an underdog team eliminating the best team in hockey in the first round; an unknown goaltender with six games of NHL experience winning the Conn Smythe Trophy as the playoff MVP; a revered French-Canadian hockey hero publicly criticizing his English-speaking coach, igniting a front-page media war with severe linguistic overtones. Then, as the final curtain fell, one of the Montreal Canadiens' all-time greatest superstars was carrying the Stanley Cup off the ice at the Chicago Stadium, his final act in what had been the final game of a now-legendary career."

Halfway through Dick's summation, any Montreal fan worth his salt realized the esteemed commentator was talking about the 1971 playoffs and a stunning triumph for the Montreal Canadiens.

The underdog team was Montreal, of course, called on to face the mighty Boston Bruins of Orr, Esposito, Cashman and Bucyk in the first round of the playoffs. The Bruins had won the Stanley

Cup the year before and would capture it again in 1972. Their 1971 squad was perhaps the strongest of the three finalists, evidenced by their 24-point lead over the Habs during the 1970–71 regular season.

Perhaps the Bruins took the Habs too lightly that spring. After all, the Bruins were the defending champions and the Canadiens hadn't even made the playoffs the previous season (even though they had accumulated 92 points).

And the Bruins were facing a rookie netminder with six games' experience under his chest protector — a tall, studious-looking ex-college player with poor eyesight. His name was Dryden — Ken Dryden.

Veteran Johnny Bucyk, who played 21 of his 23 NHL seasons with Boston, recalls approaching that series with confidence, even though, over two decades, none of the Boston teams he played on had won even a single series against the Habs.

"It was Dryden who beat us in '71," he recalled. "I know we had the better team, but Dryden got hot and beat us."

Boston superstar Phil Esposito complained that Dryden made saves that were out of this world. "The guy has arms like a giraffe," Phil testified, and when it was pointed out that giraffes were more noted for their elongated necks than their long arms, he shrugged and said, "Ah, you know what I mean. So we never had a zoo in Sault Ste. Marie, where I grew up."

Boston goalie Gerry Cheevers, who was keeping notes in his diary at that time for a book called *Goaltender*, wrote, "Dryden, the budding lawyer, appears to have awfully fast hands. We've seen him under fire now and I guess he'll be around for awhile. For one so young he has remarkable composure. And he has the best left hand I've seen since Jacques Plante's."

Cheevers and the Bruins almost lost Bobby Orr in game one at Boston. Orr was livid when he drew a penalty and growled something at referee John Ashley, who added 10 minutes to Orr's time in the box. Orr then leaped from the box ("You'd have thought somebody had lanced his ass with a six-inch needle," wrote Cheevers) and tried to get at Ashley. But the linesmen intercepted him and three or four Bruins herded him to the dressing room, saving him from a game misconduct and a suspension.

Cheevers, Esposito, Bucyk and the rest of the Bruins would later agree that game two was the turning point in the series. After Boston captured the first game, 3–1, in front of Cheevers, Boston coach Tom Johnson switched to goalie Eddie Johnston (the second-guessers said it was a big mistake) for game two. The Bruins flew into a 5–1 lead. Then Beliveau, in his final season, rallied the Habs as he had done so often in the past. Late in the second period, Henri Richard scored and there was hope. Montreal lit up the third period with five straight goals to win 7–5. Dryden made so many incredible saves that Esposito finally stood next to him, staring at him, then skated away, shaking his head in disbelief and frustration.

Backup goalie Cheevers figured Beliveau and Richard, with 74 years between them, acted like there was some kind of law against anybody but Montreal winning the Cup. "Those Frenchmen go slightly glassy-eyed when they get thinking of their tradition and their pride and all the rest of that bullshit," he said. "Then they suddenly acquire adrenaline not available to other teams."

Cheevers displayed his edginess when the series switched to Montreal. A young boy holding a dog on a leash taunted him outside the Boston team bus. "Hey, Cheevers," he said, "we gonna beat you Bruins tomorrow." Cheevers snarled back, "Shut up, kid, or I'll cut the balls off your dog."

On the Forum ice, the Canadiens won again, 3–1. Dryden made a save off Esposito that drew the ultimate compliment from the Boston sniper. "It was the greatest save anybody made off me," said Espo. "The best one ever."

Dryden, down on his knees, followed the puck across the crease to his right. Just then, Cashman flipped the puck over to Esposito standing in front of the net and Espo saw four or five feet of open net. He whipped the puck into the hole and it disappeared — right into Dryden's glove. Superman couldn't have reacted any faster. Cheevers called it "an amazing feat of dexterity."

The Bruins won game four, 5–2, and rained rubber at Dryden in game five — 23 shots in the first period, 12 in the second and 21 more in the third — as they coasted to a 5–3 victory. But Dryden bounced back with another solid effort in game six and the Habs rolled to a surprise 8–3 win to tie the series at three games apiece.

Dryden's composure throughout the series worried Cheevers. He noticed that the rookie, between flurries around his net, rested on one foot and placed the point of his goal stick on the ice. Then he rested his chin on his gloves at the knob of the stick, as relaxed as a guy watching a ballet. Cheevers would say, "Dryden picked one hell of a time to play the best goal of his life. The long-legged sonofabitch was robbing us of a lot of goals — and a lot of money."

The Canadiens went on to eliminate the Bruins, a team that had set 37 team records during the regular season, with a 4–2 triumph in game seven. It was a huge playoff upset. Cheevers was tempted to join the lineup of players shaking hands when it was over. He wanted to tell Dryden, the big giraffe, that he had done a masterful job. But Cheevers said to hell with it. He had never congratulated anyone in the past for taking money out of his pocket and he wasn't about to change his style. Instead, back in the Bruins dressing room, he took Jacques Beauchamp, a Montreal reporter, aside and said, "Jacques, you tell that kid he had a hell of a series. Give him my best."

Habs Rookies Seldom Win the Calder

Names of Montreal rookies have been conspicuously absent from the list of Calder Trophy winners in recent years. It has been more than 30 years since goalie Ken Dryden edged Richard Martin (a 44-goal scorer) of the Buffalo Sabres for the coveted Calder in 1972. Another Canadiens rookie who ended up in the Hall of Fame, Guy Lafleur, wasn't even close in the balloting that year.

Jacques Lemaire came close in 1968, only to be edged out by Derek Sanderson of the Bruins. Two Habs vied for the trophy in 1964, with Jacques Laperriere nosing out John Ferguson. Phil Esposito, who was eligible that season, scored only three goals in 27 games for Chicago.

Bobby Rousseau won it in 1962, over Boston's Cliff Pennington, who scored a grand total of 17 goals in 101 career games. Ralph Backstrom was the top rookie in 1959, beating out the Leafs' Carl Brewer, and Bernie Geoffrion took home the Calder in 1952, over Hy Buller of New York.

The first Hab to win the Calder was Johnny Quilty in 1941. Quilty scored 18 goals and 34 points in his freshman season. He never matched those totals, and within three years he was gone from the NHL.

Rocket Richard made his debut in 1942–43 but broke his ankle after 16 games. Gaye Stewart of Toronto skated off with the award, while Montreal defenceman Glen Harmon was runner-up.

The Rocket was eligible again the following season. He scored 32 goals in 46 games and no doubt fumed when Toronto's Gus Bodnar captured the award with 22 goals in 50 games. To be fair, Bodnar outpointed Richard 62–54. The Rocket didn't even finish second in the voting: teammate Bill Durnan, the Vezina Trophy winner, was next best to Bodnar in the eyes of the selectors.

When Doug Harvey broke into the league in 1947–48, the voters decided to give the Calder to Detroit's Jim McFadden. Boston's Pete Babando came in second. Harvey would go on to win seven Norris Trophies in his career.

Jean Beliveau was the odds-on favourite to win the Calder in 1954 but was often injured. He played in only 44 games, scored 13 goals and finished behind winner Camille Henry of New York and runner-up Earl Reibel of Detroit.

After Dryden, the next Hab to come close to breaking the Calder drought was defenceman Chris Chelios, who finished second to Mario Lemieux in 1985.

Scotty Bowman: Often an Enigma

A few harsh words in St. Louis paved the way for Scotty Bowman's return to the Montreal Canadiens fold. After leading the Blues to the Stanley Cup finals in each of their first three seasons (1967–68 to 1969–70), a major confrontation erupted between Bowman and the Blues' owners, and he was fired after his fourth season.

The timing was propitious. In the spring of 1971, the Habs had won the Stanley Cup under coach Al MacNeil. But MacNeil couldn't possibly survive as coach in Montreal after Henri Richard roasted him during the playoffs, labelling him "the worst coach I ever played for." The French media also made life difficult for MacNeil because he was an Anglophone.

MacNeil was dispatched to Halifax to coach the Habs' AHL farm club and before the door had closed behind him, Sam Pollock was on the phone to Scotty Bowman, his first choice to replace MacNeil.

Bowman jumped at the opportunity to return to Montreal. He had begun his front-office career with the Habs organization in 1954, working for Pollock, who was then manager of the Hull-Ottawa Junior Canadiens. Prior to the 1967–68 season, with the NHL about to double in size, Bowman moved up to the St. Louis Blues, where he soon replaced Lynn Patrick as head coach.

His greatest coaching successes came after he donned his Montreal cap. In eight seasons, his teams captured the Stanley Cup five times. From 1975–76 through 1978–79 his teams were the class of the NHL, winning 229 games while losing a mere 46. During the 1976–77 season Bowman's Habs won a record 60 games out of 80, losing only eight. It was a mark that stood until the 1995–96 campaign when the Detroit Red Wings, another Bowman-coached team, rolled up 62 wins in the 82-game schedule.

Bowman is the winningest coach in NHL history and has nine Stanley Cup rings, more than any other coach. He was inducted into the Hockey Hall of Fame in 1991 and is the only man to win the Cup with three different teams (Montreal, Pittsburgh and Detroit).

Fergie Victim of Savard's Devilish Humour

John Ferguson teed up his golf ball and stepped back a few feet. He smiled at the rest of his foursome. A few moments earlier, someone had asked him to relate the story of an incident back in 1972 — something about a practical joke involving his friend and former teammate Serge Savard. Fergie leaned on his driver and began to talk.

"Right after Team Canada beat the Soviets in 1972, I went around the dressing room in Moscow and had the players sign a special hockey stick for me. I really treasured that stick and planned to have it mounted in my den when I got home to Canada.

"Well, you'll recall the huge welcome-home reception we got when we arrived back in Canada. Prime Minister Trudeau was there to greet us, and I followed Serge Savard off the plane and through the reception line, still clutching my hockey stick. Trudeau shook hands with Savard, and I couldn't believe my ears when I heard Serge say to him, 'By the way, Mr. Prime Minister, look what John Ferguson has brought you all the way from Moscow — an autographed hockey stick.'

"Sonofabitch! Savard took the stick from my hands and placed it in Trudeau's. I was speechless. I wanted to throttle Savard on the spot. Trudeau thanked me and suddenly my prize was gone, handed over to Trudeau, and then passed along to one of his flunkies."

"You never got it back?" I asked.

"Nah. Someone from Trudeau's office called me one day. I guess he'd heard about the joke Savard had concocted. He asked if I wanted the stick back and I said I guessed not. I said Trudeau could keep it."

"He should have sent it back no matter what you said," I told him. "That stick meant a lot more to you than it ever did to Trudeau."

Fergie shrugged.

The Roadrunner Could Fly

He was just a little guy, but he had the speed of a lightning bolt, the stamina of a marathon runner and team spirit in abundance.

Yvan Cournoyer, as a 15-year-old with the Lachine Maroons, was the only Francophone on an English-speaking team. When he required a piece of equipment, he would slap the part of his body that needed protection and the trainer would hand over the appropriate item.

Though Cournoyer would soon become bilingual, his real fluency was on the ice. Few could keep pace with him when he took off like a rocket.

He played 15 seasons with Montreal and might have stayed longer but for a chronic back problem that shortened his career. He competed in 968 NHL games, scored 428 goals and 435 assists for a career total of 863 points. He lined up with the Habs in a dozen playoff years and earned a coveted Stanley Cup ring in 10 of them.

In 1972, he was a sparkplug for Team Canada in the Series of the Century against the Soviet Union — even though broadcaster Foster Hewitt could never get his tongue around Yvan's name.

Cournoyer was the Habs' leading scorer twice and had three seasons when he scored 40 or more goals. He served as team captain from 1975–76 through 1978–79, one of the most glorious eras of Montreal hockey.

A true sportsman, Cournoyer believed in playing by the rules. He accumulated a mere 255 minutes in penalties in his career, an average of less than 17 minutes a season.

His contributions to the game were recognized in 1982 when he was inducted into the Hockey Hall of Fame.

Montrealers Are Dominant in Vezina Trophy Wins

Each year the Vezina Trophy is awarded to "the goalkeeper who is judged to be the best at his position." The judges are the NHL's general managers, and the lucky winner of the award receives $10,000. Two runners-up are named, and they receive $6,000 and $4,000 respectively. Dominik Hasek captured the Vezina six times in eight seasons between 1993–94 and 2000–01.

Prior to 1981–82, the trophy was awarded to the goal-keeper(s) who played a minimum of 25 games for the team with the fewest goals scored against it. Then the Vezina rules were changed, and the William Jennings Trophy was commissioned to the stingiest goalies. The old Vezina criteria didn't make for much suspense at the annual awards banquet, since everybody knew who the winner or winners would be once the regular season ended. And once teams universally adopted backup goalies in the mid 1960s, it meant multiple names had to be engraved on the trophy each year. In 1981, *three* goalies shared the Vezina:

Canadiens Richard Sevigny, Denis Herron and Michel Larocque.

A check of the NHL's *Official Guide and Record Book* indicates that Montreal goalies have had their names inscribed on the famous old trophy on 28 occasions. George Hainsworth's name is there three times, Bill Durnan's six and Jacques Plante's seven (six as a Hab and one as a Blue). Plante won the Vezina five times in a row between 1956 and 1960 — a goaltending record.

Montreal's Charlie Hodge won it in 1964, and then shared it with teammate Gump Worsley two years later. Worsley and Rogie Vachon combined to win it in 1968. In 1973 and 1976, Ken Dryden skated off with it solo, and for the next three seasons he shared it with Michel "Bunny" Larocque. Patrick Roy was a three-time winner, in 1989, '90 and '92. The most recent winner was Jose Theodore in 2002.

Strangely, Montreal goalies have seldom been runners-up. Roy was second in 1991. Before that, a curious researcher must go all the way back to 1967 to find Charlie Hodge's name. The Habs' Gerry McNeil was runner-up to Terry Sawchuk of Detroit in 1953.

Dream Team Honoured

On Saturday, January 12, 1985, the Canadiens' all-time "dream team" was honoured in a special ceremony at the Montreal Forum. The event coincided with the team's 75th anniversary.

More than 20,000 ballots were tabulated to name the members of the team. The fans selected:

- goalie Jacques Plante, who played on five straight Stanley Cup winners from 1956 to 1960 and captured six Vezina Trophies as a Hab;
- defencemen Doug Harvey, nine times an NHL All-Star during his Montreal years, and Larry Robinson, twice a winner of the Norris Trophy;
- centre Jean Beliveau, an extraordinary playmaker and scorer for 18 seasons;
- left winger Dickie Moore, a fierce competitor and two-time NHL scoring champion in the late 1950s;

- right winger Maurice Richard, who scored 544 regular-season goals and was the first NHL player to score 50 goals;
- and coach Toe Blake, who guided the Habs to eight Stanley Cups in 13 seasons.

The second team consisted of goalie Ken Dryden, defencemen Serge Savard and J.C. Tremblay, centre Henri Richard, left winger Toe Blake and right winger Guy Lafleur, with Scotty Bowman as coach.

Special guests included Aurel Joliat, then 83 years old and the oldest living former Hab, and Bob Gainey, who was the current captain of the Canadiens.

Maple Leafs

Toronto's First Cup Champs

The inaugural season of the NHL was an agonizing one, and by the time a Toronto team, the Blueshirts, skated off with the Stanley Cup in the spring of 1918, league organizers must have been concerned about the future of hockey in Canada. Over the course of the schedule, the newly formed league had weathered a series of threats, headaches, squabbles and bewildering events.

On the eve of the NHL opener in Montreal, the owner of the Montreal Arena said he was fed up with the poor calibre of hockey displayed by the two NHL clubs based there, the Canadiens and Wanderers, and threatened to turf them both and reserve the ice for pleasure skating if the locals didn't shape up.

The Wanderers won their first home game over Toronto by a margin of 10–9. It was wartime, and soldiers in uniform were invited to fill the many empty seats for the opener. Little did the Wanderers know that their first victory would also be their last. A few days later, the Montreal Arena burned to the ground, forcing the Wanderers (with a 1–3 record and 35 goals against) to withdraw from the circuit. Prior to the season, the Quebec franchise had decided not to ice a team, so there were only three teams — the Canadiens (who hastily made arrangements to play at the Jubilee Rink), Ottawa and Toronto — left in competition.

When Ottawa's starters skated out for a game in Toronto in January, the Senators bench was empty — they had no substitutes on hand. Toronto reciprocated by emptying its own bench. It was the only NHL game ever played with the minimum of 12 players involved.

Later that month, "Bad Joe" Hall of Montreal and Alf Skinner of Toronto tried to decapitate each other in a vicious stick-swinging duel. Both were arrested and hauled into court, where a lenient judge released them with suspended sentences.

Two Toronto stars, Harry Cameron and Reg Noble, were fined $100 each by management after they refused to play in a game at Montreal in February. They had also been caught breaking training.

Toronto tough guy Ken Randall was fined $15 by the league for lambasting game officials. He was suspended until he paid the fine — plus other outstanding fines of $20. Randall grudgingly coughed up $32 in bills and some rolled coins totalling three dollars. He tossed the change on the ice, where a player whacked a roll with his stick, scattering pennies in all directions.

The Jubilee Rink was so tiny that one Montreal game was transferred to Quebec City. Canadiens scoring whiz Joe Malone, on loan from the dormant Quebec Bulldogs, scored 44 goals in 20 games, a per-game pace that remains unmatched.

Toronto and Montreal were tied in the standings, and met in a two-game, total-goals playoff. Toronto won the league championship, 10 goals to 7. Both games were described as slugfests.

Toronto went on to capture the Stanley Cup over Vancouver, the champions of the Pacific Coast Hockey Association, winning three games to two on home ice. The westerners wore very little padding and were pounded by the more aggressive Blueshirts. The fifth game was tied 1–1 in the third period when Toronto's Corb Denneny, who had tallied 20 goals in 21 league games, broke through to slam home the winning goal and become Toronto's first NHL playoff hero. The Blueshirts, soon to be known as the Arenas, became the first NHL club to win the Stanley Cup.

It wasn't the first time the trophy resided in Toronto, however. In 1914, the Blueshirts were members of the National Hockey Association, the NHL's forerunner. Playing before small crowds, the Blueshirts defeated the western champions from Victoria, British Columbia, to seal their claim to Canadian hockey supremacy.

Corb Denneny would score the goal that propelled Toronto, by now renamed the St. Patricks, into the 1922 Stanley Cup finals. After another 20-goal season, Denneny scored the decisive marker against Ottawa in the NHL playoffs, advancing the team to the finals against Vancouver of the PCHA. Toronto sharpshooter Cecil "Babe" Dye, with 11 goals in seven games, was the playoff hero as Toronto captured the Stanley Cup for the third time — the second time as a member of the NHL.

It would be another 10 years before Toronto claimed a fourth Stanley Cup. By then, the city's hockey powerhouse would be known as Maple Leafs, performing in a world-class arena before sellout crowds and guided by the firm hand of a controversial, colourful hockey visionary named Constantine Falkland Kerrys (Conn) Smythe.

Little-Known Facts About Maple Leaf Gardens

Opened in 1931 and used by the Toronto Maple Leafs until 1999, Maple Leaf Gardens possessed a heritage that today's swanky North American ice palaces will take decades to acquire, if they do at all.

The story of the Gardens' conception, its financing (it cost a paltry $1.5 million) and its rapid construction in record time (an astonishing six months), is a familiar one to most hockey fans.

But some little-known facts about the famous building may be worth revealing. For example:

The first site considered for the new arena was on the Toronto waterfront, close by Yonge Street. A second site discussed was on Spadina Crescent, north of College Street. But when residents of the area objected, that plan was abandoned.

The T. Eaton Company originally offered Conn Smythe property on Wood Street, off Yonge, a few hundred feet from the present location, but Smythe held out for the site at the corner of Church and Carlton because streetcar lines would run directly past his building.

Initially, the ice surface was to run east-west rather than north-south. There was to be a circular gallery installed, large enough to hold 5,000 spectators, but the idea was dropped before construction got under way.

A gymnasium, a billiard room and a bowling alley were also in the original prospectus. These areas were approved and installed.

Leafs star Clarence "Hap" Day, who was a graduate of the University of Toronto's pharmacy school, made a shrewd deal with Smythe and opened the Hap Day Pharmacy in a corner of the building.

Embedded in the cornerstone, laid at the southeast corner of the building by Ontario's lieutenant governor, W.D. Ross, is a manuscript that records some additional facts about the edifice.

It states that the artificial ice would be manufactured by three 60-ton machines with sufficient capacity to cover the cement floor with ice, approximately three-quarters of an inch thick, within eight hours.

Construction of the building required 750,000 bricks. One bricklayer estimated that, laid end to end, these would stretch a distance of 28 miles. Other materials included 77,500 bags of cement, 70 tons of sand, 11,000 tons of gravel, 950,000 board feet of lumber, 540 kegs of nails, more than 14 miles of conduit and more than 230,000 haylite blocks. Roughly nine miles of piping was embedded in the cement floor to carry the fluids from the ice-making machines.

The Gardens was an instant success. It was filled to capacity on opening night, November 12, 1931, when the Leafs lost to Chicago.

One month later, the arena was home to a unique church service that not only filled the seats, but forced organizers to turn away an estimated 20,000 people standing in a drizzle outside.

The Gardens was home to a broad spectrum of events, not all of them box-office successes. Professional lacrosse, pro basketball, indoor softball, soccer and dog racing were among the promotional nightmares. One night during the dog races, the mechanical rabbit broke down. The dogs skidded to a halt and wandered off, perhaps in search of hydrants.

On another occasion, the participants in a six-day bike racer suspected that the promoters were short of funds. They refused to ride until they were paid in cash.

For a rodeo in the 1960s, several tons of dirt and straw were laid over the ice surface. But getting the stuff off again in time for a hockey game with Detroit presented a formidable, time-consuming problem. It was the reason the Leafs' home game became the only

NHL match ever to be played on brown ice. That situation did not make Conn Smythe proud, for he insisted from the beginning that the Gardens should be spotlessly clean at all times. There are many bigger, fancier, more glamorous hockey arenas around, but there was no place quite like Maple Leaf Gardens.

The "Busher" Had Everything... and Lost It All

He learned to skate wearing girls skates, stumbling around the outdoor ice on Poverty Pond in West Toronto. His skates and sticks were hand-me-downs, discarded by older kids. It was the early 1920s and the kid, like most of his peers, learned to cash in pop bottles and hustle newspapers to raise some spending money.

He honed his natural athletic abilities and grew up to become one of the NHL's flashiest performers, gifted with a movie star's good looks, a player described by Frank Selke as "the classiest player of all time." He was the speediest member of the Leafs' famed "Kid Line" and a five-time NHL All-Star. His name was Harvey "Busher" Jackson.

As a teenager, he helped the junior Marlboros to three Ontario Hockey Association titles and a Memorial Cup triumph in 1929. Soon afterward, he joined the Leafs. Conn Smythe wisely placed him on a line with Charlie "The Big Bomber" Conacher and "Gentleman" Joe Primeau. The line clicked almost instantly, and would become the most famous trio in Leaf history.

Jackson earned his nickname from Leafs trainer Tim Daly. One day the surly trainer asked the rookie to help carry some sticks to the Leafs bench. "I'm not here to carry sticks," snapped Jackson. "I'm here to play hockey."

Daly snapped back, "Why, you're nothing but a fresh young busher," and the nickname stuck.

In 1932, Jackson celebrated his 21st birthday by winning the NHL scoring title with 28 goals and 25 assists. His 53 points were three more than teammate Primeau and four more than Montreal's Howie Morenz. He became the youngest scoring champion to that date. In 1980–81, Wayne Gretzky would win a scoring title at age 20.

The late Red Burnett, then a young sportswriter for the *Toronto Star*, once said of Jackson, "He had everything: appearance, stick-handling ability, more shifts than a racing car and a blazing backhand shot.

"He burst like a Roman candle on the NHL scene. Watching Joe Primeau, the clever little centre, deal payoff passes to the giant Charlie Conacher, hurtling down right wing, or Jackson, moving with the grace of a ballet dancer down the left side, is something one never forgets.

"The Busher had something special — that extra bit of speed, the size and strength, packed into an almost perfect physique."

Red Dutton, a bruising defenceman with the New York Americans, was awed by Jackson's shiftiness. "He could cut either left or right with an almost perfect fake. He had a knack of weaving past a rearguard so close that he practically brushed sweaters."

Jackson's offensive skills netted him 241 goals during a 15-year career. But the on-ice skills that vaulted him to superstardom were offset by weaknesses away from the arena. An addiction to alcohol and a hunger for the bright lights led to complaints from his hockey bosses. There were two failed marriages, a series of business failures and unsuccessful coaching stints. He died too young — at age 55, hobbled in his last few years by a liver ailment and deeply hurt by the fans and cronies who no longer cared about him or had time for him.

I would meet him occasionally in the pressroom at Maple Leaf Gardens, where he would whisper his need for "a couple of spare bucks." His sallow complexion, shabby clothes and lined features gave him the appearance of an old man. I recall the occasions when he appeared wearing a brace to protect a broken neck suffered in a fall down a flight of stairs. "And I wasn't drinking when it happened," he insisted.

This was the fabulous forward whom Conn Smythe once described as "priceless." But not so priceless that Smythe didn't shunt him off to the New York Americans in 1940. Not so peerless that Smythe didn't carry enough clout to keep Jackson out of the Hockey Hall of Fame.

Smythe once told journalist Dick Beddoes, "As long as Jackson lives, he must not be admitted to the Hall. If we gave him a Hall of Fame plaque today, he would be on the front steps of the Hall tomorrow, hocking it for booze money."

"Mr. Smythe, bar him from the Temperance Hall of Fame or even the Chivalry Hall of Fame," Beddoes responded, "but for God's sake, not from the Hockey Hall of Fame, where performance on the ice should be the important criterion."

Beddoes was echoing sentiments expressed by Jackson's linemate, Charlie Conacher. "They inducted Joe and me into the Hall and completely ignored Busher. We should have gone in together as the Kid Line. That's how we're going to be remembered."

Jackson died in the summer of 1968, with his wish to be inducted unfulfilled. Five years after his funeral, he was finally reunited with his Kid Line comrades in the Hall of Fame. By this time, Smythe's protests could be safely ignored. Beddoes wrote a fitting final paragraph: "There is no humanity in an institution which waits five years to salute an individual just to be sure he is very dead. Flowers are worthless unless you are alive to smell them."

Doraty Ends Torrid Grind

On April Fools' Day, 1933, a record crowd filled Maple Leaf Gardens for the fifth and deciding game of the semifinal playoff series between Boston and Toronto. Every inch of space in the building was packed with spectators. In the standing-room areas, some brought folding camp chairs to stand on. Others rented soft-drink crates. A few "borrowed" cuspidors from the men's rooms, turned them upside down and stood on them. Anything to elevate them a few inches in order to see over the heads of others and watch the thrilling action below. When the attendance was announced — 14,539 — many said a larger crowd would never see a hockey game in Toronto.

At the end of the amazing marathon, no one could complain they hadn't got their money's worth; the spine-tingling struggle entered the record books as an epic, a playoff game like no other ever witnessed.

The *Toronto Star*, in bold print, offered a concise synopsis of the action:

Ken Doraty Comes through with Lone Goal after Record Crowd Sits through 164.46 Minutes of Scoreless Hockey

Fans in a Frenzy as Toronto Team Triumphs in Nerve-Wracking Playoff Game

Players Troop off Ice in State of Exhaustion

Winners En Route to Meet Rangers in Stanley Cup Finals

Andy Blair Combines with Syracuse Rookie for Million-Dollar Tally

Struggle Will Go Down as Greatest in History of Professional Hockey

Conquerors Proved Themselves Men of Mettle

At exactly 8:30 p.m., referees Daigneault and Cleghorn brought the teams to centre ice for the opening face-off. At 1:48 the next morning, in the sixth period of overtime, the fans' cheers rocked Conn Smythe's new ice palace to its very foundations as little Ken Doraty whipped the puck past Bruins netminder Tiny Thompson for the only goal of the game. Until that moment, Thompson had been sensational and had faced 114 shots. His counterpart in the Toronto goal, Lorne Chabot, had faced 93 shots and stopped them all.

Blair and Doraty were two unlikely heroes. Doraty, one of the smallest players in hockey at 124 pounds, had recently been called up from Syracuse. In a previous trial, it was said that he lacked endurance and simply wouldn't make the grade in the NHL. Blair, it was reported after a recent injury, was at the end of his career.

For 164 minutes and 46 seconds the teams, comprising some of the greatest hockey players in the world, battled each other into a state of exhaustion. After the fifth overtime period had been played, some players wanted to stop, but a conference with NHL President Frank Calder resulted in the decree: "Play to a finish!"

Someone had suggested that a coin be flipped to determine a winner. "Let's play without goalies" was another proposal. Calder vetoed both suggestions. It's a wonder that no one proposed a shootout, similar to the tiebreakers that are employed in modern-day hockey.

The goat of the contest turned out to be Bruins immortal Eddie Shore, the highest-paid and most feared defenceman in hockey. Blair intercepted Shore's cross-ice pass. He threw the puck over to Doraty, who took a couple of choppy strides toward Thompson, fired the puck and scored!

Hats flew out on the ice. Programs fluttered down. The crowd was delirious with delight. Before his mates could leap on Doraty's toothpick-slim frame, he dove into the net and retrieved the puck, a souvenir of the greatest athletic feat he would ever achieve. His mates hugged and kissed him and dragged him back to the bench. One Leaf, Harold Cotton, skated around the ice kicking hats into the air. He fell down, got up and did an Irish jig. He pulled a battered derby over his head and made comical faces at the fans.

Boston coach Art Ross took the devastating loss like a champion. He embraced Leafs defenceman King Clancy and planted a kiss on his cheek. Earlier in the season, during a dispute in Boston, a snarling Ross tried to plant another kind of kiss on Clancy — using his knuckles.

The following day, Lou Marsh, the esteemed sports editor of the *Toronto Star*, wrote of Doraty's delightful deed and was widely criticized by his readers for his comments.

> The gink who breaks up these epic hockey matches is always some meek and lowly punk … some comparative non-entity who comes from behind the barrel to carve his name on the tablets of athletic fame.
>
> The gent with the ready roscoe who broke up last night's titanic struggle was the midget of the team — Ken Doraty …little undersized runt as far as big league hockey players go…lightest and smallest player on the roster…the kid who hauls down the thinnest envelope…last sub on the relief corps…the tool the master-mind uses when all others are blunted. Now get me right — I don't intend to insinuate that Ken Doraty, who played the hero's role last night, is literally a punk. He is a gallant and game young man, but he is just plain lucky to be on the Leaf payroll!

For the next few weeks, Marsh fended off fans and harsh letters. His critics objected to his use of the words "punk" and "undersized runt" to describe the 27-year-old Doraty. Many of them described themselves as "not much bigger than Doraty myself. And nobody calls me a runt!"

Ken Doraty ended the longest game ever played at Maple Leaf Gardens. Three years later, the marathon would be eclipsed by one in Montreal between the Red Wings and Maroons that would last a dozen or so minutes longer.

Doraty stayed with Toronto for the next two seasons and scored another 10 goals in 45 games. During the next season, he established a record that can never be broken. When Toronto met Ottawa on January 16, 1934, the game was tied 4–4 at the end of regulation time. The overtime rule in that era required a full 10 minutes of extra play — no sudden-death endings. Doraty rattled in three goals in the overtime frame and the Leafs won the contest 7–4. He thus became the only NHL player ever to score a hat trick in overtime.

Ace Bailey's Final Game

Ace Bailey was a superb left winger for the Leafs in the late 1920s and early '30s. Despite a career shortened by a near-fatal incident on December 12, 1933, at the Boston Garden, Bailey's solid work earned him induction into the Hockey Hall of Fame in 1975.

It was King Clancy who first gave me an eyewitness account of the infamous "Ace Bailey Incident." Another who watched in horror from near the Leaf bench that night was Frank Selke. Later, just before his death, Bailey himself provided additional details, even though he remembered little of the body check that wrote finis to his career.

Here's what happened that night at the Boston Garden.

Bruins defenceman Eddie Shore led a Boston rush toward the Leafs zone, but Clancy tripped him up at the blue line. Shore slid along the ice and waited for the referee to wave Clancy off with a penalty. When no penalty was called, Shore rose to his feet, glowering. By this time, Clancy was leading a return rush and was deep in Boston territory, fighting for possession of the puck. Ace Bailey, with his back to Shore, dropped back to the blue line to cover for Clancy. Shore wheeled up behind the unsuspecting Bailey and charged into him, striking him with such force that Bailey was thrown into the air, his body somersaulting backward.

Everyone in the arena — the players on both teams, most of the fans and the men high above in the press box — heard a crack that might be compared to the sound of smacking a pumpkin with a baseball bat. Bailey's head hit the ice and he lay on his back as though his neck were broken. His legs, bent at the knees, began twitching.

Toronto defenceman Red Horner rushed up to Shore and snarled, "Why the hell did you do that, Eddie?"

When Shore just grinned, Horner threw a punch that knocked him cold. Shore's head cracked on the ice and he lay in a rapidly expanding pool of blood. Both injured players were carried off the ice unconscious.

Conn Smythe tried to make his way to the medical room — it was actually the room used by the Bruins' minor-league team, the Cubs — to check on Bailey's condition. En route, a fan punched the Leafs owner. Smythe returned the blow. Just then, Clancy raced over, brandishing a hockey stick. "Don't touch my boss!" screamed Clancy.

Bailey came to in the small room, and for a few seconds he appeared to be all right. Tim Daly, the team trainer, offered encouragement: "Come on, Ace. You'll be back in the game. You got a bump on the head, is all. I've seen lots worse in the [boxing] ring."

Bailey tried to get up, and then slumped back. Dr. Kelley, the Bruins' team doctor, arrived and began to examine Bailey. "Get an ambulance here fast!" he ordered. He turned to Daly and added softly, "If this young man is a Roman Catholic, someone should call a priest immediately."

While the ambulance was on its way, Shore, having recovered somewhat from Horner's knockout blow, and with 16 stitches in his skull, came into the room and apologized to the groggy Bailey.

Bailey is reported to have slurred a response through trembling lips, "That's all right, Eddie. It's all part of the game."

It was an eternity before the ambulance arrived. In fact, the game was over before Bailey was finally taken to the hospital. His mates left for the train station — they had a game to play in Montreal two nights later.

Fortunately, there were in Boston at that time two neurosurgeons who were particularly skilled at dealing with Bailey's type of injury. Two delicate operations were performed seven days apart. Internal damage was so severe the surgeons offered little hope for his survival. The doctors had told Smythe his player couldn't possibly make it, and he began making arrangements to have Bailey's body shipped back to Toronto. But Bailey's fighting spirit was a factor they hadn't accounted for; besides which, as an athlete he was in the best possible physical condition to submit to major surgery. While his teammates and family held their breath, Bailey fought for his life. On one occasion, a nurse on duty rushed in to save his life when he swallowed his tongue.

One nurse took a particular interest in Bailey. Hour after hour, she held his hand and urged him to "Keep fighting, Ace. Everybody is praying for you."

It was true. All across Canada, fans were praying for his recovery. Thousands of get-well cards arrived at the hospital. There was a nationwide sigh of relief when his doctors announced that the crisis was over, and that Bailey was on his way to recovery.

In 1990, a few months before he passed away, Bailey said, "It was Dr. Munro [one of the Boston surgeons] who saved my life. He drilled a hole in each aside of my skull. There was a life-threatening blood clot in there between the brain and the skull. He went to work and removed the clot. Took him two and half hours to get it all, because it came out in pieces. He told me he was ready for a large glass of brandy when he was done.

"I was going to press charges against Shore and the Bruins, but Dr. Munro advised me against it. He said, 'Ace, you may get only $5,000 or so if you win a lawsuit. But I hear they're going to hold a benefit game for you in Toronto and you'll get a lot more money from that than you will by going to court.' So I withdrew the charges.

"Dr. Munro let me come home to Toronto, and a few weeks later I got a letter from the Boston Bruins. Guess what was inside:

60

it was a cheque for $7,800, part of the gate receipts from a game between the Bruins and the Maroons. With that money we bought some property and built a house on it. It cost us exactly $7,800 — try doing that today. Then, when they held the big benefit game for me at Maple Leaf Gardens, we received another cheque — this one for about $20,000. That money was placed in a trust company and they sent us a cheque every month for years."

It was during the Toronto game, a forerunner to today's annual All Star Game, that Bailey and Shore met again — at centre ice. When Shore offered his hand and Bailey took it, indicating there were no hard feelings, the crowd erupted in a tremendous ovation.

"I was never the type of man to hold grudges — against anybody," he told me. "With my dad, it wasn't quite the same story. My dad, after listening to a description of my injury on the radio, became distraught. Within hours he left Toronto and headed for Boston, packing a loaded gun. He vowed not to return until he'd shot the man who'd nearly killed me. Fortunately, Conn Smythe and Frank Selke got wind of it and took care of the situation."

Selke, who had returned to Toronto with the Leafs after the Bailey-Shore incident, received a phone call from Conn Smythe in Boston.

"Frank, Ace Bailey's dad is here, and the word is he's out to get Shore. Threatens to shoot him. Can you do something about this situation?"

Selke could and did. He contacted an old friend, former Boston policeman Bob Huddy, and gave him the name of the hotel in which he could find Bailey. Huddy went to the hotel, located Bailey in the bar, and befriended him. After several drinks, Bailey showed Huddy the gun he had brought with him from Toronto.

"With this weapon I'll soon make Shore regret he injured my son," vowed Bailey.

Huddy took the gun and persuaded Bailey to walk with him to the train station. There he put Bailey aboard a train bound for Canada, flashed his badge and told the conductor to make sure the old fellow stayed on the train until it arrived back in Toronto.

Bailey's career was over, but Conn Smythe hired him as a minor official for games at Maple Leaf Gardens, and he was a fixture there for the next 47 years. Harold Ballard dismissed him before he could reach the half-century mark, something Bailey remained bitter about for the rest of his life. "I didn't even get a thank-you note from Ballard for all those years I put in," he complained. "Others did when they were let go, but not me. I saw the letters signed by Ballard and I told him about it once. He said, 'Ace, I didn't send any letters.' I said, 'Oh, yes, you did. I saw your signature on them.' He said, 'Not my signature. One of my staff must have signed it.' I said, 'Harold, I know your handwriting, and it was your signature.' He snarled, 'Okay, then I lied to you.' And I said, 'Thanks for admitting it. Now you can take this job and stuff it up your keester.' "

A Night for the King

As a star defenceman, King Clancy sparked the Leafs to a Stanley Cup triumph in 1932. He retired during the 1936–37 season and coached the Montreal Maroons the following season. Then he turned to refereeing, and became one of the most respected officials in the game. He coached the Leafs from 1950 to 1953 and served the club after that as assistant general manager and, to borrow from his own self-styled job description, "vice president in charge of nothing."

Back in the mid 1960s, I prevailed upon Clancy to record some of his favourite hockey yarns for posterity. The conversations, recorded on audiotape, now repose in the National Archives in Ottawa for future hockey historians to discover and enjoy.

Here's the King, talking about a special night held in his honour at Maple Leaf Gardens.

> Whenever I think back to March 17, 1934, and recall how the Toronto Maple Leafs honoured me with a night on St. Patrick's Day, I get a lump in my throat. Remember, I wasn't a native son. I'd played nine years with the Ottawa Senators before coming to Toronto.
>
> Even so, they paid me the greatest tribute any hockey player could ever hope to get. I didn't do anything to

deserve it. I figure they just got together and said, "Why not give the old Irishman a night?"

Can you believe they talked me into getting dressed in a green uniform with a big white shamrock stitched on the back? They had me wear a long white beard, and somebody placed a crown on my head. A huge crowd filled the Gardens that night to see the pre-game shenanigans and a nasty game that followed against the New York Rangers.

First they brought Mr. Conn Smythe to the microphone, supposedly to introduce me, but he kept getting interrupted by a batch of telegrams announcing my impending arrival.

The Rangers were good sports and joined in the fun. Their big defenceman, Ching Johnson, hauled a huge float onto the ice in the shape of a potato. The crowd was sure I was inside the float. But they were fooled when it opened up and some Junior B players from St. Mike's flew out.

Then a lot of other floats appeared, and I wasn't in any of those, either. One of my teammates, Ken Doraty — he's the little guy who scored the winning goal in the longest game ever played at Maple Leaf Gardens, in the sixth overtime period against Boston — came out of a large pipe and Harold Cotton popped out of a huge top hat. Our trainer, Tim Daly, was hidden in a big bottle of ginger ale and our goalie, George Hainsworth, emerged from inside a big boot. Red Horner, the team tough guy, stepped out of a giant boxing glove, which was appropriate, and Gentleman Joe Primeau came out of a harp, of all things.

When a big shamrock showed up, the crowd roared because they thought I was inside it. But Bill Cook, a great Rangers star, stepped out and took a bow.

When my turn finally came, the lights in the building were dimmed. Then, wearing my royal robes, my crown and my scraggly beard, I was ushered in on a makeshift throne, pulled along the ice by my pal Hap Day. When the float reached centre ice, I stepped down. Then everything went black because either Charlie Conacher or Day threw a mittful of chimney soot in my face. They showed no respect for royalty at all. So when the lights came up, I stood there looking like a king, all right, except that my face was pitch black. It took me two or three days of hard scrubbing to get the darn stuff off.

But it turned out to be a fantastic night and I have wonderful memories of it. They gave me a grandfather's clock which still keeps real good time. And a silver tea service for my wife. I think I was the first Leaf player ever to be given a night, and the prime movers behind the salute were Mr. Smythe and Mr. Selke. It was one of the greatest things that ever happened to me in sports.

Anyway, I wore my green uniform for the first period of the game that followed. During the intermission, Lester Patrick, the Rangers coach, told me I'd better change back to a blue shirt because the green sweater with the shamrock on back was confusing to the other players.

I didn't play well that night. I was just too emotional after all those ceremonies. I was too wrought up to even make a proper speech when they threw a microphone in front of me. I was absolutely tongue-tied, and that's quite an admission for an Irish gabber like me.

When I look back over the years to that St. Patrick's Day in 1934, to that night of mine and all the nights of hockey that went before it and came after it, I realize it's the friends I've made that count. After all, having a lot of good friends and making sure you get along with people is what life is all about, isn't it?

Hockey's Most Incredible Comeback

Old-time Leafs fans will never forget the Stanley Cup final series in 1942. It matched the Leafs, coached by Hap Day, against Jack Adams' Detroit Red Wings. There has never been a series quite like it.

For starters, the Leafs were fortunate to be in the finals. In the first round of the playoffs against New York, the NHL's top team, it took a goal by Nick Metz with seven seconds left in the deciding game to propel the Leafs into the final series.

Playing for the Cup against the Detroit Red Wings, the Leafs were odds-on favourites. Hadn't they finished the regular season with eight more wins and 15 more points? But the Leafs stumbled through the first two games on home ice and lost them both. Then they dropped the third game back in Detroit. Leafs fans were frustrated and furious, sneering at Day's name and saying he was no coach. The Toronto sportswriters were similarly merciless in their criticism of the coach and the players. Andy Lytle of the *Toronto Star* wrote, "Except for the gate receipts and the records, there is little apparent use in prolonging this series."

Hap Day told the Maple Leafs directors that Detroit's style had his team buffaloed. It marked the first time a team had consistently shot the puck into the Leafs zone and flooded in after it. In those days there was no centre-ice red line. The Wings simply worked the puck over their blue line and then fired it into the Toronto zone. Day told the directors that defenceman Bucko McDonald was worn out and that Gordon Drillon's talents weren't suited to the Wings' shoot-and-chase style.

"Are there any other players available?" he was asked.

"Well, yes, there's Ernie Dickens and Don Metz," he replied. "They're green, but I'll work them in and drop McDonald and Drillon. We'll also change our style and play the same way the Red Wings are playing. Maybe we can beat them at their own game."

Don Metz was an unlikely replacement for Drillon, the team's leading scorer. Metz had scored only two goals all season while Drillon finished eighth in the NHL scoring race with 23 goals and 41 points. Ernie Dickens was another two-goal man; a lad who'd played only 10 NHL games in his brief career.

In game four at Detroit's Olympia, Nick Metz, the brother of Don, got the winner in a 4–3 victory, forcing the Red Wings to put the champagne back in the cooler. Their coach and manager, Jack Adams, also required some cooling down. He was suspended for the rest of the series after he leaped onto the ice after the game and attacked referee Mel Harwood. The official was badly mauled in a free-for-all triggered by Eddie Wares and Don Grosso of the Wings.

In game five, Don Metz scored a hat trick, Syl Apps picked up a pair of goals and the Leafs romped to a 9–3 triumph. Andy Lytle wrote: "This series gets curiouser and curiouser. Only Alice in Wonderland would believe it from beginning to end."

It was back to Detroit for game six, in which Toronto goalie Turk Broda had a hot night and blanked the Red Wings 3–0. For game seven, the fans almost broke down the doors at Maple Leaf Gardens in their frantic efforts to see the game. A record crowd of almost 17,000 witnessed the culmination of the most incredible comeback in playoff history. It ended when the Leafs' Sweeney Schriner scored two third-period goals and Pete Langelle added a bit of insurance in a 3–1 Toronto triumph. Hap Day and his weary men, blistered for their incompetence a few days earlier, were now the toast of the nation. Day had captured his first Stanley Cup as Maple Leafs coach. Many more would follow.

Day Rewrites the Record Book

By the end of the 1948–49 NHL season, coach Clarence "Hap" Day had an enviable coaching record in hockey — in fact, a record-breaking one. In nine seasons behind the Leafs bench, he had captured five Stanley Cups.

In 1941–42, Day's Leafs made history by losing the first three games of the finals to Detroit, only to storm back to take four in a row to capture the Cup.

In 1944–45, Day used only "11 good men and true" to end the Montreal Canadiens' reign.

Then came his grand slam feat with victories in 1947, '48 and '49.

If the Leafs had won again in 1950, Day might have been the first coach to lead his team to five consecutive Cup triumphs, as Toronto won again in '51 on Bill Barilko's memorable overtime Cup-winning goal. But the Leafs finished third in the standings in 1949–50, behind first-place Detroit and runner-up Montreal. The Wings' big line of Ted Lindsay, Sid Abel and Gordie Howe finished one, two and three in the scoring race, with Lindsay taking the Art

Ross Trophy. The Leafs trounced Detroit 5–0 in the opening game of the semifinals, a game in which Howe suffered a devastating injury. When Ted Kennedy slipped away from a Howe check, the big right winger slammed headfirst into the boards and suffered a concussion, a broken nose, a scratched eyeball and a broken cheekbone. Despite the loss of Howe, the Wings fought back and eliminated Toronto in seven games. They went on to edge the Rangers in the finals.

By then, Hap Day had had enough of the pressures of coaching. He quit as bench boss in 1950 but stayed with the team for another seven years as an assistant general manager and GM. He wasn't entirely happy in either role; his self-esteem suffered because Conn Smythe made most of the major decisions. Day was never comfortable in a subservient role, so he walked away from the Leafs in 1957.

"I was glad to get away from it," he said at the time. "I would have dug ditches rather than stay with the game."

Day was one of the toughest coaches ever to handle the Leafs. His training camps were described as prison camps. Pity the poor Leaf who made a mistake in practice. His players may have cursed him — behind his back, of course — but they agreed that he knew what he was doing at all times and was able to get the best out of them. What better endorsement can a coach receive? Day kept his promise to forget hockey when he left the Leafs. He purchased a company that produced axe and tool handles and swept those memorable championship seasons almost completely out of his mind. He was inducted into the Hockey Hall of Fame in 1961.

Triumphs and Troubles of the Turkey Man

Leafs owner Conn Smythe once said, "If we had to play one game with everything at stake, Turk Broda would be my goaltender."

Smythe first saw Broda play goal in the spring of 1936. Smythe had watched in disgust as Leafs goalie George Hainsworth gave up nine goals in a playoff game to Detroit. He decided it was time to find a replacement for the beleaguered Hainsworth. He stayed over in Detroit to scout Earl Robertson, a Detroit substitute netminder with a can't-miss reputation. Robertson was playing for the Detroit Bulldogs in a game against the Detroit Olympics. During the contest, it wasn't the Bulldogs' Robertson who impressed Smythe; it was the burly goalie for the Olympics — a 21-year-old from Brandon, Manitoba, named Walter "Turk" Broda. The nickname, Smythe soon learned, came from Broda's childhood pals, who claimed his freckles reminded them of a turkey egg.

The Red Wings said they'd be happy to part with Broda for the sum of $8,000. If Smythe couldn't see that Robertson was a much better prospect, that was his problem; the Wings' Jack Adams had no qualms about taking money from a blind man. Smythe anted up and bought himself a future Hall of Famer.

At first, Smythe's cronies questioned his decision. Broda, they pointed out, looked and acted kind of funny. He was a yappy guy with the appetite of a horse. Now that he's earning a big-league salary, they warned, he'll eat his way out of the league in no time. Really, Conn, the man is fat! Look at that body! A few more donuts and he won't be able to lace up his skates.

Conn Smythe smiled and said, "Let's just wait and see."

It didn't take long for the roly-poly Broda to establish himself as one of the game's best puck stoppers. At the same time, he became one of hockey's most popular players. From 1936 to 1952, he played in 628 games for the Leafs and recorded 62 shutouts. He played in 101 Stanley Cup playoff games, a record at the time, and chalked up 13 playoff shutouts, another record. He won the Vezina Trophy twice, with a 2.06 goals-against average in 1940–41 and a 2.38 average in 1947–48. His 1948 Vezina prevented Montreal's Bill Durnan from capturing the trophy seven times in a row.

Broda led the Leafs to five Stanley Cups, including four in five years in the late 1940s. His work in the playoffs was often spec-tacular, and even today he is named by old-timers as one of hockey's greatest "money" goaltenders.

In the 1949 Stanley Cup finals against Detroit, Broda allowed just five goals in four games as the Leafs swept the Red Wings aside for their third straight Cup triumph.

In 1951, at age 37, he allowed just nine goals in eight games as Toronto won the Cup again.

Smythe held a night for Broda on December 22, 1951. Only one other Leaf, King Clancy, had been honoured in such a manner. It was Broda's last season. He played in only one game during the regular schedule, but after Al Rollins lost the opening game of the playoffs against Detroit, Turk got the call. In game two, he played brilliantly, only to lose 1–0 in his 100th playoff start. He started again in game three against the Wings, and was shelled 6–2. Rollins finished up as the Leafs bowed out in four games.

In retirement, Broda turned to coaching. His travels took him to Quebec City, Moncton, Charlotte, North Carolina, and Newmarket. He found his coaching niche in junior hockey, and his Toronto Marlboros won two Memorial Cups in the 1950s. He yearned for a crack at the NHL, and it was thought he might find himself behind the Leafs' bench one day. Three times the position became open, and three times he was said to be "not quite right" for the job — he was passed over in favour of Howie Meeker, Billy Reay and Punch Imlach.

In his 50s, his health began to fail. His marriage came apart. His final and biggest thrill in hockey was being named to the Hockey Hall of Fame in 1967, Canada's centennial year. Five years later, he died of a heart attack.

Sportswriter Rick Boulton tells the story of Broda's daughter and some of her friends returning from a rock concert one night, a few weeks before he passed away. "Mr. Broda," said one of the teenagers, "you never heard such a noise at Maple Leaf Gardens."

"Oh yes, I have," he grinned in reply.

Triumph to Tragedy

High on the list of Toronto Maple Leaf players who've achieved instant hero-status is the name Bill Barilko. Barilko's golden moment in the Stanley Cup playoffs thrilled a full house at Maple Leaf Gardens on April 21, 1951. It occurred in sudden-death overtime against the Montreal Canadiens. People still talk about that goal over fifty years later. And the photo of it, snapped in all its beauty by ace lensman Nat Turofsky precisely when the puck entered the Montreal net, is perhaps the most famous playoff photo of them all.

After 2:53 of extra time in game five of the finals, Barilko, never one to hesitate when boldness was called for, dashed boldly in from his defence position, and while falling through the air, whacked the puck at Gerry McNeil in the Montreal goal. His aim was true, the rubber whizzed by a startled McNeil, the red light flashed and the Leafs had captured the Stanley Cup.

While McNeil turned in dismay, disgusted at himself for falling too early on the play, Barilko and his mates began a wild celebration of their fourth Cup victory in five years. The Barilko goal ended a five game final series that required overtime in every game before it was settled.

After mobbing their grinning teammate, the Leafs hoisted Barilko to their shoulders. He was accorded a thunderous standing ovation from the Toronto fans. Owner Conn Smythe, who had earlier warned Barilko to "Stay back" and "Don't take too many reckless chances," skidded across the ice to pump his hand.

Later, Bill's mother Faye, using a soup spoon, helped hockey's newest celebrity sip champagne from the bowl of the Stanley Cup. This beaming woman had fled the Russian Revolution in 1924 to begin a new life in Timmins, Ontario. Losing her husband in 1946 had been a terrible blow but on this night she was ecstatic, the proudest mother in Canada. To think her 24-year-old son, so handsome, so talented, was the object of everyone's attention left her all but speechless.

Her joy would be short-lived. A few weeks later, back home in Timmins, she would suffer another devastating loss.

One weekend, against his mother's wishes, son Bill flew off with a dentist friend on a fly-in fishing trip to some remote northern lake. Later, through her tears, his mother would say, "Oh, I made such a terrible mistake that day, letting Bill go, not kissing him goodbye, being angry with him for leaving, not telling him I loved him."

Barilko and his friend flew 300 miles north to the rivers that flow into James Bay where the fishing was superb. Two days later, with the plane's pontoons loaded with fish, they started back. The dentist pilot had difficulty getting the Fairchild off the lake and into the air. But he finally managed and the plane disappeared over the treetops. It never arrived back in Timmins. Somewhere along the way, the plane went down without a trace.

A massive search was organized. Hundreds of private planes and at least 17 RCAF aircraft crisscrossed thousands of acres of dense bush. Day after day the flights took off. None reported any sightings. Months went by, then years, and the disappearance of the popular hockey star and his friend remained a baffling mystery.

Then, in 1962, helicopter pilot Garry Fields spotted the reflection of the sun glinting on a piece of metal buried in the deep bush about 50 miles north of Timmins. He marked the spot with some toilet tissue thrown into the tree branches. A few hours later he led a search party into the area and located the missing Fairchild. The skeletal remains of Bill Barilko and his pilot friend were found inside.

Punch Imlach's Biggest Thrill

When a relatively unknown hockey vagabond named George "Punch" Imlach was hired as assistant general manager of the Toronto Maple Leafs in 1958, the job description puzzled him. He had nobody to assist, because the club had no general manager. King Clancy was in the executive suite, but he, too, bore the title of assistant general manager. And Clancy made it clear he had no ambitions to become anything else. Newcomer Imlach and old-timer Clancy both might have been assisting Billy Reay, who had coached the Leafs to a dismal last-place finish in his rookie season in 1957–58. But when owner Conn Smythe had offered Reay the GM's job a few weeks earlier, Reay had turned it down.

"I'd rather be the team coach," explained Reay. "I've got something to prove here."

Imlach quickly found out how well known he was around Maple Leaf Gardens. When he went to the office receptionist and asked her to find Billy Reay, she said, "He's not in yet, sir. Care to take a seat and wait?"

The Leafs players didn't know much about Imlach, either. They'd heard that some bald, 40-year-old former senior player who had been working in Springfield had been hired in an executive capacity, but they had no inkling what an impact he would soon have on their lives and careers.

When the Leafs won only five of their first 16 games in 1958, Imlach was asked by the Silver Seven, the "hockey committee" that ran the team, to explain the reason for the poor start. His response so impressed them that Imlach was asked to step right into the general manager's job. The team promptly lost four more games, and Imlach decided he had no choice but to fire Reay, even though the coach was a favourite of team owner Conn Smythe.

He decided to coach the team himself, at least on an interim basis, and after a 2–1 loss to Chicago the following night, the players picked themselves up and went on a six-game undefeated streak. Imlach began telling everyone who would listen that his last-place team was now inspired and would make the playoffs. Most of his listeners scoffed at the words of this cocky little optimist.

Imlach still considered himself a fill-in coach, and within days he had offered the job to former NHL star Alf Pike. But Pike wanted certain conditions written into his contract, demands that took him out of the running and convinced Imlach he should remain behind the bench.

The new coach was pleased with his goaltending, having signed Johnny Bower to a contract as one of his first moves after joining the Toronto organization. Bower, acquired from Cleveland in the off-season, was proving to be a standout at age 33. Imlach bolstered his defence by turning Carl Brewer pro and picking up Allan Stanley from Boston in return for Jim Morrison. Midway through the season, the Bruins placed Larry Regan, a former rookie of the year, on waivers and Imlach claimed him. Regan, a clever playmaker, became the ideal centreman for Dick Duff and George Armstrong. He traded minor leaguer Willie Marshall to Hershey for Gerry Ehman, who had scored 40 goals for Imlach in Springfield the year before. Ehman turned out to be a very productive forward.

Despite the canny moves, by mid March Imlach's Leafs were still long shots for a playoff berth. Time was running out and they were nine points behind the fourth-place New York Rangers. A reporter asked Rangers coach Phil Watson, "Is there any chance the Leafs can overtake your club in the race to the playoffs?" Watson scowled and said, "Young fella, there's no way that's gonna happen. No way! And you can tell Imlach his club will never put my team out of the playoffs. In fact, I'm going to keep his team out of the playoffs. And that's the truth!"

The NHL offices, then located in Montreal, began releasing possible playoff matchups for the television people and the newspapers. There was no mention of Toronto in any of the groupings. Obviously, even the league executives thought it was preposterous to consider the Leafs for any postseason activity.

With two weeks to play in the regular season, the Leafs met the Rangers in back-to-back games. On Saturday, March 14, at Maple Leaf Gardens, Toronto blanked New York 5–0 and then held on the following night to win a 6–5 thriller back in New York. Both were "must-win" games for Imlach and the Leafs. Now Toronto was only three points behind Watson's club with three games left to play.

The following Thursday, the Leafs went into the Montreal Forum and defeated the Canadiens 6–3. Now they were only one point back of New York; the Rangers had lost to the Bruins the previous night.

On the last weekend of the schedule, the Rangers regrouped on Saturday night and beat Detroit 5–2 to re-establish a three-point cushion over Toronto. But the Leafs downed Chicago 5–1 on home ice, which meant the race would go down to the final Sunday — with Toronto at Detroit and New York hosting Montreal.

Imlach had spent a sleepless night on the train ride to Detroit for the final encounter. At the old Olympia before game time, his heart flipped when he learned that the Rangers had jumped into an early lead over Montreal in their clash at Madison Square Garden. His pulse almost returned to normal when a follow-up report indicated the Habs were leading 2–1 after goals by Moore and Beliveau.

His next jolt came after the puck was dropped in Detroit. Two Red Wings, Norm Ullman and Marcel Pronovost, scored first-period goals against his Leafs to open up a 2–0 lead. By then the final score had come in from New York: Montreal 4, Rangers 2. Punch rejoiced. There was still a chance. A Toronto win would cap one of the most incredible seasons in hockey history.

While he paced nervously outside the dressing room after the first period, Imlach was approached by Stafford Smythe. "Well, our boys gave it everything they had," said Smythe. "They've got nothing to be ashamed of."

"Stafford, don't be stupid," snarled Imlach. "We're not through yet. We're not going to lose this game. There's still 40 minutes left."

Regan scored a pretty goal early in the second period and then Baun batted one in — his first goal of the season. Ullman scored another Red Wings goal, his second of the game, but Brewer quickly tied it with a blast. Then Regan, enjoying the best game of his career, put the Leafs ahead 4–3. But Pronovost made a nifty rush and fired the puck off Bower's glove into the net. With 20 minutes to play the score was tied 4–4.

In the third period, Regan displayed some marvellous stick-handling and set up Dick Duff for his 29th goal of the season as the Leafs took a 5–4 lead. Regan said later, "I told Duffie I'd set him up for the winner." The insurance marker was engineered by another smooth stickhandler, Billy Harris. Harris maneuvered the puck to Baun, who fired it toward the Detroit net. Harris deftly tipped it out of the air and into the cage to complete the scoring. Toronto 6, Detroit 4. The Leafs were in the playoffs, edging the Rangers by a single point.

Imlach always claimed it was one of the greatest games he'd ever been involved in. "People love to see a team come from nowhere to accomplish something and that's what we did in my first year with Toronto," he said. "They called us the Cinderella Leafs because we got off the floor and started winning and we refused to quit. People love that sort of thing."

When the playoffs got under way, Imlach predicted his Leafs would win the first round against Boston and they did, even after falling behind 2–0 in games. Gerry Ehman scored six goals in the seven-game series.

But Imlach's crystal ball let him down in the finals against Montreal. His team came close, posing a constant threat to the mighty Habs, a club that was establishing a streak of five consecutive Stanley Cup triumphs. Montreal won the first two games on home ice by 5–3 and 3–1 scores. Back in Toronto, the Leafs captured game three, 3–2, and might have won game four but for an unfortunate twist of fate, a bizarre playoff oddity. George Armstrong's hard shot went right through the webbing in Jacques Plante's net and the light failed to go on. Had the Leafs won that game (they lost 3–2) they would have returned to the Montreal Forum tied 2–2 in games instead of down 3–1. The Habs won game five and the Stanley Cup by a 5–3 score.

By then Imlach was not only a fixture in Toronto, he was famous. He would be back to lead his Leafs to the Stanley Cup four times in the 1960s. But even after those stirring triumphs, he would often look back with pride on the 1958–59 season and the dramatic victory over Detroit that won his team a surprise playoff berth.

"I can recall how every one of those goals was scored that night," he'd tell reporters. "Those goals, that game and that season, provided me with the greatest thrill I've ever experienced in hockey."

Brewer Had 'Em in the Palm of His Hand

One night during the 1959–60 season, Leafs defenceman Carl Brewer said a few unkind words about referee Eddie Powers. Powers overheard every adjective and sentenced Brewer to the penalty box to cool off. The period ended with Brewer still serving his time. But when the penalty timekeepers got up to leave the box, they got a big surprise: Brewer had locked the penalty box door and refused to let them out. Hot words were exchanged and a scuffle ensued. Brewer's behaviour was noted on the referee's report to NHL headquarters, and it cost him a stiff fine.

It was a Brewer brainwave that led to the insertion of a new rule in the referee's handy guide to officiating. After a battle on Toronto ice one night, referee Vern Buffey spotted a pair of unusual gloves on the ice, tossed there by one of the combatants. The palms had been removed from each glove, and when Brewer skated over to retrieve them, Buffey had the answer to a long-standing mystery. How, he had often wondered, had Brewer been able to throw opposing forwards off stride so easily when they fought for space near the Leaf goal crease? The answer lay in the palmless gloves. Brewer simply reached through the holes, clutched an opponent by the jersey and tossed him around like a rag doll.

For the following season, there was a new rule in the book. Players could no longer perform with palmless hockey gloves.

Brewer was not the first defenceman to cut holes in the palms of his gloves. Former Rangers defenceman Ivan Irwin used "doctored" gloves to clutch unwary opponents many years before Brewer arrived in the NHL.

Had Brewer not been such a rebel, and had he played longer in the NHL, he might easily have compiled career benchmarks that would have led to his entry into the Hockey Hall of Fame. But his major contribution to hockey, and every player should thank him for it, was his stubborn resolve to battle the league over millions of dollars in pension funds owed to retired NHL players. It was a battle the players eventually won.

The Leafs of the Sixties

How can anyone who saw the Toronto Maple Leafs compete in the 1960s not feel he or she watched some of the most spectacular hockey ever played?

At Maple Leaf Gardens, each week brought new thrills, produced by players representing six clubs with lengthy traditions, players whose names and numbers were familiar to millions of Canadians. These were not faceless strangers with unusual names, performing as Ducks or Sharks. These weren't skaters we saw just once each season. These were men whose linemates we could name, whose stats we could recite, whose styles we critiqued. Their heads and faces, unprotected by padded helmets and shiny visors, were as familiar to us as our co-workers, our cousins, and our classmates. Everyone knew the NHLers of the '60s!

At least seven times a year, and more at playoff time, the Leafs would host five bitter old rivals at the Gardens, the yellow-brick House that Smythe Built. One challenge would come from the hard-shooting Blackhawks, with Bobby Hull, Stan Mikita, the Scooter Line and hot-tempered Reg Fleming, a crew-cut battler who once accumulated 37 penalty minutes in one game! In goal would be durable Glenn Hall, whose nervous stomach caused him to upchuck before every contest — and often between periods! "Oh, gross!" our sisters and girlfriends would say. Hall played in 502 consecutive games, an iron-man streak that ended when he was forced to limp to the bench in his 503rd. That was on November 7, 1962. It's one hockey record that is safe for all time.

One night, Hall stopped a Leaf shot with his chin at the north end of Maple Leaf Gardens. He turned his head into a rising shot and was gashed for 26 stitches. He staggered and fell, blood dripping from the wound onto the Indian-head logo that decorated his jersey. Slowly, he skated off to the medical room. Ten minutes later he was back, patched up and ready to play again.

All NHL goalies could recount similar tales of cuts and concussions, kayos and blows that forced them to leave games for bodily repairs. Most times they managed to come back to finish the contest. Late in 1959, Montreal's Jacques Plante, his nose bloodied by an errant slap shot, refused to come back unless he could wear a protective mask he'd invented. On that night Plante changed goaltending forever.

Perhaps the next Leafs home game would feature the Red Wings and a potent lineup that included "Terrible" Ted Lindsay, Gordie "Mr. Hockey" Howe, Alex "Fats" Delvecchio, slick playmaker Norm Ullman and the master of the shutout, goalie Terry Sawchuk. Sawchuk's stern mug bore more stitches than an old quilt. One night, Howie Young, a noted Red Wings reprobate, appeared with his head shaved Mohawk-style. More frightening than his looks was his penchant for dispensing two-handers to any Leaf who crossed his warpath.

The New York Rangers would be the next visiting club, led by handsome Rod Gilbert, Jean Ratelle, Harry Howell, Leapin' Lou Fontinato and that popular and irrepressible pug-nosed puck-stopper, Lorne "Gump" Worsley. "What team gives you the most trouble, Gumper?" someone would ask. "My own," was his famous reply.

A Boston invasion usually meant a high-scoring performance by the Uke Line of Horvath, Bucyk and Stasiuk. But the Bruins, like the Rangers, despite an interesting mix of players, seldom struck fear into the hearts of the Leafs. Only in the late '60s, when a kid named Orr signed on, would the Bruins move to the front of the NHL class.

Best of all would be the seven matches at Maple Leaf Gardens each season against the Montreal Canadiens. On those nights, there would be enough electricity in the building to light up Yonge Street all the way north to Barrie.

Those clashes guaranteed incomparable, crowd-pleasing hockey. Bower against Plante, Keon and Kelly versus Beliveau and Richard, and the genius of veteran coach Toe Blake — wearing the black fedora — pitted against the savvy and bravado of newcomer Punch Imlach (wearing the white). One night, Punch started his own son Brent at centre ice to face Beliveau! What chutzpah! Another time he started five defenceman against the Habs.

Fans who have witnessed modern-day hockey's many dramatic changes fondly recall those glory years of Toronto hockey — Original Six hockey. Not just the four Stanley Cup triumphs, but the abundant skills of individual favourites as well. There are memories of ancient Allan Stanley forcing slippery Henri Richard to the outside, then slamming the gritty little Hab into the side boards; Tim Horton, the strongest Leaf, outmuscling anyone who challenged him in the slot, a big brother protecting agile but fragile Johnny Bower, the stingy netminder who patrolled his crease with tight-lipped determination; Bob Baun, a fearless defender, blocking shots and bouncing intruders from *les glorieux* off his massive chest; Carl Brewer, a sly opportunist, snaring the loose puck and racing nimbly away with it, deking and darting with nifty little moves, and then throwing a perfectly-timed pass across ice to speedsters Keon or Duff.

Sometimes in these confrontations there would be a dozen future Hall of Famers on the ice at the same time. But nobody knew that way back then.

When the Habs added John Ferguson to their winning mix, tempers were bound to explode whenever Eddie "The Entertainer" Shack or Orland Kurtenbach dared to block Fergie's path to the goal mouth. Fergie came at the Leafs like an enraged bull. Some spectators swore they saw steam emerging from Fergie's generous nose. If he failed to score, he'd charge through the players guarding Bower's crease, stick high, elbows flailing. His message was clear: "Get out of my way or I'll skate right over you!"

Mike "Shakey" Walton, who joined the Leafs in '65, recalls Fergie running over him three times in one game. Finally Walton drummed up enough courage to do something about it. "The next time he came at me I whacked him with my stick," he recalled. "Cut him for about six stitches. Geez, was he mad. He grabbed me by the throat and then everybody piled in. He had me down on the ice and he was shouting, 'Shakey, I'm gonna kill you!' Geez, was I scared!"

Oh, there were some dandy punch-ups in the days when clubs met 14 times a season and there were no rules covering "third men in." "They're clearing the benches!" Bill or Foster Hewitt would shout into their microphones, and a vast *Hockey Night in Canada* audience would sit a little closer to their black-and-white Motorola TV sets as a dozen players from each team leaped over the boards into the battle.

A few years ago, there was a mini hockey reunion in the Hot Stove Lounge at Maple Leaf Gardens. John Ferguson, Frank Mahovlich, Eddie Shack and Johnny Bower were there, discussing the '60s and some of those memorable Leaf-Canadiens battles.

"They were more than battles," declared Ferguson. "It was more like war, a heck of a war. It was like no other game when we played the Leafs." Over the decades, Fergie has mellowed. In his playing days, and for some time after, he considered it sinful to fraternize with players from a hated rival. On this occasion, in the company of three former enemies, he seemed to enjoy looking back on a marvellous era.

"Somehow the intensity was higher for our games with Montreal," Mahovlich said. "The fans knew they were assured of a good night's entertainment. And it was always a sellout crowd."

"I remember it as very, very exciting hockey," said Bower. "I used to go to church with George Armstrong before those games with Montreal and I'd say a little prayer. And I often said another prayer on the ice during those matches."

Fergie recalled visiting the Toronto Stock Exchange on game days when the Habs came to town. "Yeah, I'd drop by the exchange and sit in the gallery. First thing you know, the brokers on the floor would spot me and the hollering would begin. The whole floor would be booing me."

The restaurant emptied, goodbyes were said, and only Shack and Ferguson lingered. They sat at a table having lunch — right across from each other. It was a sight as rare as a hole in one. Two players who had fought and bruised and cursed each other when they played, reminiscing over a steak sandwich. Photos should have been taken. Ripley should have been there.

"Remember when we'd sometimes be on the same train," Ferguson said, "and we had to walk through the Leaf car to get to the dining car? Geez, I hated that. I never spoke to one of you guys. I never even looked at one of you."

"Yeah," laughed Shack, "and when you'd get past me, I'd throw something at you, trying to get you to react."

Ferguson grinned. But there was a hint of danger in the air. If Shack should say the wrong thing, if a 40-year-old feud should be rekindled because of an ill-advised remark, a couple of waiters and a busboy wouldn't have been able to keep them apart.

Ferguson kept smiling, however, as another thought came to mind. "After a game in Toronto one night," he said, "Toe Blake was looking for a pair of socks. Some joker had cut the feet out of his socks. We must have won the game, because no player would dare fool around with Toe if we'd lost. So the trainer brought him a pair of white socks with a small Maple Leaf logo on them. Blake threw them aside and said disgustedly, 'I'll never wear bleepin' Leaf socks.' He slipped his bare feet into his loafers and left the building."

Hockey fans recall the '60s as being very special. It was a decade when everything stopped on Saturday night for *Hockey*

Night in Canada, with a cast that included Foster and Bill Hewitt, Jack Dennett, Eddie Fitkin and Ward Cornell. Murray Westgate, everyone's friend, with his gravelly voice, his broad grin and his Esso service station coveralls, would invite everyone to "Fill 'er up at the Esso sign" and enjoy "Happy motoring."

As one of the TV pioneers, I recall the beginning of the decade, when there were no instant replays, no highlights from out-of-town games, and no long delays for in-period commercials. And everyone stayed tuned for the Three Star selections. Fans almost always argued over the choices. Foster was often accused of choosing "the two goalies and Keon."

Any player who scored 20 goals in a 70-game season was a star in those days. It wasn't until 1968–69, after the NHL had doubled in size, that three of hockey's best scorers — Phil Esposito, Bobby Hull and Gordie Howe — surpassed the 100-point barrier. By then, teams were playing 76 games. Leaf fans would wait another six years before Darryl Sittler became the first Leaf to reach the century mark.

In the early '60s, there were no curved sticks in the Leafs' stick rack, no names on the backs of jerseys, no player agents, no helmets, no talk of adding franchises or European players to the mix. Backup goaltenders, like Plante's face masks, were relatively new to the NHL. As recently as 1957–58, goalie Ed Chadwick had played in all 70 games — the last Leafs netminder to perform without anyone to back him up. If Chadwick was injured, a team trainer or a junior goalie seated in the stands would have been pressed into service.

Most NHL goalies were reluctant to follow Plante's lead and don facial protection. They feared that coaches like Imlach would question their courage if they hid behind a mask. So they would offer an excuse. "Too hard to see the puck at my feet," they'd say. Or "It gets too hot under that mask." In time, common sense prevailed and all began to wear masks — all but the one holdout, Gump Worsley. Eventually, he too succumbed.

For four of the first seven seasons of the 1960s, the Montreal Canadiens finished atop the NHL standings. The Canadiens' success rankled the other clubs, especially the Leafs. The Leafs and their fans were weary of Montreal's dominance. They'd seen the Habs powerhouse wrap up five consecutive Stanley Cups from 1956 to 1960 and it disturbed them to think a similar streak would highlight the new decade.

But under George "Punch" Imlach, the Leafs were gaining strength. In 1959–60, toiling for the new man at the throttle, the Leafs won 35 games, lost 26 and tied nine. It was their first winning record in half a dozen years.

Imlach became a master at reclaiming other team's rejects, and when he landed veterans like Allan Stanley, Bert Olmstead and Johnny Bower, age became irrelevant. For the record, it was Billy Reay, the coach Imlach fired, who recommended that Bower and Olmstead be signed to Leaf contracts.

Horton was quick to test Imlach's sense of humour. A holdout at training camp one year, Horton signalled his willingness to resume contract discussions in an impish way. He sent Imlach a box of doughnuts — the stalest, moldiest doughnuts he could muster. Inside was a note: "Dear Punch. Do you think a man who can turn out a superior product like this needs to play hockey for a living?" A few days later, Horton was in camp, signed and satisfied.

The Leafs breathed a sigh of relief when Rocket Richard, holder of 17 league records, announced his retirement in September 1960. They were glad to see the last of the Rocket. Now they would have to contend with only one Richard — the Rocket's kid brother Henri — who was given a catchy nickname, "the Pocket Rocket," a fitting sobriquet for a player en route to 11 Stanley Cup triumphs.

Those were the days, my friend.

An Ankle Injury Leads Kelly to Leafs

Throughout the 1950s, Leonard "Red" Kelly of the Detroit Red Wings was arguably the NHL's top rushing defenceman. He was a fixture in Detroit, a Norris Trophy winner and a three-time winner of the Lady Byng Trophy, and his name had been etched on the Stanley Cup on four occasions.

During the 1959–60 season, Kelly suffered an ankle injury that slowed him down. His boss, Jack Adams, asked him to hide the injury and Kelly obediently refrained from discussing it. Later, Adams concluded the popular redhead was just growing old. Now would be a good time to trade him. The Rangers were interested and coughed up Bill Gadsby and Eddie Shack for Kelly and Billy McNeill.

But Kelly refused to accept the deal and retired instead of reporting to New York. Two days later, he was out of hockey, having accepted a job with a firm in Detroit.

NHL President Clarence Campbell called him. "You'd better reconsider, young man," he told Kelly. "If you don't report to New York, you'll be blackballed from hockey forever."

Campbell should have known better than to threaten a stubborn Irishman "That's fine, Mr. Campbell," said Red "I've had a dozen good years in the game and that should be enough for anyone."

The next day, there was a call from King Clancy of the Leafs. "Red, Punch Imlach has always liked you and we've got permission from Mr. Adams to talk to you. How about coming to Toronto for a meeting with Imlach?" Clancy's gift for the gab soon had Red wavering on the idea of retirement.

Red agreed to travel to Toronto incognito. Clancy promised to meet him at the airport.

When Kelly arrived, Clancy almost missed him. Red's copper-coloured hair was hidden under a bowler hat and his coat collar was turned up. Clancy chuckled at the disguise and hustled Kelly to Maple Leaf Gardens in a limousine. Later that day, Kelly agreed to the generous offer Imlach placed on the table. Imlach phoned Adams, who had already agreed to take journeyman defenceman Marc Reaume for Kelly if the redhead decided to join the Leafs. Adams was told the deal was a go.

Adams hung up, failing even to wish Kelly good luck.

Later still, Kelly, Imlach and Clancy headed for a downtown restaurant. A few blocks from the Gardens, Jim Vipond, the sports editor of *The Globe and Mail*, passed within a few feet of their limo but he failed to see the famous occupant sitting in the back seat. He missed the scoop of the season.

At a secluded table in the restaurant, Kelly discovered he wasn't the only hockey notable in the establishment. Toronto had a home game against the Canadiens the following night and, to everyone's surprise the entire Montreal team, led by Rocket Richard, filed in and seated themselves nearby. Richard spotted Kelly and came over to say hello. But he quickly sensed that something important was going on. The Rocket smiled and placed a finger to his mouth, as if to say, "My lips are sealed."

The next morning, the acquisition of Kelly was front-page news. At the morning skate, he posed for photographers wearing jersey number 4. His wife, Andra, flew in from Detroit for the game with Montreal. She told me recently, "I couldn't believe the reception Red got from the Toronto fans. All that day, on the street, in the hotel, everybody was talking about my husband. Everybody seemed to know him. I was newly married and didn't realize what a big hero he was. I'd never seen anything like it."

Red said, "When Punch sent me over the boards to take my first shift, the ovation I received was incredible. Punch played me at centre that night and I made up my mind I wouldn't let Beliveau beat me on the face-off. I won it cleanly and flipped the puck into the Montreal zone. I charged after it, right into the Montreal goal crease. Their goalie must have seen the look in my eye because he took a dive and I did a full somersault right over him. Andra often talks about the somersault that got me started as a Leaf."

The deal for Kelly was the best trade Imlach ever made — by a long shot. The redhead went on to help the Leafs win four Stanley Cups at an age when he should have been over the hill. He was inducted into the Hockey Hall of Fame in 1969. He even found time to combine hockey with politics, serving as a Member of Parliament, which required incredible energy and stamina.

Shack Gets a Nickname

Some time ago, Eddie Shack was one of the guest speakers at a banquet in Hamilton, Ontario. He entertained the crowd with the following presentation.

People often ask me how I got the name "Clear the Track." When I was with the Leafs, we played New York one night and I smacked Rod Gilbert and another Ranger — both at the same time. They hit the ice and rolled around and I didn't even get a penalty. The late Paul Rimstead wrote about me in the paper the next day, and the headline read, "Clear the Track, Here Comes Shack."

Then Brian McFarlane, sittin' over there, made up a song to go along with the name. He must have said, "Holy sheepshit, maybe I can do somethin' with this." You know, he's supposed to be a writer and he's got some books to prove it and all that. I don't think he knows shit about music, but anyway he did it and it went to number one on the hit parade for the next few weeks.

It went like this:

Clear the track, here comes Shack,
He knocks them down; he gives 'em a whack,
He can score goals; he's found the knack,
Eddie, Eddie Shack.
He started the year in the minors,
And almost gave up the game,
Then boom! He's back with the big club
And the Leafs haven't quite been the same.

There was a lot more, but that gives you the idea. Hey, it was true. I always spent the beginning of the year in the minors. With Imlach, if you misbehaved you were sent to the minors for a couple of weeks. So I was always going down. It was absolute hell playing for Imlach. The lines were Keon, Armstrong and Duff. Then it was Kelly, Mahovlich and Nevin. Then it was Olmstead, Stewart and somebody else. After that it was always Shack and Harris and whoever the hell wants to play with them. That was Imlach. I didn't score many goals because I was always sitting on the bench. If I squawked, Imlach would say, "For Christ's sake, shuddup, Shack, or it will cost you 10 bucks for a ticket to get in and watch the game."

Even so, the game of hockey has been great for me. I got to play with so many clubs. My little wifey — she's such a sweet little thing — told me we could make more damn money on our real estate deals moving from city to city than we could from hockey. She used to say, "Shackie, you better act up again and tick somebody off so we can get the hell out of here."

Hockey is fabulous. When I was with the Leafs and we were playing Montreal, we always anticipated a scrap or two. The team was always up for those games — well, most of us. I'd have to get Frank Mahovlich up for them because Frank could be in a bit of a cloud. I mean he's a great guy and everything, but Jesus Christ! Get up, Frank! And Imlach would love me for that.

In some of those games I picked on their smallest guy, like Henri Richard. When you're a Ukranian from Sudbury and you see a French guy out there, well, you just don't like him, see. You don't like the way he talks, you don't like how short he is, you don't like how fast he skates and you absolutely want to kick the shit out of him. So I get a hold of Henri, and remember, the rule was the third man in is thrown out of the game. That was a great deal for me, especially with Ferguson always hanging around. While I'm throwing Henri around — and he's a tough little son-ofabitch — who comes nosing around but Ferguson. He wants to get at me. I can't shake Richard so I say to myself, "Let's see if the little bugger can take it." So I bonked him with my head. Boom! I hit him just above the eye and now the blood is coming down and the worst language is coming out of him — "Shit de shit de goddamn. My brudder from Two-and-a-'Aff Rivers will kill you, Shack."

Now we have to go back and play at the Forum again and I'm a nervous wreck. In the warmup there's a guy blowing a big horn and chanting, "Shack the nose! Shack the nose!" And Fergie is shouting nasty things at me. I'm praying for a tie score because I know if one side grabs a big lead, Imlach is going to be saying, "All right, Shack and Harris and whoever the hell wants to go out there with them."

After the period, we go through the exit, and who the hell is sitting up there but Maurice Richard, Henri's big brother. You know, the guy who got two minutes for looking so good on television. He cups a hand and yells at me: "Shack, thank God you didn't hit my brother with your big nose. You would have split him in two."

I don't know if the kids today have the fun that we did. Hockey is a fun game. When I opened a hockey school I told the kids to push, grind and shoot the puck. I told them to hold the stick with both hands and skate with your head up. Of course, I never did it myself, ha, ha, but I told them to do it.

I also told them that when I grew up in Sudbury, Tim Horton and I were good friends. Timmy wound up a great career in Buffalo and he was playing against the Leafs one night nursing a broken jaw. He was taking a lot of pills for it. He had a couple of drinks after the game, and on his way back to Buffalo at four in the morning, Timmy was driving too fast and flew off the road. They'd even set up a roadblock trying to slow him down. His car flipped and he was killed. I learned from that that drinking and driving is wrong. So please be careful out there. Thank you.

Shack was never at a loss for words on the ice. One night at the Montreal Forum, after a scrap with the Pocket Rocket that earned them penalty time, he told the fuming Richard, "Henri, don't get so upset. It's not your fault that God gave all the hockey talent to your big brother."

Stump your friends with the following trivia: Name a player who scored 20 or more goals with five different NHL clubs. The answer is Eddie Shack. He scored 26 for the Leafs in 1965–66 (the year we wrote the song about him), and more than 20 with the Bruins, Kings, Penguins and Sabres later in his career.

George Armstrong, the Native Son

In the days when racist barbs were common in sports, George Armstrong, the captain of the Leafs, was often taunted about his Indian heritage. He was, after all, half Ojibwa and a proud honourary chief of the Stoney Tribe (named Big Chief Shoot-the-Puck).

During one game, Armstrong heard one too many insults about his aboriginal roots. After the contest, he skated over and addressed the loudmouth fans.

"You guys aren't so smart. Think about this. When you white people came to this country, the Indians knew how to run things. We paid no taxes. We had no debts. The women did most of the work and we menfolk spent all our time hunting and fishing. How can you beat a system like that?"

Armstrong combined great leadership with a captivating sense of humour. Johnny Bower, his roommate on road trips, was often the victim of an Armstrong prank. In the Leaf dressing room, Bower habitually placed his dentures in a small plastic cup before skating out for a game or practice. One day he returned to the room and popped in his teeth, but they failed to click into place. Frustrated, he pulled them out and examined them. "What's this?" he muttered. "These aren't my teeth." Some joker had substituted another set of false teeth during his absence. He looked across the room at Armstrong, who was straining to hold back his laughter.

"Damn you, Chief," fumed Bower. "You did this. Where'd you get these dentures — from a dentist?"

"No way," laughed Armstrong. "You know I live next to a funeral parlor. I got them from an undertaker."

It was Armstrong who scored the goal that wrapped up the last Toronto Stanley Cup triumph in 1967. With the Leafs leading the Canadiens three games to two (after Montreal had ridden the crest of a 15-game undefeated streak into the finals) and nursing a 2–1 lead into the final minute of play in game six, Armstrong scored into an empty net with 47 seconds left on the clock to assure a Toronto victory and the city's 11th Stanley Cup.

Armstrong played 20 seasons in Toronto and scored 296 goals in a team-record 1,187 games. He was captain of the Leafs for more than 10 years, longer than any other Leaf. Throughout his career, he was associated with champions. He played on a Memorial Cup winner, an Allan Cup winner, a Calder Cup winner (as American Hockey League champion, with the Pittsburgh

Hornets) and four Stanley Cup–winning teams. In 1975 he became the first Native player to be inducted into the Hockey Hall of Fame.

Spoiling Montreal's Planned Party

It was Canada's centennial year, 1967, and the Montreal Canadiens planned to celebrate the momentous occasion with a Stanley Cup triumph. The eyes of the world would already be on Montreal that summer, as it was hosting Expo 67. How much better it would be if Montrealers could bask in the glow of having won Lord Stanley's old silverware!

The Toronto Maple Leafs, easily the oldest team in the league that season, appeared to have nothing left in the tank when they faced rookie goalie Rogatien Vachon and the Habs at the Forum. Leafs coach Punch Imlach won few friends in *la belle province* when he squawked, "Don't tell me they're starting some Junior B goalie against us." Game one was a slaughter, a 6–2 Habs victory. Mrs. Imlach, watching on TV, became so angry at the Toronto broadcast crew's description of the shellacking that she was tempted to kick in her TV set.

The Toronto writers were much more caustic. One said it was like a battle between jet fighters and Sopwith Camels. Vachon said, "Maybe Punch will call me a Junior A goalie now." Terry Sawchuk was banged up so badly in the opener that Johnny Bower started game two. Amazingly, he shut out the Habs 3–0 and showed great poise, even though he was belted three times by John Ferguson, who stampeded through his crease like an angry bull.

Back in Toronto for game three, Bower ignored his swollen nose (whacked by Ferguson's stick) and stopped 60 shots in a game that went into sudden-death overtime. The overtime was packed with thrills, drama, pressure and close calls. Finally, Bob Pulford slipped the game winner behind Gump Worsley at 28 minutes, 26 seconds of extra time.

Bower drew the starting assignment in game four, but a pulled muscle in the warmup sent him limping off and forced Sawchuk to come in cold. But the old warrior played poorly and once again gave up six goals in a 6–2 loss.

For the second time in the series, Leafs fans and members of the media tumbled off the bandwagon. Critics declared the Leafs all finished, game old codgers but shooters of last bolts.

Bower, it turned out, was through for the year and Sawchuk looked like a survivor of a train wreck. The Habs couldn't wait to start peppering the man they'd beaten 12 times in two games. But Sawchuk, who had recorded his 100th career shutout earlier in the year, played near-perfect hockey in game five. He allowed just one goal — a deflection — and skated off with a 4–1 victory.

For game six, Imlach dressed Bower as backup, even though the future Hall of Famer could barely walk. Imlach didn't plan to use him — he had a third goalie, Al Smith, half-dressed and waiting in the Leafs dressing room — but he wanted Bower to share in the glory if the Leafs should win the Stanley Cup. He was also thinking of the expansion draft, and how it would rob his team of many of his favourite players. It was the end of an era for his Leafs, and he was determined it would end with memories that would last a lifetime. He even wore a new green-checked suit that night, one he'd purchased in Montreal after the humiliating defeat in game one. He'd told Tony the tailor, "I'll be wearing this suit on the night we win the Cup. You watch for it on TV." Tony had laughed at Imlach's optimism.

Once more, Sawchuk reached back and found a way to match some of his best playoff performances from the past. Ron Ellis and Jim Pappin scored for the Leafs. Dick Duff, the ex-Leaf, spoiled Sawchuk's shutout bid.

With the Leafs leading 2–1, the game came down to the final minute of play. There was a face-off to the left of Sawchuk in the Leafs zone. Imlach surprised everyone by sending out his old-timers in this crucial situation. There was Allan Stanley, Tim Horton, George Armstrong, Red Kelly and Bob Pulford in front of Sawchuk. Stanley was told to take the face-off against Beliveau. "Great," said the defenceman. "I can't remember when I last took a face-off. And the way I take them is illegal."

The puck was dropped and Stanley stepped into Beliveau and held his stick. The puck went to Kelly, who moved it up to

Pulford. Pulford sent a perfect cross-ice pass to Armstrong, who was moving up the right boards. The Leafs captain, from long range, calmly drilled the puck into the empty Montreal net to guarantee the victory. Meanwhile, Beliveau was screaming "face-off interference" at the referee. But the noise created by thousands of jubilant fans drowned out his words. Beliveau shrugged and conceded defeat. The Leafs had captured the Stanley Cup and spoiled the Habs' plans for a Centennial celebration of their own, with the Expo grounds the site of their grand soiree.

The Final Goal of the Original Six Era

When the Montreal Canadiens clashed with the underdog Toronto Maple Leafs in the Stanley Cup finals of 1967, it marked the end of the "Original Six" era in the NHL. By the time the following season rolled around, six new clubs — expansion teams in Los Angeles, Minnesota, Oakland, Philadelphia, Pittsburgh and St. Louis — would be in the league.

On May 2, 1967, the final goal was scored. It entered an empty net at Maple Leaf Gardens in Toronto, and Foster Hewitt, the legendary broadcaster, was on hand to describe it:

> The crowd can hardly contain themselves during this dramatic struggle. It has been a terrific game all the way. Now someone has thrown what appears to be an egg on the ice and the scrapers are coming out. It is rather unusual for any object to be thrown on Gardens ice, but the delay may be a great help to both clubs because all players seem to be almost exhausted.
>
> Beliveau has been the Montreal leader while Davey Keon for the Leafs has been here, there and everywhere. Both [Montreal goalie Gump] Worsley and [Toronto netminder Terry] Sawchuk have been outstanding, the latter truly sensational.
>
> There are only 55 seconds of regulation time remaining. Toronto leads two goals to one. The hometown

crowd is anticipating a Stanley Cup victory in this sixth game, while Montreal Canadiens are using every strategy to get the tying goal and push the game into overtime.

With less than a minute remaining, Leafs are called for icing and the referee calls for a face-off to the left of Sawchuk. There's a delay in play, and Montreal goalkeeper Gump Worsley doesn't know whether or not coach Toe Blake wants him to come out of the net. Now Blake has decided to remove Worsley. He's going to the bench. With 55 seconds to play, Montreal will use six attackers and their goal is empty.

Canadiens intend to shoot the works. [Jean] Beliveau is coming on the ice; so are [Jimmy] Roberts, [Yvan] Cournoyer, [John] Ferguson, Henri Richard and [Jacques] Laperriere. It's all or nothing for them now.

Leafs, too, are making changes. [Toronto coach Punch] Imlach is making his stand with an all-veteran lineup of [Allan] Stanley, [Tim] Horton, [Red] Kelly, [Bob] Pulford and [George] Armstrong. Sawchuk, of course, is in goal. Beliveau will face-off for Montreal and Stanley for Toronto.

Referee John Ashley is growing impatient. Ferguson skates over to talk to Beliveau. Stanley is hesitating, now he comes into position. This face-off is vital.

They're all set. The puck is dropped. Stanley gets possession; he snaps the puck to Kelly and Kelly kicks it up to Pulford. Pulford passes to Armstrong, who is driving hard. Army shoots toward the empty net. He's on target. It's in! *He scores!!* Armstrong has scored the insurance goal. It's now Leafs three, Canadiens one. Toe Blake's strategy has backfired and that shot just about decided possession of the Stanley Cup. Canadiens had to gamble everything and lost. Time of the goal was 19:23 — only 47 seconds left in the game.

Worsley has returned to the Montreal net and play has resumed... Now there are seven seconds left, six, five, four, three, two, one. The game is over! Leafs have won the Stanley Cup! The crowd is going wild. There's no use trying to talk against that uproar. By their well-earned victory, the Toronto Maple Leafs are Stanley Cup champions for 1966–67, their fourth triumph in six years. A truly great record.

Another Classy Captain

Like other Leafs captains before him, such as Ted Kennedy, Syl Apps and George Armstrong, Dave Keon could do it all. He was a gifted goal scorer, a tireless skater, a relentless checker, a superb playmaker and a leader who avoided the penalty box.

In 1960, he jumped to the NHL and won the Calder Trophy as rookie of the year in 1961. In his second season, he played on a Stanley Cup winner, his biggest thrill. His second biggest was capturing the Cup a fourth time in '67 and being named MVP of the playoffs. He remains the only Leaf to win the Conn Smythe Trophy. "It was a wonderful time to be a Leaf," he says, "playing in the '60s and winning four Stanley Cups."

One of only five Leafs to play more than 1,000 NHL games, Keon set team records with 365 goals and 858 points. Both marks were later erased by another great captain, Darryl Sittler. Keon was twice awarded the Lady Byng Trophy for his gentlemanly play and he rarely visited the penalty box. When Bobby Hull was barred from Team Canada in 1972 because he had jumped to the WHA, there was a storm of criticism. The furor over Hull's omission overshadowed the anger of Keon fans, who felt this great little player who excelled in "European style" hockey should have been selected. Jim Proudfoot, writing in the *Toronto Star*, said, "Keon was the most talented individual omitted from Team Canada."

McKenny's Memories

Jim McKenny was a colourful and often comical defenceman who played for the Leafs from 1965–66 to 1977–78. Since retiring from the game he has become a popular television sportscaster in Toronto, and is as famous on the air as he was on the ice.

In his playing days, *Hockey Night in Canada* commentators could always count on McKenny to come through with a good quote and a funny story. Asked once about his views on violence in hockey, he quipped, "I always felt the violence made me play better. I never skated so fast in my life as I did when the game got violent — just staying away from it.

"One night we were playing against John Ferguson and the Montreal Canadiens. What a tough bird that Fergie was! I'm standing at the blue line, and Fergie is carrying the puck down the ice. Just then Billy MacMillan, one of our forwards, cuts him off, gets a shoulder into him and knocks him flat. Geez, did he land hard. Billy must have been crazy to do it. When Fergie staggered to his feet, his nostrils flaring, the first Leaf he saw was me. I knew right away he thought I'd flattened him. So for two periods he's chasing me all over the ice trying to kill me and MacMillan is loving it. Finally I had to scream at Fergie over my shoulder, 'For God's sake, Fergie, get off my case. It was MacMillan who hit you, not me. Go chase him!' On the next shift, he grabbed MacMillan and beat the crap out of him. I felt badly about tattling on a team-mate. But I thank God it wasn't me that Fergie drilled.

"During the 1973–74 season, the Leafs made a good deal, getting Timmy Ecclestone from Detroit in exchange for Pierre Jarry. I loved Tim because of his sense of humour. We were in Philadelphia one night. Tim and I were sitting on the bench, not playing too much. Now Flyer tough guy Dave Schultz, a guy who's been in a million fights, skates by our bench and Timmy yells at him, 'Hey, Schultz, you asshole, you're going to get yours tonight.' That broke me up and I started laughing. Then Schultz stopped and shouted back, 'I'll break your face, you little faggot!'

"I turned and said, 'Tim, did you hear what he said to you?' But Tim wasn't there. He was crouched over, pretending he was lacing up his skates. So Schultz assumed it was me who'd challenged him. I paid for that one big time, with Schultz whacking away at me every chance he got. Of course, Timmy thought it was hilarious.

"One more Tim Ecclestone story, okay? We were playing at the Montreal Forum one night and the Habs hadn't lost at home for something like 38 games. Or maybe it was 38 months. That was the night a guy came into our dressing room before the game and said, 'Gee, it's quiet in here.' I told him, 'You'd be quiet, too, if you knew you were going to get the shit kicked out of you in the next couple of hours.' Anyway, we were playing brutal hockey. Our coach, John McLellan, a real good guy, gave us a pep talk before the game. He said, 'Come on, guys, my ass is on the line. Looks like I'm going to be fired pretty soon, so give it your best shot out there tonight.'

"Our best wasn't very good, because we came back into the room trailing 2–0 and we'd been outshot like 21–1. McLellan was fuming. He said, 'One shot! One goddamn shot! You guys make millions to play hockey and all you can manage is one shot. I can't believe it!' And he began to tear the room apart, kicking waste-baskets and throwing towels around. Then he went outside to cool off, slamming the door behind him.

"That's when Tim stood up and faced his teammates. 'Okay,' he said, 'Who's the wise guy?' "

Pal Hal's Most Outrageous Acts

On April 11, 1990, Harold Ballard, the irascible owner of the Toronto Maple Leafs since 1972, died peacefully in his sleep. His body succumbed to diabetes, kidney failure and a weak heart. He was 86. He fought with his players, his family, sportswriters and broadcasters, the Soviets and anyone else who wanted to scrap. His Toronto teams were often woefully weak, and finished .500 or better in only six of the 18 seasons he was in charge. They never finished higher than third in any division of the NHL. If someone were to prepare a "top 10" list of Ballard's most bizarre moments, it might look like this:

1. In 1928, Ballard appears at the Winter Olympics in Switzerland as Canada's assistant hockey coach. A non-competitor, he talks his way into becoming the flag bearer in the Olympic parade, depriving a bona fide athlete of the honour. Later, he steals an Olympic flag. Four years later, he takes his Sea Fleas team to the

world hockey championships in Prague. His undisciplined players are involved in many brawls, on the ice and off. Ballard is thrown in jail after a fracas in Paris. His Sea Fleas become the first Canadian team to lose a world title.

2.   In 1965, Ballard brings the Beatles to Maple Leaf Gardens. On a blistering hot summer day, he turns up the heat in the packed building, cuts off the water flow to the drinking fountains and holds the show up for more than an hour. Hundreds of parched fans pass out while hundreds more line up for soft drinks, which are sold in large cups only. Ballard books a second — unauthorized — show for the same day, and when the Beatles' manager protests, Ballard says, "They'd better perform, or the fans who've bought tickets will tear them apart."

3.   In 1972, Ballard is charged and found guilty of 47 counts of fraud and theft totalling $205,000. He is sentenced to three concurrent three-year terms and serves several months in jail.

4.   In 1973, released from prison on a three-day pass, he tells reporters that Millhaven Penitentiary is akin to a country club, with steak dinners and colour TVs available to all the inmates. His comments anger Canadians from coast to coast and are discussed in Parliament.

5.   In 1974, Ballard rents the Gardens to Johnny Bassett and the Toronto Toros of the WHA for $15,000 per game. But the arena is in semi-darkness for the Toros' home opener. "The TV lights will cost you extra," he tells an enraged Bassett. The additional cost is $3,500 per night. He also removes the cushions from the team benches. "Let 'em buy their own cushions," he mutters.

6.   In 1978, Ballard buys the Hamilton Tiger-Cats football team for $1.5 million. During his stint as owner, attendance drops 42 percent. He loses $20 million on the

venture and sells the team 11 years later to the City of Hamilton for one dollar. He tells journalist Dick Beddoes, "What can you say about those city clucks running Hamilton? One guy over there is growing marijuana [an alderman had been charged with growing the plants in his cellar] and all the others are smoking it."

7. In 1985, Ballard quarrels with all three of his children and denounces them through the media. They object to his relationship with Yolanda MacMillan, a 49-year-old divorcee who served time in prison for conspiracy to commit fraud. Ballard cancels a minor team's hockey game scheduled at the Gardens when he discovers his daughter's son is on one of the teams. "Sometimes I think I'm surrounded by lunatics," he says. "Them and her."

8. Ballard fires his son, Harold Jr., from his job at Davis Printing, a Gardens-owned subsidiary, after he learns that his son told a CBC reporter, "My dad once stuck my finger in a light socket when I was young. Then he told my mother he was 'just giving the kid some juice.' "

9. In 1979, Ballard orders Foster Hewitt's famous gondola taken down and incinerated to make room for high-priced luxury boxes. Ballard announces he has saved Foster Hewitt's chair from the gondola. He rounds up several old chairs and has them painted red with Foster Hewitt's name emblazoned across the back. He tells reporters he sold all the chairs at five bucks apiece. (Author's note: In all the years I worked with Foster Hewitt in the gondola at Maple leaf Gardens, I never noticed that he had a special chair. He certainly didn't have his name painted on any of them.)

10. In 1979, Ballard is interviewed on Barbara Frum's CBC radio show *As It Happens* and implies that women are best in one position — on their backs. He doesn't actually say as much, but the inference is clear. He also says,

"They shouldn't let women on the radio. They're a joke." A few days later, a group of women picket the Gardens. They shout, "Down with sexist Harold." Women who call him personally to complain hear him ask, "What's the matter, baby? Can't you find yourself a man? You want my body?"

Harold Ballard was inducted into the Hockey Hall of Fame as a builder of hockey in 1977. Some people ask why.

Bruins

Adams Brings Big-League Hockey to Boston

Born in 1876, Charles Francis Adams, a poor boy from Newport, Vermont, never owned a hockey stick as a youth. But he was adept with a broomstick, working his way around the potato sacks, the feedbags and other merchandise in the corner grocery store where he first was employed as a chore boy. The proprietor, noting the meticulous attention young Adams gave to sweeping up the dust and debris, said, "That lad shows a lot of promise. He'll probably be running his own store some day."

It was the start of a brilliant career in the grocery business, one that would propel Adams all the way to the chairmanship of First National Stores, one of the major chains in the United States. The same unique, visionary qualities that made him hugely successful in business also served him well in the world of sport. A horse racing enthusiast, he was the founder, president and owner of Suffolk Downs, and he was instrumental in getting pari-mutuel betting legalized in Massachusetts. In the mid 1930s, he was principal owner of the Boston Braves of baseball's National League and used his powers of persuasion to get Sunday baseball approved in Boston.

"Where he got his interest in sports I don't know," his son Weston once said. "As a young man he worked so hard he had no time to play games himself."

When young Adams moved from Vermont to Brookline, Massachusetts, he discovered hockey and was hooked for life. He and Weston attended most of the club games played at the Boston Arena, and in time he even sponsored a team, the Irish-Americans.

In 1924 Adams journeyed to Montreal to see the Stanley Cup finals and became even more enthused. "Those pros in the NHL can really play this game," he told his business associates. "I'm determined to get a team for Boston."

Weston would say, "When Dad got an idea in his head there was no stopping him. He gambled all his life on the things he believed in. And he had a strong belief in the future of hockey."

Adams applied for an NHL franchise at a meeting in Montreal on October 12, 1924, and was told that a man named Thomas Duggan had been granted two franchises on the condition they be placed in major U.S. cities. Adams snapped up one of the franchises for a fee of $15,000. Requests for franchises also came from Pittsburgh and Philadelphia, but these applications were shelved. Adams hired veteran hockey star Art Ross to run his team and to serve as governor. The Bruins played home games at the Boston Arena, which soon proved to be too small to house his new team. The Boston Garden, which opened in 1928, would not have been constructed if Adams had not guaranteed $500,000 rental for five seasons.

Charles Adams enjoyed the thrill of three Stanley Cup championships. The first came the year the Garden opened, with the Bruins defeating the Rangers in a best-of-three final series. A decade later, in 1939, the Bruins defeated Toronto for the Cup, and two years later they ousted Detroit in the finals.

Adams was elected to the Hockey Hall of Fame in 1960 as a builder, indicating the high esteem in which he was held by his peers and associates in the game.

Following his father into the Hockey Hall of Fame in 1972 was Weston Adams, who had been associated with the Bruins since his father purchased the NHL franchise in 1924. Weston played goal at Harvard, and in 1932 he took over as president of the Boston Tigers, a Bruins' farm club. He succeeded his father as Bruins president in 1936, served with distinction with the U.S. Navy in World War II — rising to the rank of commander — and returned to play a key role in a merger of the club with the Boston Garden Arena Corporation. He became chairman of the board of Boston Garden in 1956 and two years later was elected chairman of the Bruins as well. By 1964 he was club president again and remained in office until 1969 when he retired in favour of his son, Weston Jr.

Bruins Win Their First Stanley Cup

When the 1928–29 NHL season opened, the Boston Bruins presented a formidable lineup. A new goaltender, Cecil "Tiny" Thompson, had moved in to replace the aging Hal Winkler. Eddie Shore and Lionel Hitchman were at their peak on defence. Ralph "Cooney" Weiland, called up from Minneapolis of the American Hockey Association, joined Aubrey "Dit" Clapper and Norm "Dutch" Gainor on a line. The trio would soon become known as the "Dynamite Line."

During the season, the Bruins introduced George Owen, a Harvard grad, to the lineup; along with the former Dartmouth star Myles Lane, acquired from the Rangers. The club traded Frank Fredrickson to the Pittsburgh Pirates; Fredrickson, in a display of class, wrote a letter of thanks to the Bruins for their treatment of him. The letter, published in a Boston paper, included the words; "I will always cherish the privilege of having the opportunity of knowing something about Boston and Bostonians."

The Bruins tied a league record for most wins in a season, with 26, and led the NHL in goals (89). They finished two points behind the Canadiens in the overall standings and faced the Habs and their record-setting goaltender, George Hainsworth (22 shutouts in 44 games), in the first round of the playoffs. Hainsworth had allowed only 43 goals all season — an average of less than one per game. Why the two top clubs met in the first round in those days remains a mystery, one of the biggest bonehead decisions of the era.

While Hainsworth was brilliant in the first two games, Boston's Tiny Thompson was even better. He produced back-to-back 1–0 shutouts in games one and two, played in Boston. These stunning victories were followed by a 3–2 Bruins win at the Montreal Forum in which Eddie Shore scored the winning goal. The Bruins were led by captain Lionel Hitchman, who played throughout game three with blood flowing from a huge gash in his head. At the final buzzer, Howie Morenz was the first Montreal player to race over and congratulate the Bruins.

When the train carrying the winners arrived back home, the team was accorded the greatest reception yet seen for a Boston team. And they were still a series away from the Stanley Cup!

The best-of-three final series was historic because, for the first time, two American teams, the Bruins and the New York Rangers, were to play for the Stanley Cup. Boston captured the first game, on home ice, 2–0, behind Thompson's superb goaltending. It was his third shutout of the playoffs. Two nights later, at Madison Square Garden, Dr. Bill Carson of the Bruins scored with less than two minutes to play in regulation time, giving Boston a 2–1 victory and the Stanley Cup.

Rookie netminder Tiny Thompson had played in all five games, recorded three shutouts, and given up only three goals — an average of 0.60.

Another wild celebration greeted the Bruins on their return to Boston, and a few days later, at a gala affair in the Swiss Room of the Copley Plaza Hotel, the players gathered for a victory party. Team president Charles F. Adams divvied up $35,000 in bonus money, while the players in turn surprised Adams with an unusual present: a two-foot-high bronze bear imported from Russia. Manager Art Ross, who received a set of golf clubs, expressed his appreciation for the loyalty his players had displayed all season: "There has never been a professional team where there has been less bickering, fewer jealousies and better spirit. All season long, that has been the case." He paid special tribute to Hitchman, an original Bruin, calling him "a cornerstone of the franchise."

Ross also remembered ex-goalie Hal Winkler, arranging for his name to be inscribed on the Cup, even though Winkler's NHL career had ended the season before.

The Eddie Shore–Ace Bailey Incident

December 12, 1933, was a black day in the history of Boston hockey. A check delivered in anger — and from behind — by Bruins tough guy Eddie Shore ended an opponent's career and left him near death with a fractured skull. It remains one of hockey's greatest tragedies.

There was little evidence of Christmas spirit in the stands or on the ice that night. The largest crowd of the young season howled for blood as they watched the Bruins and the Leafs pound each other from the opening whistle. Before long there would be pools of blood on the ice and many would be forced to turn away, sickened at the sight.

In the second period, Eddie Shore made one of his patented rushes and was tripped up by King Clancy at the Toronto blue line. Clancy grabbed the puck from Shore and made a dash of his own into the Boston zone. Meanwhile, Shore had jumped to his feet and targeted the nearest Leaf for a return check. The innocent opponent was Ace Bailey, who had his back to Shore.

Frank Selke, Toronto's assistant general manager, was sitting in the front row of the press box, in perfect position to see what happened next. He would write in his memoirs, "Shore arose and slowly started back for his end of the playing arena. He was behind [Red] Horner and Bailey. Whether he mistook Bailey for Clancy, or whether he was annoyed by his own futility and everything in general, nobody will ever know. But we all saw Shore put his head down and rush at top speed. He struck Bailey across the kidneys with his right shoulder and with such force that it upended Bailey in a backward somersault, while the powerful Shore kept right on going."

Bailey's head hit the ice with terrific force, fracturing his skull in two places. An awestruck hush fell over the arena. Everyone realized immediately that Bailey, his knees raised, his body quivering, was very badly hurt. Clancy would say, "I had many battles with Shore but I never thought he was a vicious player. He wasn't out there to maim anybody. But that night he certainly hit Bailey as hard as he could. It was a shocking thing to see."

Toronto's Horner, a muscular, fearless defenceman, skated past his unconscious teammate, and then made a beeline for Shore, who stood as though stunned. Horner shook Shore by the shoulders, and then pole-axed him with a right to the jaw. Shore collapsed to the ice, out cold. Blood flowed freely from a deep cut to his head and spread across the ice.

Bailey and Shore were carried to their respective dressing rooms. In the visitors' room, Bailey began convulsing. His head was packed in ice and then, barely conscious, he was rushed to a Boston hospital. Two delicate brain operations in the next ten days were necessary to save his life. Even when the crisis passed, doctors were concerned about permanent damage to the brain that might result from such a severe concussion. The Leaf forward never played hockey again, but he made a satisfactory recovery and lived to a ripe old age.

While the two injured players were being carried off that night, the Boston crowd, for no good reason, became ugly. Many left their seats and jammed the corridors. Toronto manager Conn Smythe, taunted by some as he fought his way to the dressing room, lashed out and punched a fan. Smythe was later hauled into court, charged with assault. But a sympathetic judge ruled that his actions were the result of great stress and all charges were dismissed.

Back in Toronto on the night of the incident, Bailey's father, having listened to Foster Hewitt's description of the incident on the radio, grabbed a revolver and hopped a train to Boston. He fully intended to shoot Eddie Shore — if he could find him. But Smythe and Frank Selke, his assistant, had a friend intercept the elder Bailey and ply him with liquor until he was in no condition to shoot anybody. The friend relieved him of his gun, and then slipped him aboard a train headed back to Canada.

Shore's head wound required several stitches. He left for Bermuda a few days later, after learning that he had been suspended for 16 games.

Two benefit games were held for Bailey. The Bruins announced that all the profits from a Boston–Montreal Maroons game on December 19 would go into a fund for Bailey. But a modest turnout at the gate produced little more than $6,000. Two months later in Toronto, a game between the Bruins and the Leafs brought the stricken star over three times that amount.

"I bought a house with that money," Bailey once told me, "and had plenty left over."

It was during the pre-game ceremonies at the benefit game in Toronto that Eddie Shore approached Bailey for the first time since the incident at Boston Garden. Tentatively, he skated up to Bailey and offered his hand. Bailey smiled; his firm handshake convinced the crowd that he held no grudge against his adversary. Shore was forgiven. The Toronto fans roared at this display of sportsmanship. At rinkside, a number of Toronto's finest sighed in relief; they had anticipated an ugly demonstration, perhaps even a riot.

Shore wasn't much use to himself or his teammates for the rest of that season. In fact, almost a year passed before he displayed his old dynamic fury.

James Hendy, a writer of that era, once said of Shore, "It is doubtful that any player will ever equal Shore's efficiency in capitalizing on his bad man reputation. The NHL fixed an annual salary maximum which many players have exceeded, but Shore is the only one who forced the league to wink at more than double the figure."

Eddie Shore's Quirks

Defenceman Eddie Shore's reputation as a player who marched to his own drummer followed him throughout his NHL playing career and stuck with him long after he discarded his Boston jersey.

When he bought the Springfield hockey club in the late 1930s, he became known for running the club in a unique fashion.

Don Cherry, who played under Shore, tells some fascinating stories about the owner's quirks and bizarre behaviour. As the owner, player and coach, just before game time Shore could be seen parking cars outside the Springfield Arena. Then he'd dash inside, suit up and play for his team.

There's a story, difficult though it is to believe, that Shore instructed his players never to tip a cab driver more than 15 cents. Soon, cabbies in Springfield tried to avoid picking up hockey players. If a player had a bonus clause for scoring 30 goals, Shore would bench him when he neared the mark.

Shore insisted that his players practice tap dancing in hotel lobbies and ballet moves on the ice. He assured one player that he would score more often if he combed his hair differently. He tied one player's legs together because he felt the player was skating with his legs too far apart. He tied his goalies to the crossbar in order to teach them how to remain upright during game action. At least once he locked a referee in the officials' dressing room because he felt the man had done a poor job during the game.

He told his players that he had cured himself of cancer and had survived eight heart attacks in efforts to promote his special treatments and home remedies to sick or injured players. He enjoyed displaying his chiropractic skills. "You'd ache for a week after he finished working on you," says Cherry. "Some players were terrified to get on that medicine table."

Once, Shore invited all of the players' wives to the arena. They dressed for the occasion, thinking that he had planned a surprise party for his team. When the women arrived, Shore sat them down and preached to them his views on sex. He instructed them to "be celibate until the playoffs are over," because "too much sex" was the reason for the Indians' poor play.

He destroyed the dream of many players, men who quit the game rather than play for him. Players around the league referred to Springfield as the Siberia of hockey. When they signed their contracts with other clubs, they added a clause that prohibited a trade to Springfield.

Once, Shore desired a goalie by the name of Smith. He made the trade and awaited the arrival of the newest member of his team. When Smith entered the Springfield dressing room, Shore asked, "Where are your goalie pads?" The puzzled Smith replied, "But, I'm not a goalie, I'm a forward." Leave it to Shore to trade for the wrong Smith.

Leafs Hall of Famer King Clancy enjoyed telling a story about a famous playoff incident that involved Shore.

"In March of 1936 we played the Bruins in the playoffs. In those days it was a two-game [total-goals] series. Well, the Bruins blanked us 3–0 in Boston and in the second game back in Toronto they jumped to a 1–0 lead. It looked like curtains for the Leafs.

"Shore was the big cheese of the Bruins so I decided to try a little goading. I told my mates when we left the dressing room for the second period, 'Don't worry. I got Shore in my hip pocket.' After the period started, Shore was caught for some infraction and that infuriated him. He was headed for the penalty box when I intercepted him and said, 'Geez, Eddie. That was a rotten call. Are you gonna let the referee get away with that?'

"My words must have influenced him because he wheeled around, laid his stick on the puck and fired it at the referee, Odie Cleghorn. Cleghorn wouldn't stand for that sort of nonsense and sent Shore off with an additional 10-minute misconduct penalty. Boston was a different team without him. By the time he got back, we'd tied the score overall and eventually went on to beat the Bruins 8–6 on total goals.

"Another time," adds Clancy, "I nailed Shore into the boards and he didn't like it one bit. He turned in a flash and raised one big mitt, ready to let me have it. I grabbed his glove and pumped his arm up and down. I said, 'Hello, Eddie. How are you tonight?' And he mumbled, 'Pretty good, King. Pretty good.' "

Clancy continued. "Did you know Shore used to come out on the ice for the warmup in Boston wearing a long gold dressing gown over his uniform? And the music would blare out 'Hail to the Chief' while he pranced around with those long strides of his. The Boston crowd loved it. One night I skated up next to him and said, 'I hope you're gonna wear that gown in the game tonight, Eddie. You look so lovely in it. Trouble is, you'll probably get all tangled up in it, fall into the boards and then start crying for a penalty.'

"He just glared at me and said, 'I'll kill you tonight, Clancy.'

"I laughed and said, 'You try it, Eddie, if you don't mind taking a good licking right in front of all your fans.'

"How I loved to needle Shore. He was a fabulous hockey player, and later on he became a good friend of mine."

Milt Schmidt Signs with Boston

Milt Schmidt first attracted interest from the Boston Bruins when he was a naive 17-year-old living in Kitchener, Ontario. After being invited to the Bruins' training camp, the first thing Milt did was write a letter to Bruins manager Art Ross saying that he would get a summer job to pay for the trip from Kitchener to the team's training base in Quebec. He didn't know the team would pick up all expenses.

"Oh, I was green all right," Schmidt told me recently. "Especially when Ross called me in to sign my first contract with the Bruins. He offered me something like $3,000, and I told him I'd like $3,500. Well, he raised his eyebrows and said that was more than he'd been authorized to give me. He said he'd have to go down the hall and discuss my request with the team owner, Mr. Adams. So I waited patiently while he went to see Mr. Adams.

"In a few minutes he was back, and he had a grim look on his face. 'Sorry, Milt,' he said, 'I fought for you, but Mr. Adams wouldn't budge on the $3,000 offer. He told me you could take it or leave it.'

"So I reached for a pen and signed the contract. On my way out of the building, I passed Mr. Adams' office. I said to myself, 'I think I'll go in there and ask Mr. Adams why he wouldn't give me the extra 500 bucks I requested.' So I entered the office and encountered Mr. Adams' secretary.

" 'Yes? Can I help you?' she asked.

" 'Hi, I'm Milt Schmidt. I just signed with the Bruins and I'd like to see Mr. Adams, please.'

"She smiled and said, 'I'm sorry, but Mr. Adams isn't in today. He won't be in all week.' "

Milt turned to me. "Brian," he said, "they lied to me from day one, and they have been lying to me ever since."

Milt Was a Superstar

Herb Cain, who played for the Boston Bruins from 1939–40 through 1945–46, says that many players of his era would have selected Milt Schmidt as the best all-round player in the NHL.

"Schmidt was a terrific player," Cain said. "In fact, he was the best player I ever played with or against. He could slow a whole team down all by himself. I never saw a forward who could body-check the way he could. I remember one night we were playing the New York Americans, and by the end of the second period Schmidt had put three guys out of the game with his crushing checks. Finally, Flash Hollett, a teammate, nudged him on the bench. 'Milt, stop bodychecking, for Pete's sake, so we can get the damn game over with.'

"Schmidt often skated with his head down, so you'd think he was going to get clobbered. I mean, hockey's supposed to be a heads-up game, right? Then, all at once, he'd leave his feet and spring at the guy who was going to lay a big hit on him. Schmidt would nail the fellow before he was ready, and the guy's stick would go one way and his body the other. I never saw anyone like him. I've seen many a fellow he hit stagger back to the bench like a guy coming home from an Irish wedding.

"The thing is, Milt wasn't that big — maybe 175 pounds. It's funny — you'd go for a walk with the guy and he'd wear glasses and move so slowly you'd think he was a preacher. But as soon as the puck was dropped, he was a regular tornado. When they name the all-time best of the Bruins, old Milt has to be right at the top of the list."

Fiery Ted Lindsay agrees. The Hall of Fame left winger says, "Milt Schmidt was the greatest competitor I ever played against. He was a tremendous team player and a great skater. They can talk about the wonderful skaters in the game today all they want, but those people never saw Milt in his prime. And tough! Why, he would come down on the right side and if he didn't make it through he would turn and come down on the left side. And if you stopped him there, he'd grab the puck again and this time he'd come down the middle and skate right on top of you. And he would hurt you. There were some jarring collisions when he did that. It took a brave person to stand in his way."

Schmidt played 16 years with the Bruins, beginning in 1936–37 and retiring on Christmas Day 1954. He quit to become coach of the Bruins, a position he held until 1960–61. He returned as coach in 1962–63, and stayed behind the bench until 1965–66. He was later GM of the Bruins and the expansion Washington Capitals. In 776 regular-season games, he scored 229 goals and 575 points. He was elected to the Hockey Hall of Fame in 1961.

Mel Hill Earns a Nickname

In the mid 1930s, a 140-pound right winger from Glenboro, Manitoba, tried out unsuccessfully for the New York Rangers. The Rangers coaching staff said he was too light and didn't have enough talent, but what Mel Hill lacked in size and skill he made up for in clutch ability.

Hill was not discouraged by the Rangers' rejection — in fact, he expected it. He was, after all, a flyweight battling middleweights and heavyweights. He played senior hockey in Sudbury and minor-pro in Providence, put on a few pounds, and by 1938 he caught on as a regular with the Boston Bruins. At the season's end it still looked as if the rookie was not ready for the fast pace of the National Hockey League. Hill had managed only 10 goals in 46 games. Amid such take-charge teammates as Eddie Shore, Dit Clapper and Milt Schmidt, he seemed out of place. He considered himself fortunate indeed to hold down a spot on the Bruins roster.

When the Bruins rolled into the playoffs that season, Hill was determined to make some kind of mark. He figured that a couple of solid postseason performances would go a long way toward ensuring future employment. Boston met New York in the semifinals, and Hill thirsted for revenge on the club that had coldly turned him away a short time earlier. In game one, Hill scored a dramatic overtime goal to finish off a six-period marathon. In game two, Hill again scored in overtime to give the Bruins a 2–0 lead in the series. Boston took the third game in regulation time to grab a commanding lead in the seven-game series. But the Rangers, finally awake and furious, fought back with three straight victories to force a deciding game, which would be played at Boston Garden.

Game seven, a tight-checking, low-scoring affair, produced the most thrilling hockey of the series. The score was tied 1–1 going into overtime. Every Bruins fan in the building began to keep a close eye on Hill, hoping he would strike one more time with his overtime magic.

The first two overtime periods resolved nothing. Late in the third extra frame, Hill took a pass from Bill Cowley and slapped the puck past Rangers goalie Dave Kerr. Incredibly, he had done it again. His third overtime goal had captured the game *and* the series. By the next day, reporters and broadcasters across North America were referring to the previously unheralded John Melvin Hill, the little winger from Glenboro, as Mel "Sudden Death" Hill, the scoring hero of the Stanley Cup playoffs. The nickname would stick with him for the remainder of his life.

Hill's Bruins went on to win the Stanley Cup that year, defeating Toronto four games to one in the finals. When NHL President Frank Calder presented the Stanley Cup to Art Ross and the Bruins on the Boston Garden ice, the fans roared for Eddie Shore, who had suffered a broken nose and a black eye in an encounter with the Rangers' Muzz Patrick. The second-loudest ovation went to Mel Hill.

He pocketed $2,000 for the Stanley Cup win, and a special bonus of $1,000 for his three overtime goals. The bonus money matched his regular-season earnings of $3,000. Not only did Hill gain his revenge on the Rangers, he doubled his income in the process.

Mr. Zero Makes a Sensational Debut

When the Boston Bruins sold goalie Tiny Thompson to Detroit in 1938, some of the Bruins thought it was a shame, a boneheaded mistake. Thompson, a 10-year veteran, had won four Vezina Trophies and was extremely popular with the fans and his teammates. Defenceman Dit Clapper, Thompson's roommate, was so incensed when he heard of his pal's departure that he threatened to quit the game on the spot.

"Art Ross will never be able to replace Tiny," the skeptics agreed. "The man must be losing his marbles."

But the replacement Ross had in mind, a kid from Minnesota named Frank Brimsek who had been playing in Providence, made such a sensational debut in the Boston goal that, within days, fans and players alike agreed — grudgingly — that he was even better than Thompson.

In his third game against Montreal, Brimsek was unflappable, making a dozen brilliant saves. Still, the Bruins lost, 2–0. In his next seven starts, Brimsek embarked on a streak that astonished the hockey world. It began with a 5–0 shutout of the Blackhawks in Chicago. Two nights later, he again blanked Chicago, by a 2–0 margin. He followed up with a 3–0 shutout against the Rangers. In his seventh NHL game, he broke Thompson's record for shutout minutes when the Bruins edged Montreal, 3–2. And over the three games that followed, he was unbeatable, blanking the Canadiens, 1–0, the Red Wings, 2–0, and the Americans, 3–0.

By now, Boston fans has started calling Art Ross a genius and had picked out a proper nickname for their new goalie: Mr. Zero. It would stick with him the rest of his life.

After compiling six shutouts in seven games, Brimsek and the Bruins were themselves shut down, 1–0 against the Rangers.

But Brimsek's amazing start was no fluke. He went on to win the Calder Trophy that season, with 10 shutouts and a 1.59 goals-against average over 43 games. He also captured the Vezina Trophy and a berth on the First All-Star Team, and saw his name engraved on the Stanley Cup when the Bruins eliminated the Toronto Maple Leafs, four games to one, in the finals.

Wartime robbed Brimsek of two NHL seasons, 1943–44 and 1944–45, during which he tended guns instead of goal nets on a patrol boat in the South Pacific. He wasn't as sharp when he returned, because "walking those decks for two years was hard on my feet. My legs were never the same again after the war."

Harold Kaese, then a Boston columnist, wrote glowingly of Brimsek: "If all the pucks stopped by Frigid Frankie were stuck together, they would form a solid rubber hose, three inches in diameter, that would stretch from Boston to his home in Minnesota."

His home was in Virginia, Minnesota, five miles from the site of the U.S. Hockey Hall of Fame in Eveleth, where a plaque honours his memory and his achievements. He was also inducted into the Hockey Hall of Fame in Toronto in 1966.

Mr. Zero died of a heart attack while preparing to shovel snow on November 11, 1998.

Bruins Capture '41 Cup in Record Time

On April 12, 1941, the Boston Bruins established a new Stanley Cup record with an easy victory over Detroit in the Cup finals. The Bruins won in four straight games, an unprecedented accomplishment. And they did it without the services of Bill Cowley, their star player, the league's leading scorer and most valuable player in 1940–41. Cowley suffered a knee injury during the playoffs and took park in only two semifinal games.

The Bruins prepped for the playoffs by running up a 23-game undefeated streak during the regular season. After dropping a 2–0 decision to the Rangers on February 25, which ended the streak, the Bruins went undefeated in their remaining eight games.

The Bruins met Toronto in a semifinal playoff round and ousted the Leafs in seven games. Herb Cain had two game-winning goals and Mel Hill scored the winner in game seven, a 2–1 victory at the Boston Garden.

In the finals against Detroit, after the Red Wings suffered through three consecutive losses by scores of 3–2, 2–1 and 4–2, Red Wings fans showed little support for their team for game four at the Olympia. Only 8,125 showed up — half as many as witnessed the first two games at the Boston Garden. They were distressed when Red Wings enforcer Jimmy Orlando took a second-period penalty and the Bruins promptly pumped in two goals while he rested in the box. The final score was 3–1 for the Bruins. It was the second time in three years that Boston had captured the Cup, and the first time a best-of-seven series had been completed in the minimum number of games.

There was a brief presentation at centre ice following the game. Handshakes were exchanged and then the champions headed for the railroad station, where they caught the train back to Boston.

Talking with Topper

On the golf course, Jerry Toppazzini is a delightful companion. Over 18 holes in a charity tournament in Toronto he has lots of time to talk hockey — and his career with the Bruins (from

1952–53 through 1963–64, with brief stops in Detroit and Chicago).

"Did you know the Bruins alumni honoured me at their golf tournament in New Hampshire one summer?" he says. "All the old Bruins show up every year, and each year they pick one guy who they feel represented what a Bruin should be. It felt good when Milt Schmidt, a man I'd played with, a man who'd coached me, came across the room and shook my hand. 'Jerry, you really deserved it,' he said. 'You were one of the most honest players I ever worked with.' "

"Did you have to make a speech?" I ask.

He laughs. "No way. They know I'm a man of few words. Actually, they knew if they asked me to speak they'd never get me to sit down."

Jerry, you never won a Stanley Cup ring, did you?

"No, but there's an Englishman who may think I did."

What do you mean?

"Henri Richard and I were playing golf one day with the president of this big company, a man from London, England. He didn't know that Henri Richard had won 11 Stanley Cups with Montreal. In fact, he didn't know much about hockey at all. On one hole he said to me, 'Jerry, how many Stanley Cup teams did you play on?' And I said to him, 'Well, between Henri Richard and myself, it was 11.' "

Topper does have a way with words. I remind him that I interviewed him on TV at Boston Garden for CBS back in 1960. I asked my first question and never got to the second. He rambled on about the Bruins for at least three minutes and was still talking when the TV producer frantically began calling for a commercial break. Before throwing the cue, I said, "Jerry, you are without doubt the easiest player to interview I've ever encountered."

Now, almost 45 years after that interview, he tells me a story that's a complete surprise.

"I was at the NHL meetings in Montreal one summer — it was 1973 — and I didn't have a job in hockey. But I was hoping for something. The Bruins at the time were trying to hire Don Cherry as their new coach, but Cherry was reluctant to move to Boston. He owned 25 percent of the Rochester franchise and he was really popular there.

"I got a call from Lynn Patrick, who was then general manager in St. Louis. He said, 'Listen, Jerry, it's obvious Cherry is not going to Boston. You'd be ideal for that job. I spoke to Harry [Sinden] about you. Are you interested in coaching the Bruins?'

"I said, 'You kidding? Of course, I'm interested.'

"So Lynn called Harry, and that day I got word that Harry wanted to see me. I met with Harry and he told me Cherry wasn't taking the job, that he wanted me to take it. He told me not to say a word to anybody about the job for a couple of days. He told me he'd meet me in his office back in Boston. 'We'll work out all the details then,' he said. 'We'll arrange a press conference and you'll be the next coach of the Boston Bruins.'

"Boy, was I happy. Wow! Coach of the Bruins. Thank you very much, Harry.

"That night we went out for some drinks. Don Cherry was in the group and I started telling him how stupid he was not to take the Boston job. Hey, what do I care now that Harry's chosen me for the role? The more we drank the more I told him what a dummy he was to stay in Rochester.

"I was living in Springfield then, and the next morning I was driving back home with my good friend Walt Atanas. At noon, we stopped at some roadside joint and went inside for a bite to eat. Over coffee, Walt says, 'Jerry, I'm worried about you. No job, no prospects. I wish I could help you land something for the winter.'

"Of course, I hadn't told Walt about my conversation with Harry. I'd promised not to breathe a word of it. I just grinned and said, 'Walt, don't worry about Topper. I always land on my feet. I'm going to be just fine. You're going to be reading a lot about me in the next few days.'

"I was about to order a sandwich when I looked up at the TV set on the wall and there was a sports bulletin. The announcer says, 'Don Cherry has just signed a contract to coach the Boston Bruins.'

"Well, shit. I turned to Walter and I said, 'Walter, on the other hand, I might be able to use all the help I can get this winter.'

"And that's a true story."

When I stop laughing, I ask Jerry if there was a single perform-ance as a Bruin that stands out in his memory.

He grins. "Well, not many people know this but I'm the only player in history to score four goals in a game — one that ended in a 2–2 tie."

What?

He begins to laugh. "One night I scored two goals against Montreal and two goals against my own team. The last two were accidental, of course. But that's one helluva record, isn't it?"

Did you have a rocky start to your career with Boston?

"Hell, no. I had a nervous start because I was called up from Hershey and the first game was in Montreal — at the Forum. I'd never seen the inside of the Forum and now I was going to be up against the Rocket, Doug Harvey, Jacques Plante, Boom Boom Geoffrion and all those great players. Sure, I was nervous.

"And then our coach, Lynn Patrick, took me aside and said, 'Jerry, I want you to check the Rocket tonight. Make sure he doesn't score.' So I checked the Rocket and I kept him off the score sheet. Meanwhile, I got a goal and an assist, and we won the game 4–2. Now, there were 30 seconds left to play and by then I was pretty cocky. So I skated up to the Rocket and I said to him, 'I don't know why I'm checking you. You should be checking me.'

"Geez, his eyes lit up and his hair stood straight up in the air and he said, 'You flash in the pan!' For the rest of his life he called me 'flash in the pan.'"

"I just thought of another record I might hold," he continues. "It was my second or third game in the NHL and we were playing in Chicago. Sugar Jim Henry, our goalie, took a shot in the nose, and both his eyes closed tight. There were about nine minutes to play and Hal Laycoe said to our coach, 'I'll finish the game in goal.' Lynn Patrick said, 'No, you're too valuable. You might get hurt. Toppazzini, you play in goal.'

"So I finished the game and didn't give up a goal. Stopped some pretty good shots, too. I actually played in three different games in goal. Must have played 15, 16 minutes in all. And never was scored on. I made a brilliant save one night. Frank Martin let a shot go from the blue line and I made a sensational glove save. I still haven't seen the shot, but I stopped it.

"Another funny thing happened to me during my final season in hockey. After a game, a father approached me and asked me to sign his son's program. While I'm signing, the kid looks up at me and says, 'How old are you, Mr. Toppazzini?' Well, I was 35 years old, but I said to the kid, 'Son, how old do you think I am?' He stared up at me and said, 'Maybe 45?'

"I said, 'Son, you're out by 10 years.'

"And he said, 'You mean you're 55?' "

You're a funny man, Topper.

"Me? You want funny, you should talk to Leo Labine. He had the guys in stitches at the golf tournament."

The NHL's First Black Player

They called him the Jackie Robinson of hockey when the Boston Bruins called him up on January 18, 1958. He was Willie O'Ree, a fleet left winger from Fredericton, New Brunswick, and the first black player in the NHL.

O'Ree was given a chance that had been denied another black player a few years earlier. A Toronto youth, Herb Carnegie, should have been an NHLer. Everyone said so. Toronto owner Conn Smythe once told him, "Herb, I'd sign you in a minute if I could turn you white." So Willie O'Ree, and not Carnegie, became the player who broke the NHL's colour barrier.

O'Ree was born in 1935 and he began skating at the age of three. In junior hockey, playing for the Kitchener-Waterloo Canucks, he was struck in the face by a puck and lost 95 percent of the vision in one eye. He turned pro in 1956–57 with the Quebec Aces, signing for $3,500. He neglected to tell his employers he was legally blind.

O'Ree's first stint with the Bruins amounted to a mere two games, a home-and-home series with Montreal in January 1958. He recalls, "We beat the Habs at the Forum, 3–0, and back in Boston the following night, they beat us 6–2. That was it — my two-game trial. By Monday, I was back in Quebec City, playing for the Aces, coached by Punch Imlach. I waited three and a half years before Boston called again."

During the 1960–61 season, O'Ree was back with the Bruins, this time for 43 games. He scored four goals and added 10 assists.

The major difference between the NHL and the Quebec league was the number of racial slurs hurled at him by fans and other players. One night in Chicago, he struck a Blackhawk over the head with his stick, and a dozen fans sitting nearby threatened to lynch him.

"It started when Eric Nesterenko gave me a butt-end — right in the face. I spit out a couple of teeth and then nailed him over the head with my stick. The referee threw both of us out of the game, but I needed police protection to get to the Boston dressing room. Those Chicago fans were livid. They were ready to murder me.

"They were mean to me in places like Detroit and New York, too. But never in Boston. I'll never forget how my teammates there — men like Johnny Bucyk, Doug Mohns, Charlie Burns and Don McKenney — took care of me. They accepted me totally. All of them had class."

What did the first black player in the NHL earn? Not much. O'Ree recalls signing with the Bruins for an annual salary of $3,500 — precisely his salary in Quebec — plus the promise of a $200 bonus if he scored 20 goals.

And his best memory of the big league? "That's easy," he said. "I scored the winning goal against the Canadiens on January 1, 1961 — New Year's Day. I'll never forget the reception I got from the Boston fans when that puck went in." The ovation lasted for more than two minutes, a well-earned salute to the first black player to score a goal in the NHL.

At the time, it appeared that Willie was on his way. Milt Schmidt called him "one of the fastest skaters in the league." Lynn Patrick took him aside after the season and said, "Go home and have a good summer, kid. We'll see you in training camp."

Six weeks later, a reporter called. "Willie, what do you think about the deal?"

"Deal? What deal?"

"You've been sold to Montreal."

"Oh, no," groaned Willie. "Montreal is loaded with wingers. I'll never make that team."

And he never did. But he was a minor-league star for years, and he twice won the Western Hockey League's scoring crown, in 1964 and 1969.

"To this day a lot of people don't realize I played for 20 seasons while blind in one eye," he says.

On January 17, 1998, during ceremonies that were part of the NHL All-Star Game, the league honoured Willie O'Ree for his pioneering efforts and named him director of youth development for the NHL/USA Hockey Diversity Task Force. He now travels all over North America, helping kids from various backgrounds with their hockey skills and other life skills.

When Laycoe and the Rocket Collided

Hal Laycoe had always liked Rocket Richard. Before joining the Boston Bruins during the 1950–51 season, Laycoe had played for the Montreal Canadiens. He and Richard often played tennis during the off-season, and they got along splendidly.

But during a game between the Habs and Bruins at Boston Garden on March 13, 1955, any goodwill between them was lost forever in a few violent seconds. "I hate to rehash the incident," Laycoe would say in retirement. "There was never anything like it. Ever."

Before his death at age 75 on April 28, 1998, Laycoe told Tom Hawthorn of the Victoria *Times Colonist*, "The Rocket started the melee by pitchforking me in the face with his stick. I wore glasses, and that's what saved me from a bad cut. I reached up, and *ding*, I got him right in the back of the head. I remember Rocket touched his head. He saw blood, and boy, did he come at me."

At that point, Laycoe dropped his gloves and prepared to duke it out with the fiery Richard. But the Rocket had something else in mind. He swung his stick, nicked Laycoe's ear with it, and crashed it down on the Boston player's shoulder. The stick splintered. Then Richard grabbed another stick and broke it over Laycoe's back. Finally, he picked up a third stick and attacked Laycoe, who later said, "I was standing there like John L. Sullivan, fending off sticks with my hands and arms. The Rocket was relentless."

When linesman Cliff Thompson intervened, Richard punched the official twice.

The latter attack prompted NHL President Clarence Campbell to suspend the Montreal superstar for the rest of the season (three games) and the playoffs, a penalty that infuriated Richard's countless fans. When Campbell attended the Canadiens' next home game against Detroit, he was attacked by fans and pelted with debris. A tear gas container was thrown and exploded inside the Forum, the building was evacuated, and Detroit, leading 4–1, was awarded the victory. As the fans streamed out of the Forum, an angry mob indulged in a frenzy of looting and vandalism along St. Catherine Street. It was the blackest hour in Montreal hockey history.

Richard's suspension cost him his only chance to win the NHL scoring crown. Teammate Boom Boom Geoffrion overtook him in the final week of the season to edge him, 75 points to 74.

Even without the Rocket, the demoralized Canadiens were able to oust the Bruins in five games in the semifinal round. Laycoe was vilified by Habs fans in the games played at the Forum and was told that the Montreal police were concerned about death threats against the Bruins defenceman. "I sat on the bench with a big Number 10 on my back," Laycoe told Hawthorn. "If there was a nut with a gun in the stands, he'd have had a pretty good target."

In the finals, the Habs lost to Detroit, four games to three. With the Rocket in the lineup, they might have won the final series. If so, they would have embarked on a string of six consecutive Stanley Cup triumphs, since they went on to rule as hockey's greatest team from 1956 through 1960.

Undoubtedly, Montrealers with long memories still swear the loss in '55 was all Hal Laycoe's fault.

Horvath Battles Hull for the Art Ross Trophy

On March 20, 1960, the Bruins and Blackhawks met at the Garden in the final match of the season. Bruins centre Bronco Horvath, the playmaker on the prolific Uke Line, had grabbed the hockey spotlight and was on the verge of snaring the Art Ross Trophy as NHL scoring champion. With 60 minutes to play in the regular season, Horvath led Chicago superstar Bobby Hull by a single point in the race for the Ross.

120

Horvath, who had never been in such lofty company before and never would be again, knew it might be his only chance to capture one of the NHL's top prizes. At age 30, he desperately wanted to beat the 21-year-old Hull and win that trophy.

But his hopes took a header shortly after the opening face-off. Midway through the first period, Boston defenceman Bob Armstrong wired a shot from the blue line that hit Bronco squarely in the jaw. Horvath flopped to the ice, unconscious. He was carried off and rushed by ambulance to the hospital. On the way, Horvath recovered sufficiently to begin screaming, "Go back! Go back! I want to play! I want to play!"

At the hospital, he refused to take off his uniform while doctors hovered over him. X-rays were taken, and there was a delay while the medics examined the film. They finally concluded that Bronco's jaw was severely bruised, but not broken.

Bronco bolted for the door. He was rushed back to the Garden, threw on his skates and played the final few minutes of the third period. By then, his slim lead in the scoring race had evaporated. While he was away, Bobby Hull had recorded two points in a 5–5 tie to win his first scoring crown.

A disconsolate Horvath had to settle for the runner-up spot. And he would never challenge again. The following year he slumped to 15 goals and 30 points — 50 fewer than his banner season. He often wondered what might have been if his teammate hadn't kayoed him in that final game of the 1959–60 season.

A hockey oddity earlier in that season also contributed to Horvath's missing out on the scoring crown. Playing against the Blackhawks on November 8, Bronco was tripped from behind on a breakaway. Referee Dalt McArthur awarded a penalty shot to the Bruins, but in a bizarre interpretation of the rules, he allowed the *Blackhawks* to nominate a Bruin to take the shot. Chicago coach Rudy Pilous chose a utility forward named Larry Leach to take the free shot, and he missed.

McArthur should have allowed the Bruins to pick the shooter. Had he done so, Horvath would have been their choice. The missed opportunity may have cost Horvath a tie with Hull in the scoring race. McArthur's glaring gaffe cost him his job; his contract was not renewed.

Unbelievable! A Defenceman Wins the Scoring Crown

Prior to the 1969–70 season, hockey people and fans alike thought it impossible for a defenceman to win the individual scoring title in the NHL. By the end of that season, Boston's multi-talented Bobby Orr had changed their thinking by changing the face of hockey — and the role of the defenceman — forever.

With 120 points, 21 more than teammate Phil Esposito, Orr shattered the long-standing myth that defencemen were supposed to be guardians, not goal scorers. Coaches of the day expected their blueliners to stay at home, to know their place. But Orr was a mold breaker, a visionary. Over the next four years he finished second in the scoring race three times and third once (all four times behind Esposito).

Then, in 1974–75, he zoomed right to the top again, capturing his second Art Ross Trophy with 135 points. No defenceman has won the scoring title since. Orr's fantastic point production proved that he was a gifted offensive player, and it could be argued that his offensive stats overshadowed his defensive skills. How good was he from the blue line to his own net? One of Orr's most amazing stats is his career plus-minus rating. Over his 657-game career, Bobby amassed an amazing aggregate rating of plus-597. In 1970–71, he was an astonishing plus-124.

A Night for the Chief

During the 1967–68 season, the Boston Bruins held a night for one of their most popular players, veteran left winger Johnny Bucyk. Bucyk had played spectacular hockey for the Bruins for the past decade as a member of the Uke Line. Now it appeared as though he was beginning to lose his touch: his goal production had slipped to 18 in 1966–67. Perhaps he should consider retirement while he was still on top, thought some observers. Bucyk was given a new car, an outboard motor and other gifts, as well as much praise for serving the Bruins so well and for so long. At the end of the on-ice ceremony, it seemed that everyone expected Bucyk to announce that he was in his final year of hockey.

But that was never his intention. At the age of 32, Bucyk had no plans to buy a rocking chair, to fish from his new boat or to whack golf balls into the sunset. In 1967–68 he recorded a 30-goal season. Then, playing as if rejuvenated, he scored 24, 31 and, incredibly, 51 goals at the age of 35. He became the only player of that vintage to score 50 or more goals in a season, and in the 33 seasons since then, no one older has ever scored 50.

Even then, Bucyk gave no thought to retirement. Five years after that 51-goal campaign, he connected for 36 goals. Only when he turned 43, more than a decade after his night, did he decide it was time to step aside — after a "disappointing" season in which he scored a mere 20 goals. By that time, the car and the boat's motor had long since worn out. During those years, Johnny helped the Bruins to a pair of Stanley Cup victories and had received several individual honours, including a pair of Lady Byng trophies. He had scored an incredible 319 goals since his "retirement party" and 556 in all, making him the fourth-leading scorer in NHL history at that time.

When it comes to durability, the man they called the Chief ranks right up there with Gordie Howe.

Espo Almost Missed Out

It's difficult to believe that one of hockey's greatest scorers was such a late bloomer. Phil Esposito, with more than 700 career goals in the NHL, was 19 years old before he caught on with a Junior A club. Espo, who led all NHL scorers on five occasions, almost got shuffled onto the discard pile as a teenager.

As an 18-year-old, he failed a tryout with the Chicago Blackhawks' Junior A club in St. Catharines, Ontario. He was told to drive a few miles down the road, to Niagara Falls, where the Bruins had a junior affiliate. Maybe there would be room for him on that team, he was told.

Hap Emms, the manager in Niagara Falls, took one look at the gangly youngster lumbering around the ice and said, "Kid, if you can't make it with St. Catharines, we don't want you here."

"Hap could see that I was a terrible skater," Esposito recalls. "Geez, my brother Tony was a better skater than I was, and he was a goalie."

The dejected centreman finally caught on with a Junior B team in Sarnia, making $15 a week. It's a wonder his big-league dreams weren't squashed then and there. Only one or two rookies made the leap to the six-team NHL each year, amid the fierce competition for a handful of job openings. Junior B graduates? They weren't even considered.

Espo's skating improved in Sarnia, and he finished second in the scoring race to a future NHL player and coach, Terry Crisp. His performance earned him another chance with St. Catharines in 1961, but the critics were still around and the jibes didn't stop.

"Hey, Fatso!" were among the first words he heard from coach Rudy Pilous in training camp. "Lose 20 pounds and I'll keep you around."

Espo lost the weight and gained a spot on the roster. After scoring 32 goals in 49 games, he broke his wrist during the OHA playoffs, but that didn't prevent him from turning pro with his hometown team, the Soo Thunderbirds. The next season, however, the team moved to Syracuse, where it sometimes played before 50 people. The franchise then transferred to St. Louis in midseason.

Phil couldn't shake the feeling that he'd been branded a bush leaguer and would probably remain one for the rest of his career. But despite his misgivings, he ran up 90 points, earning him a look with the parent Chicago Blackhawks. At training camp it was concluded that he needed further seasoning, but when he scored 80 points in only 43 games with St. Louis, they gave him a second chance.

Espo was shocked when he discovered how miserly the Hawks were when it came to wages. "Their offer was so low, I almost quit the game," he says. "I knew I could make as much driving a truck back home in the Soo."

Still, the game was fun — more fun than driving a truck — so he decided to stay with it. He turned in seasons of 23, 27 and 21 goals and threw passes onto the stick of a kid named Bobby Hull, who converted those passes into 39-, 52- and 54-goal seasons.

Espo began to feel he had become a fixture in Chicago. He began to feel appreciated, especially when he talked management into laying out considerably more money for his services. Then, during the summer of 1967, after recording a career-high 61 points, he was shocked to hear he had been traded to Boston.

"Geez, it was the last place I wanted to go," he says. "The Bruins were awful — always in last place. They were tail-enders for six of the last seven years and second-last the other year.

"And the Hawks showed no class in announcing the deal. They left it up to Don Murphy, the publicity guy, to tell me. He never did get to me, so he left a message with my wife. I made sure the folks in Sault Ste. Marie knew all about it. I went on the radio myself and said, 'Hi, folks. Here's a hockey scoop for you. Phil Esposito has just been traded to Boston, along with Ken Hodge and Freddie Stanfield. In return, the Hawks will get Gilles Marotte, Pit Martin and goalie Jack Norris. This is no hoax.' "

Later, still angry with the Hawks, he left for Boston, determined to turn the moribund hockey team into a winner. And with the help of Hodge and Stanfield, Bobby Orr and Johnny Bucyk, that's exactly what he did.

Today, almost four decades later, whenever people discuss the most lopsided deals in NHL history, the Esposito-to-Boston trade is at or near the top of the list. And the verdict is always the same: big advantage to Boston.

The Green-Maki Incident

For some reason, the preseason exhibition games in the autumn of 1969 were rampant with brawls. The most serious flare-up occurred on September 21, during a game in Ottawa between the Boston Bruins and St. Louis Blues.

Early in the game, Ted Green, a veteran Bruins defenceman, and Wayne Maki, a swift but unspectacular winger with the Blues, collided in the Boston zone. Linesman Ron Finn, officiating in only his fourth NHL game, was close by when they bumped — close enough to feel the breeze when Green turned and swung his stick viciously at Maki, missing him by a few inches. Maki retaliated instantly with a stick swing of his own, catching Green flush on his unprotected head. Green dropped to the ice and lay there, bleeding and barely conscious.

"I could see right away that Green was badly hurt," said the late Dan Kelly, the longtime broadcaster for the St. Louis Blues. "When he tried to get up, his face was contorted and his legs began to buckle under him. It was dreadful. I almost became physically ill watching him struggle because I knew this was very, very serious."

As Green fell back, unable to help himself, Finn and the other officials waved for the trainer and a doctor. They, too, knew instantly that Green was in serious trouble.

Bobby Orr leaped off the bench and smacked Maki. Then Garnet "Ace" Bailey belted him. But the sight of Green lying on the ice knocked the will to fight out of all the players.

Bruins centreman Derek Sanderson, who was sidelined with a sore knee, was watching from the stands. He recalls saying to himself, "Here's the toughest guy on skates and he's in big, big trouble." He also recalls a conversation with Green before the game. "You won't see me hitting anyone out there tonight," the blueliner said. "I'm still negotiating a new contract. When I'm signed, then I'll hit."

Green was rushed to hospital, where surgeons operated on his brain for five hours. A few days later, more surgery followed, including the insertion of a metal plate in his skull.

After the game, Ottawa police charged Green and Maki with assault. The NHL suspended both players and fined them $300 each. In retrospect, the suspensions and fines seem ludicrous, although a league official at the time called them "the stiffest in league annals." Maki was suspended for 30 days, while Green was to sit out 13 games "if and when he returns to hockey."

Weeks later, both men were exonerated after testifying in an Ottawa courtroom. A year later, Green made what was called "a miraculous comeback" and played effectively for the Bruins. In 1971–72 he was a key performer on Boston's Stanley Cup–winning team. Then he jumped to the WHA and played until 1978–79. When he left the game, he spoke out against violence in hockey and asked the owners to put an end to it.

In the 1980s and '90s, Green had a long association with the Edmonton Oilers as an assistant and head coach, and was later an assistant with the New York Rangers.

Even though the incident, which came a little more than a year after the death of Bill Masterton of brain injuries suffered during a league game, shocked most NHL players, they still weren't prepared to adopt helmets to protect themselves from similar injuries. Boston coach Milt Schmidt went out and bought two dozen helmets, which he issued to his players. When he showed up for practice the next day, none of the Bruins were wearing them. He ordered them to don the headgear or leave the ice. All eyes turned to Bobby Orr, who, his head down, skated slowly off the ice. His teammates followed, Schmidt decided not to make an issue of it, and the helmets were put in storage.

Ironically, Maki's NHL career was cut short by a brain tumor, discovered while he was playing for the Vancouver Canucks in 1972. He died in the spring of 1974.

Espo's Wild Ride

It was a Ron Harris check that put Phil Esposito and the Boston Bruins out of the 1973 playoffs. Harris, a tough Ranger defenceman, sent Esposito to a Boston hospital, where doctors treated him for torn knee ligaments.

The next morning, when his teammates came to his room to visit, they told him they were planning a windup party at a nearby tavern.

"Gee, I wish I could make it," Espo sighed, "but the doctors tell me I'm going to be in here for a few more days."

"Oh, you're going to make it, all right," laughed Bobby Orr. "We're coming back to get you."

That evening, the Bruins paid Phil another visit. This time, they had a plan. They distracted the nurses on duty with a wild story about a man outside who had reportedly been riddled with bullets. The nurses scurried around looking for the wounded man while the Bruins went to work. Orr and Dallas Smith wheeled Esposito's bed out of the room and pushed it down the corridor to the service elevator.

Down on the main floor, they ran into a problem. The metal railing on Espo's hospital bed made it too wide for the exit ramp. The players quickly dislodged the railing and tossed it aside. They were on their way to the party.

The Bruins hurried down the street, some pushing, some pulling on the bed and its famous patient.

As they reached an intersection, Orr shouted, "Signal a left, Phil. Signal a left!" And Esposito's arm shot out from under the sheets to make the appropriate gesture.

Arriving safely at the party, Esposito became the centre of attention. His mates poured him a little refreshment to fortify him for the return trip.

The party over, the Bruins wheeled Esposito back to the hospital, where they found staff members milling about. One of them had discovered the broken railing and had compiled a bill, amounting to hundreds of dollars, for damage to hospital property.

"Who's going to look after this?" the man asked.

Orr and Smith examined the bill, then looked down at Esposito, who had nodded off to sleep. Gently, they slipped the invoice into his pyjama pocket.

Don Cherry's Memories of Orr

Don Cherry was one of the most popular coaches the Bruins ever hired, the only Boston coach to win the Jack Adams Trophy as NHL coach of the year. He captured that award in 1975–76, after his rookie season behind the bench. When Harry Sinden fired him after a dramatic playoff loss to Montreal in 1979, his Boston record stood at 231–105–64.

You wanna know about Bobby Orr? How long is this book? I got so many Bobby Orr stories.

I know this will really surprise you, but at first I couldn't stand Bobby Orr. That's right. He stood for everything I was against. I was a big defenceman, and I would see him on TV sometimes, and I would think that this guy isn't a defenceman; he doesn't stay back. This guy is a rover. He's all over the place.

I was playing for the Rochester Americans and we played an American League game in Boston one night. Well, we had a practice the next morning at Boston Garden, right after the Bruins practice. So I walked in early, and you have to remember that I've seen Gordie, I've seen the Rocket, I've seen 'em all. I'm like an old horse trainer — you can't fool me. So I walked in and I saw Orr practicing and my mouth fell open. I could not believe it. It must have been like Sunny Jim Fitzsimmons when he saw Seabiscuit for the first time. I was mesmerized by the things he was doing. I had never seen anything like it and he was just jerkin' around. Nobody ever skated like him or handled the puck like him and he was just jerkin' around.

Little did I know that four or five years later that I'd be coaching him. And you know what happened when I was coaching the Bruins? If we fell behind, we always knew Orr would be back to pop a couple in, and if we were ahead, he'd be there to slow the game right down. When he was killing a penalty, he could kill the whole penalty himself. He was incredible! You saw these guys chasin' him. He would go in behind the net, and when they chased him in behind the net, he scooted out in front! He made monkeys of people.

The best goal I ever saw him score was when we were playing the Flames and Bobby had the puck behind our net. No one would go in after him because they knew he'd make them chase him out in front and they would never catch him. So they left him alone because they were tired of chasing him all game. Bobby came out from behind the net, real slow, and started up the wing. He got to just inside their blue line and he began to pick it up — you know, he had four different speeds. Then, for some dumb reason, they all ran at him and he sifted by them all. Now he went behind their net and their goaltender made a stab at him and kinda fell down! Bobby slipped out in front and back-handed the puck into the net while they were all laying on the ice.

And the type of guy he is, he's not a hot dog, he puts his head between his legs as if to say, "Sorry, guys." And if you look at every goal he scored, it was almost as if he would be saying under his breath, "Sorry, guys. I really didn't mean to embarrass you like that."

Now, this is another true story. I know it's hard to believe, but it's true. The Bruins had flown out to L.A. and we were going on the ice to get a little sweat, shoot a few pucks, just get the jet lag worked out. Carol Vadnais was the first guy out, and it was dark because they didn't have all of the lights on. So he was the first one out and I was the second. We were just skating around, waiting for the guys. Then Bobby came out.

Now, there were a bunch of pucks in the corner, just behind the goal line, and Bobby took a puck, flicked it in the air, and didn't even look at the net at the far end, just flicked it and it landed in the top corner. Almost 200 feet away!

I didn't know if I saw what I thought I saw, so I went up to Vadnais and I said, "Did you see what he did?" And Carol said, "Geez. Grapes, I'm glad you said something, because I don't believe it either."

Orr was supernatural.

Serge Savard said it best when he said, "There are players, there are stars, there are superstars, and then there is Bobby Orr." Bobby Clarke said he thought they should have had another league for him to play in and Terry O'Reilly once said they should pass him around from team to team each year — just to keep things fair.

The Irascible Irishman

One of the most colourful players ever to wear the Bruins jersey during the 1970s and '80s was Terry O'Reilly. With an Irish name and a hell-bent style of play, along with some scoring talent, O'Reilly became an overnight hometown favourite. The fans named him "Taz," after the Tasmanian Devil, a cartoon character who trampled everything in his path.

Off the ice, O'Reilly displayed a quiet, caring, intellectual side. He volunteered for charity work in the community. He loved good books and collecting antiques. Family was important to him.

When Don Cherry's son Tim underwent a kidney transplant, O'Reilly was one of the first of several Bruins to donate blood.

On the ice, he was Cherry's kind of player, skating recklessly up and down his wing, crashing and bashing anyone who dared to get in his path. If an altercation broke out, he never backed down. When challenged, he often let his opponent take the first shot. Or he'd let them get set to take it. Cherry would shake his head and say, "O'Reilly, you're too nice to be known as a tough guy."

His style of play sometimes landed him in trouble. During the seventh and deciding game in the 1982 conference semifinals against Quebec, he was ejected from the game for punching a referee. The Bruins lost the game and the series. After a review of the tapes, O'Reilly was suspended for the first 10 games of the following season by NHL executive vice president Brian O'Neill.

In a game against Minnesota on October 26, 1977, O'Reilly received a minor penalty for tripping. He appeared to deliberately bump into referee Denis Morel to argue the call. Then he threw his gloves at the official in disgust and skated off the ice. Morel ejected him from the game and the league followed up with a three-game suspension.

In 1977–78, O'Reilly became the first player in NHL history to finish among the top 10 scorers and collect more than 200 penalty minutes. Only two other players have matched his feat — Kevin Stevens in 1991–92 and Brendan Shanahan in 1993–94.

During his career, he amassed 606 points (204 goals, 402 assists) and a staggering 2,095 minutes in penalties in 891 regular-season games — still a club record. He ranks eighth overall among Boston's all-time point scorers in regular-season play.

In 1986, after his playing career ended, O'Reilly was invited to coach the Bruins and he held the position for three seasons. He finished with a respectable record of 115 wins, 86 losses and 26 ties in 227 regular-season games.

Nobody calls him Taz anymore. The name only seemed fitting when he had skates on his feet and a piece of lumber in his hands.

Cashman: A Ruffian and a Rogue

In past years, the Boston Bruins have employed some wild characters. But despite the antics of Derek Sanderson, Mike Walton and others, the zaniest — if not the meanest and toughest — member of those teams they called the Big Bad Bruins was Wayne Cashman.

"I knew I'd never be a 50-goal scorer, so I spent my career doing what had to be done," Cashman told *Sports Illustrated* in the twilight of his career.

He played left wing on one of Boston's most prolific lines, with Phil Esposito at centre and Ken Hodge on right wing. He was counted on to do the dirty work in the corners and get the puck, by fair means or foul, to Espo in the slot. Goaltender Gerry Cheevers says, "Cash was the greatest of all the guys from our era when it came to digging in the corners and along the boards. And if someone gave Orr or Espo a cheap shot, Cashman would be there in an instant, throwing punches, exacting revenge."

When he retired in 1983, Cashman had served 1,041 penalty minutes to rank third among Boston sinners behind Terry O'Reilly and Keith Crowder. At 38, he had served the Bruins well in 1,027 games, second only to Johnny Bucyk's club record of 1,436. When veterans Serge Savard of the Winnipeg Jets and Carol Vadnais of the New Jersey Devils bowed out of NHL hockey a few days before Cashman's final game, it made the Bruin left winger the last survivor of the six-team NHL.

Off the ice, he was a master of mischief. Once, he broke his foot while swinging on a chandelier. In Los Angeles one night, when the anthem singer was about to perform before a critical playoff game, Cashman spoiled the soloist's rendition by impishly cutting the microphone cord with his skate. And in 1970, after the Bruins won the Stanley Cup, he played traffic cop during the celebrations that followed, standing in a Boston intersection and waving cars in all directions until there was a mammoth snarl.

Reluctantly, the cops arrested him and brought him to the station, where he was told he could make one phone call. Did he phone his lawyer? No, his call was to a restaurant — for an order of Chinese food.

Cashman, like millions of others, was stunned to learn on the night of November 7, 1975, that the Bruins had traded his best pal Phil Esposito, along with Vadnais, to the hated New York Rangers in exchange for Brad Park, Jean Ratelle and Joe Zanussi. He organized a going-away party for his former mates in a Vancouver hotel room, and before it was over the players had done $2,000 worth of damage.

The next season, he assumed the Bruins captaincy and the high jinks became less prevalent. Johnny Bucyk, who had been wearing the "C," returned from an injury, saw the leadership that Cashman was providing, and told him to keep the job. Manager Harry Sinden would say, "I don't think I could have dreamed of Cashman becoming such a leader."

He was durable enough to play in more than 1,000 games and with 793 points he ranks sixth on the list of Boston's all-time scorers.

A great player? Yes. A different kind of guy? You bet.

Even as a child he was unpredictable. One day, on the family farm near Kingston, Ontario, where he grew up, he acquired a new pair of skates. Told by his parents not to wear them outside until the weather warmed up, young Cash waited until his parents went off somewhere. Then he opened all the windows, hooked up a hose and flooded the kitchen floor with an inch of water. "When it freezes," he reasoned, "I'll skate inside."

Red Wings

Big Jim Norris Steps In

James D. Norris, the czar of the multimillion-dollar Norris Grain empire, was a benevolent despot who loved hockey. He even had a small rink built on his estate in Lake Forest, Illinois, where his kids learned to play and enjoy the game. If someone interviewed for a job as the Norris chauffeur or butler, one of the first questions asked was, "Can you skate?" because their duties included playing shinny with the Norris offspring.

For a couple of seasons, Norris sponsored an outlaw team in Chicago that competed with the NHL's Blackhawks for fan support. In 1932, when he noticed that the Detroit franchise was floundering financially, Norris stepped in and bought the club. The franchise, established in 1926 and known as the Cougars, had been playing its home games across the river in Windsor, Ontario, until a new home, the Olympia, was completed in 1927. Prior to the 1930–31 season, the name of the team was changed to the Falcons. Jack Adams, an employee since day one, was the coach and general manager.

After taking over, Norris called Adams into his office and barked, "You've got one year to make something of this. You're on probation. I'll give you the money, you build me a team."

Adams grinned and said, "Yes, sir." He knew he was talking to a man whose personality and hockey ambitions matched his own.

"Another thing we're gonna do," added Norris, "is change the name of this team. Forget about names of animals and birds like Cougars and Falcons. From now on, it's going to be the Red Wings."

Norris, a Montreal native, had grown up following the famed Winged Wheelers of the Montreal Amateur Athletic Association, the same team to which the Stanley Cup was first awarded in 1893. He liked the image of a wheel, and felt it would be an ideal logo for Detroit, the automotive capital of the world.

Dipping into the immense Norris fortune, Adams began building a hockey dynasty. His team tied for the American Division title in 1932–33, won it outright a year later, and captured the Stanley Cup in 1936, defeating Toronto three games to one.

His team suffered an extraordinary number of injuries in 1936–37 but still managed to finish atop the NHL standings. Going into the finals against the New York Rangers, Adams had only a dozen healthy players. Out with a broken leg was Larry Aurie, who had led the league in goals with 23, while Vezina Trophy–winning goalkeeper Normie Smith had a severe elbow injury. The Rangers turned down Adams' request for permission to fill some roster slots with players from other teams.

"Why should we grant such a request?" asked Rangers manager Lester Patrick. "We'd be jeopardizing our own Cup chances." Despite the manpower shortage, Adams' team stubbornly made its way to a Cup victory in five games, becoming the first NHL club to win both the league title and the Stanley Cup in consecutive years. By then, Adams' "probation" had long since been served.

The Strange Career of Norman Smith

Normie Smith was having a good first season in the NHL, until he ran into Howie Morenz — or rather, Morenz ran into *him*. The rookie goaltender had broken in with the Montreal Maroons in 1931 and played 20 games before Morenz, the dazzling star of the Canadiens, was sent flying into the Maroons net, crashing into Smith and injuring him so badly that he sat out the rest of the season.

Smith spent the next two seasons in the minors, learning how to handle rebounds. He also discovered that wearing a peaked cap over his eyes cut down the glare from the overhead lights, allowing him to follow the play more easily. In 1934, Jack Adams signed him. At first, Adams was not satisfied with Smith's play and brought in John Ross Roach to take over for the second half of the season.

Smith got a second chance in 1935–36 and was in the Detroit goal for one of the most remarkable hockey games ever played. After the Wings and Maroons finished atop their respective divisions (Detroit with 56 points, the Maroons with 54), they met in the first round of the Stanley Cup playoffs. On March 24, 1936, Smith and Lorne Chabot were the opposing goaltenders when the teams faced off at the Montreal Forum before more than 9,000 fans. Many of those in the crowd would not be around for the end of the match; they would be back home and fast asleep when the Wings' Mud Bruneteau scored the game's only goal at 2:25 a.m., at 16:30 of the *sixth* overtime period. Norm Smith recorded a shutout in the longest NHL game ever played — 176 minutes and 30 seconds.

Smith would later reveal that Jack Adams supplied his boys with a few sips of brandy between periods to give them energy. Later still, the editors of the *Guinness Book of World Records* sanctioned the 92 saves Smith made in the game as a world record.

Smith's mastery over the Maroons continued into game two of the series, played two nights later on the same ice surface, when he chalked up his second consecutive shutout as the Red Wings outscored the Maroons 3–0.

In game three, back in Detroit, the Maroons' Gus Marker finally put a puck past Smith in the first period, ending the shutout streak at 248 minutes and 32 seconds. But Johnny Sorrell and Scotty Bowman (not to be confused with the legendary coach of the same name) replied for the Wings, who won the game 2–1, ending the series.

Detroit went on to defeat Toronto in the finals, three games to one, and skated off with the Stanley Cup.

The next year, thanks largely to Smith, who won the Vezina Trophy, the Red Wings repeated as league champions. In the playoffs that spring, Smith suffered an elbow injury in game three against the Canadiens and was forced to the sidelines. He came back for game five and was in the net for a Detroit win that required 52 minutes of overtime.

"Rocket" Richard joined the Canadiens for the 1942-43 season. He was the first player to reach 50 goals in a season, the first to score eight points in one game and earned a place in 14 consecutive All-Star games. He will always be remembered as one of Montreal's most beloved stars.
Imperial Oil-Turofsky/Hockey Hall of Fame

Goalie Jacques Plante popularized the goalie face mask. Plante helped guide the Habs to five consecutive Cup wins from 1956-1960.

Imperial Oil - Turofsky / Hockey Hall of Fame

Defenceman Serge Savard enjoyed a Hall of Fame career with the Habs. Later he served as general manager of the club.

Robert Shaver / Hockey Hall of Fame

Maple Leaf Gardens, built in six months (in 1931) at a cost of one million, five hundred thousand dollars, was home to the Leafs throughout the Original Six Era.
Imperial Oil - Turofsky / Hockey Hall of Fame

Bill Barilko's stunning goal in overtime gave the Leafs the 1951 Stanley Cup. Barilko was killed in a plane crash later that year.
Imperial Oil - Turofsky / Hockey Hall of Fame

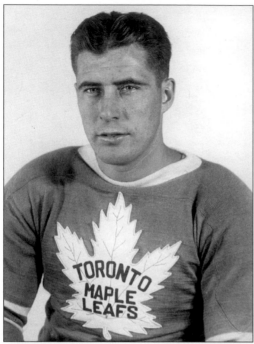

Handsome Harvey "Busher" Jackson, a member of the famous Kid Line had everything—and lost it all.
Imperial Oil - Turofsky / Hockey Hall of Fame

Goalie "Turk" Broda, shown here accepting the Vezina Trophy from NHL president Clarence Campbell, was known as hockey's best "money" goaltender.
Imperial Oil / Hockey Hall of Fame

Coach Hap Day chats with team owner Conn Smythe in the Leaf dressing room.
Imperial Oil - Turofsky / Hockey Hall of Fame

Controversial George "Punch" Imlach was manager-coach of the Leafs when they captured four Stanley Cups in the sixties.
Credit: Robert Shaver / Hockey Hall of Fame

Defenceman Bobby Baun is forever remembered for scoring an overtime goal that kept the Leafs in the Stanley Cup hunt—while playing on a broken leg.
Graphic Artists / Hockey Hall of Fame

The Bruins' famous Kraut Line of Bobby Bauer, Milt Schmidt and Woody Dumart. In 1939-40 they finished one-two-three in NHL scoring. Schmidt collected 53 points, Bauer and Dumart each finished with 43.
Hockey Hall of Fame

Boston's Eddie Shore won the Hart Trophy four times. Shore's vicious check from behind ended the playing career of Toronto star Ace Bailey.
Hockey Hall of Fame

Bobby Orr joined the NHL prior to the 1967-68 expansion. He led the Bruins to a pair of Stanley Cup wins and led the league in scoring twice.

Graphic Artists/Hockey Hall of Fame

Gordie Howe joined the Detroit organization at age seventeen, lured by the promise of a Red Wing jacket.
Robert Shaver / Hockey Hall of Fame

Terry Sawchuk remains the all-time shutout leader in the NHL with 103. He died mysteriously in 1970.
Graphic Artists / Hockey Hall of Fame

"Terrible" Ted Lindsay, a fiery left winger, was banished to Chicago by manager Jack Adams after Lindsay founded a players association.

Frank Prazak/Hockey Hall of Fame

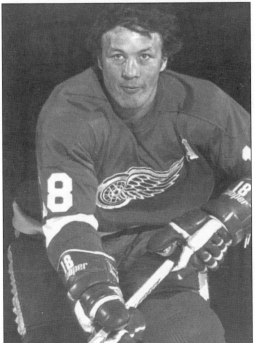

Bryan "The Pest" Watson made his mark with Detroit by shadowing the opposing team's star players.

Graphic Artists / Hockey Hall of Fame

Alex Delvecchio played for the Red Wings for 24 seasons and later coached the club.
Robert Shaver / Hockey Hall of Fame

Coach Lester Patrick, in his mid-forties, tended goal for the
Rangers in a 1928 playoff game—and won!
Hockey Hall of Fame

Andy Bathgate was a Hart Trophy winner for the Rangers in 1959.
James McCarthy / Hockey Hall of Fame

Babe Seibert. The man who blamed himself for ending the career of Howie Morenz.
Imperial Oil / Hockey Hall of Fame

Coach Charlie Conacher meets with his players. Bill Gadsby and Gus Bodnar (*back row*), Bob Goldham, (*far right*) Emile Francis (*middle of pack*) Johnny Mariucci, (*front left*)
Imperial Oil - Turofsky / Hockey Hall of Fame

Defenceman Pat Stapleton claims he has the puck Paul Henderson slipped past Tretiak to score the winning goal over the Soviets in 1972. But Stapleton is also known as a kidder...

Graphic Artists / Hockey Hall of Fame

In the finals against the Rangers, his sore elbow acted up, keeping him on the sidelines. Rookie netminder Earl Robertson took over and played a starring role as the Red Wings won their second consecutive Stanley Cup.

The Wings slipped badly in 1937–38, missing the playoffs and plummeting to the basement of the American Division, and Jack Adams threatened a wholesale shakeup. Smith was to absorb much of the blame; he played only four games for Detroit in 1938–39, and then bolted from the team one night after a game in New York. Adams suspended him and quickly acquired veteran Tiny Thompson from Boston to replace him. Smith resigned himself to the fact his NHL career was over.

But was it?

Five seasons went by and, desperate for goaltending help during World War II, Adams remembered Smith and invited him back. He played five games in 1943–44 and one more the following season, and then was discarded.

Norm Smith's NHL career wasn't long — it lasted only 198 games. But he did win a Vezina Trophy and two Stanley Cups, and he'll always be remembered as the winning goalie in the longest game ever played.

Wings Were First with Firewagon Hockey

During the 1940–41 season, Detroit coach Jack Adams found himself with a team of aggressive players who checked with a vengeance. They might not have been as skilled or speedy as their NHL rivals, but their rambunctious play soon changed the face of the game. Montreal coach Dick Irvin would later adapt the Red Wings' style to his Canadiens and give it a name: firewagon hockey.

Adams, who had a lean centreman and determined forechecker named Don "The Count" Grosso, decided to build his team's offensive strategy around him. Every time the Red Wings whipped the puck into the opposing team's zone, all five skaters would pour into the attacking zone. Other teams had used this "every man up" strategy on the power play, but the Wings began to do it all the time.

With Grosso leading the way, the Wings created trouble for everyone. Speedy centres like Toronto's Syl Apps or Boston's Milt Schmidt would circle behind their net, preparing for a rink-length rush, only to find Grosso and company blocking their way.

At first, the so-called experts jeered the Wings. Toronto fans and players called it "hooligan's hockey." The critics were less vocal two years later, when Detroit's new style brought them a Stanley Cup in a four-game sweep of the Boston Bruins.

This aggressive forechecking resulted in one of the most important rule changes of the century: the introduction of the centre red line. "Too much of the game is being played in the defensive zones," Rangers coach Frank Boucher explained. "If teams can pass all the way up to the new red line, it'll take the pressure off. It'll help them cope with the strong forechecking of the Red Wings."

Stewart, Orlando in Bloody Battle Royal

On November 7, 1942, the Red Wings visited Maple Leaf Gardens in Toronto for a game with the defending Stanley Cup champions. One of the best of the Leafs was winger Gaye Stewart, who was to win the Calder Trophy that season, outshining Montreal defenceman Glen Harmon and a future legend, Maurice "Rocket" Richard.

On defence for Detroit was the belligerent Jimmy Orlando, who was then playing his final season in the league. The Montreal-born Orlando was a tough guy who took great joy in levelling opposing forwards — especially brash newcomers like Stewart.

During this first meeting of the season between the archrivals, Stewart dashed down the boards, only to be dumped heavily into the corner by Orlando's solid check. Stewart jumped to his feet and nailed Orlando with a two-handed slash with his stick. Orlando laughed as referee King Clancy blew his whistle and ordered Stewart to the penalty box.

Orlando describes what happened next.

"There he is in the penalty box, fuming like an enraged bull. Stewart was so mad he couldn't sit down. When play resumed I could hear him hollerin' at me, so I hollered a few things back, and he didn't like that one bit. Then — can you believe it? — he jumped out of the box and raced toward me. I'd never seen anything like it. The guy still had over a minute to serve in his penalty. Anyway, I saw him coming so I dropped my gloves and nailed him a good one, sending him sprawling to the ice. Clancy didn't see this because he was way up the ice with everybody else. Then Stewart jumps up, takes his stick and smashes me right across the skull — a vicious blow that cut me for 23 stitches, I found out afterwards. I was in no man's land for the next few minutes, so I never got to smack him back with my stick, much as I would have liked to.

"Clancy gave us both match penalties and the league fined us each $100. I was suspended from playing in Toronto the rest of the season and Stewart was banned from playing in Detroit, but somehow these suspensions were rescinded. By the way, somebody took a photo of me being led off the ice and it looks like I'd just been hit by a bus. Hockey was a tough game in those days."

Howe's Life-Threatening Injury

Gordie Howe blossomed into a true superstar during the 1949–50 NHL season. He led the Red Wings in goals, with 35, and he finished third in the league in total points behind teammates Ted Lindsay and Sid Abel. His Red Wings led the league standings with 88 points — the most in NHL history to that date — and were favoured to oust Toronto in the first round of the playoffs.

The opening game was played at the Olympia on March 28, 1950, and it was a double disaster for the Wings, who lost the match 5–0 and almost lost their brilliant right winger forever.

Fists flew early in that game as Howe battled tough guy Bill Juzda of the Leafs. Meanwhile, the Production Line of Howe, Lindsay and Abel, who had scored 92 goals between them in regular-season play, were stymied by the tight-checking Leafs and the goaltending of Turk Broda. The Wings had lost 11 straight playoff games to Toronto, and midway through the third period it became apparent the string would be extended to 12.

Suddenly, there was a terrible accident on the ice. Leafs captain Ted Kennedy, stickhandling along the boards through the neutral zone, was taken out of the play by both Howe and rugged defenceman "Black Jack" Stewart.

"I was going to run Kennedy into the boards," Howe recalls. "I was leaning forward, my head low to the ice, when Kennedy passed the puck to Sid Smith. Kennedy came around with the stick and spiked me right in the eye. The blow didn't lacerate the eye, but it did some damage. The real damage came a second later when I crashed into the boards."

The crowd gasped as Howe nose-dived into the boards and collapsed to the ice, unconscious. It was obvious to all that he was badly injured. Moments later, he tried to get to his feet, and then slumped back to the ice. Someone called for a stretcher and an ambulance. In the meantime, doctors and trainers diagnosed a broken nose, a possible broken cheekbone, damage to one eye and a serious concussion. Howe was immediately taken to Harper Hospital.

"I'll never forget that horrible ride," Howe would say. "People around me were saying, 'You're okay, Gord,' but I didn't feel okay. I felt terribly sick. At the hospital, someone gave me a drink of water and I vomited. They rushed me into the operating room and I remember getting upset when they shaved my head. Even though the anesthetist was there, I recall the shock of having a drill put to my skull and feeling the pressure and hoping they knew what they were doing and when to stop the drill."

Dr. Frederic Schreiber, a brilliant neurosurgeon, drilled a small opening in Gordie's skull, above his right ear, to relieve the pressure on his brain. Dr. Schreiber would later tell Ted Lindsay that if it had taken just 30 minutes longer to tend to Howe, he could easily have lost his life.

The Red Wings arranged for Gordie's mother and sister Gladys to fly from Saskatoon to Detroit. Mrs. Howe suffered from airsickness all the way — it was her first flight. She found her son weak but conscious, and with his sense of humour still intact.

"I told her she looked so ill from the trip that I'd better get up and let her take the bed," Gordie quipped.

Dr. Schreiber predicted a full recovery for his star patient and said Gordie could expect to play hockey again the following season.

Back at the Olympia, the incident was not being forgotten quickly, and some nasty accusations were aired. Red Wings coach Tommy Ivan denounced referee Georges Gravel for not calling a penalty on the play. Ivan claimed Kennedy had deliberately butt-ended his star forward. Gravel said he hadn't seen any infraction of the rules.

Kennedy went so far as to offer to swear an oath that he had not intended to harm Howe. "I didn't even know he was hurt until I turned to come back down the ice and he was lying there, blood all over his face," the Leafs captain said.

"We had to get our act together for game two," Lindsay said. "It was a game we had to win, and even though I hated Kennedy personally, I respected him as a player. He was a great one. We couldn't worry too much about getting even. Not then."

Late in the second period of game two, Lindsay was mugged by the Leafs' Gus Mortson. No penalty was called. Then Lee Fogolin of the Wings was sent off for tripping Kennedy. A furious Lindsay hauled Kennedy's skates out from under him and a dandy free-for-all broke out. Mortson whacked Lindsay, Fogolin attacked Mortson, and Bill Barilko tossed punches at Marty Pavelich.

Kennedy found a new foe in big Leo Reise and speared him. Reise used his stick to drop Jim Thomson with a head blow, then ran the stick across Kennedy's neck. By then, Lindsay was on the loose and he charged into Kennedy, nailing him hard. Meanwhile, Mortson and Sid Abel squared off and belted each other.

Tempers flared again later in the game. With Detroit leading 3–1, Bill Ezinicki assaulted Lindsay, crosschecking him to the ice. Lindsay jumped up, dropped his gloves and charged Ezinicki. They fell to the ice, with Lindsay on top. Meanwhile, Vic Lynn decided he would test mild-mannered Red Kelly and received quite a drubbing. When Bill Juzda saw a chance, he belted Lindsay and sent him to the ice.

When the dust had cleared, the Red Wings had evened the series. They went on to eliminate the Leafs, propelled by Reise's overtime goal in the seventh game, and to win the final series over the Rangers, who hung on into double overtime in game seven before the Red Wings' Pete Babando scored the winner at 8:31, starting the celebrations. The crowd at the Olympia immediately began chanting, "We want Howe!" and, moments later, Gordie emerged from the players' entrance, his head swathed in bandages. He received a tumultuous welcome. With tears in his eyes, he reached out to touch the Stanley Cup. It would not be the last time he placed a hand on it.

Was Howe Tough? I'll Say

When Gordie Howe was a young fellow, his dad gave him some good advice: Never take any guff from anybody. One day, in a Saskatoon pool hall, Gordie witnessed first-hand what he meant. A guy was annoying his father by tapping his hand with a cue whenever he lined up a shot, so the senior Howe straightened up and socked the joker, knocking him cold with the butt of his big hand.

Perhaps Gordie had his father in mind whenever he ran into troublemakers on the ice. Instead of dropping his gloves and fighting, Gordie would let them know he was peeved by giving them a taste of his stick. He'd crack his stick over an opponent's head — bonk! — and the challenger, dripping blood, would be helped off the ice for stitches. Son Marty says his dad could inflict varying degrees of damage — a three-stitch cut here or a five-stitch wound there — depending on how much he wanted to hurt a guy.

During a brawl in a WHA game, Marty found himself underneath a bigger, stronger opponent. One of Marty's teammates skated over and told the player holding Marty down to "Let him up!" The player laughed and refused to let go.

Then big Gordie skated over and delivered the same message: "Let him up!" He was greeted with a stream of obscenities. Howe removed one glove, reached down, and pushed two fingers up the tough guy's nostrils. While the player screamed in pain, Gordie lifted him off his son.

Marty recalls the player bouncing to his feet, shouting, "I'm up! I'm up!" Only then did Gordie remove his fingers and push the player away. The bully went to the penalty bench, nursing a head that felt like a bowling ball.

Some injuries that slowed Gordie down — but not for long — can be listed: a broken wrist; broken fingers; broken ribs; a broken collarbone that went undiagnosed for a year; a broken toe that got in the path of a Bobby Hull slap shot; carpal tunnel syndrome; broken nose (14 times); broken cheekbone, scratched eyeball and severe concussion in the Ted Kennedy incident; a broken foot; a hernia; torn knee cartilage; and sundry wounds to the face requiring a total of 500 stitches.

The Octopus Tossers

What kind of fans would stuff a slippery sea creature with eight sucker-bearing arms into a paper bag and take it to a game? Detroit Red Wings fans would. They've been doing it for more than half a century.

Tossing a dead octopus onto the ice during Detroit playoff games has become a bizarre tradition that can be blamed on (or credited to) the brothers Cusimano. In 1952, Pete and Jerry Cusimano, whose father was a fishmonger, took a dead octopus to the Olympia for what turned out to be the final game of the Stanley Cup playoffs between the Red Wings and Montreal Canadiens. The brothers reasoned that the eight tentacles of the octopus represented eight playoff victories, and since the Wings had already won seven consecutive playoff games — four over Toronto and three more over Montreal — the splat of an octopus hitting the ice would inspire them, or bring them luck, or shock or jinx the Habs. Well, it seemed like a good idea at the time, if only to the Cusimanos.

But it worked. The Red Wings won the Cup with a 3–0 victory that night (although a more fitting score might have been 8–0). The octopus was given a bit of credit for the victory, and the Cusimanos enjoyed some backslapping from their friends at the fish market the next day.

"Too bad," said former NHL referee Red Storey after the octopus tossing had become an annual rite of spring. "Those guys started a tradition that always made us officials a little uneasy during Detroit games. That damn thing would come flying out of the stands sometime during the first five minutes of play. I'd have to keep one eye on the game and the other on the stands, wondering when those little buggers were going to throw that ugly thing. As a result, I seldom called any penalties early in the game. I was on octopus watch.

"Pick the damn thing up? Not me — I never went near them. Somehow, Marcel Pronovost got to be the picker-upper. It didn't bother him at all to scoop one of those weird-looking things off the ice and toss it in the nearest garbage bin."

Little Tony Lights It Up

Little Tony Leswick was not a happy hockey player in the spring of 1954. He wore a deep frown despite the fact that his Red Wings had finished with 88 points, seven more than second-place Montreal and 10 up on third-place Toronto, to wind up on top of the NHL standings.

Tony was worried because, on a personal level, it had been the least productive of his nine NHL seasons: just six goals in 70 games. Hadn't he scored 15 goals as a Rangers rookie in 1945–46, and in only 50 games? Hadn't he followed up with seasons of 27 and 24, and averaged close to 20 per season?

As the playoffs began, the rugged little winger — all five feet, six inches and 160 pounds of him — set out to redeem himself.

And he did. He scored goals in games one and three as the Red Wings ousted Toronto in the semifinals. But his biggest marker was yet to come.

The final series against the Montreal Canadiens was a thriller that seesawed back and forth en route to a seventh and deciding game. A record crowd of 15,791 turned out for the season finale at the Olympia, and they were rewarded with a brilliant display of speed and skill.

The Canadiens jumped to an early 1–0 lead on Floyd Curry's goal. Red Kelly tied it for the Wings in the second. Then the teams checked fiercely through the third period, and on into overtime.

Montreal goalie Gerry McNeil, sidelined since February 11, had replaced Jacques Plante for games five, six and seven, and had proven to be every inch the equal of Detroit's Terry Sawchuk. Then, shortly after the four-minute mark of overtime, the Red Wings got a break. Lanky centre Glen Skov dashed to the end boards behind McNeil, then turned and whipped a pass out to Leswick, who was waiting in the face-off circle about 30 feet to the goalie's left. Leswick pounced on the rubber and drilled it high and hard at McNeil. Almost miraculously, it wound up in the Montreal net. Leswick's stunning goal gave the Red Wings the Stanley Cup.

Later, Montreal's great defenceman Doug Harvey blamed himself for Leswick's winning goal. "I was in front of Leswick when he shot," said Harvey. "I reached up for the puck, intending to knock it away. But the damn puck struck my glove and caromed in past McNeil."

None of the Red Wings — least of all Tony Leswick — cared how the puck went in. They had won the game and all the laurels. Leswick was mobbed by his mates as fans leaped over the boards and onto the ice. There was a long delay while the ice was cleared for the Cup presentation. NHL President Clarence Campbell turned the Stanley Cup over to Marguerite Norris, the team's president, and a beaming Jack Adams, the general manager.

By then, the Montreal players had left the ice. None of them stayed around to congratulate the winners, and they were roundly criticized in the Detroit press for their poor sportsmanship.

Tony Leswick's winning goal assured each of his mates a playoff bonus: the winners' share of the postseason loot. He would play a couple more seasons in the NHL and enjoy many other satisfying moments, but none so much as the shot that lit the light behind Gerry McNeil on that muggy night of April 16, 1954, to bring the Cup to Detroit for the sixth time in franchise history.

Bonin the Bear Wrestler

When Marcel Bonin joined the Detroit Red Wings in 1952, he wanted to make a good impression. So he decided to entertain them. He did some amusing things, like pushing a needle through the skin in his arm and chewing on particles of glass.

"He made an impression all right," says former Red Wing Johnny Wilson. "One of the first questions our trainer asked him was, 'What size skates do you wear?' And Marcel says, 'Eight-t'irty. I wear eight-t'irty.' I guess he meant eight and a half."

Bonin's reputation as a bit of a character preceded him to Detroit. His friend Marcel Pronovost had made sure all the Wings were aware that he was a fearless bear wrestler from Quebec.

"That's true, I was a bear wrestler," says Bonin. And he tells the story.

"It started when Joe Louis, the old boxer, took a job with the Barnum and Bailey circus. His job was to referee wrestling matches with a big brown bear and anyone who wanted to fight him — try to put the bear down, eh? The circus came to my hometown, Joliette, one day, and I wasn't afraid of that bear. I was a tough kid of 16 or so and I jumped in that ring and wrestled that bear. We put on a big show. I didn't put that old bear down, but you could call the match a draw, eh? Okay, the bear he wore a muzzle and he had no claws but still everybody talked about how young Marcel fought the big bear. It was in all the papers.

"Naturally, they wanted me to wrestle him again, and I did. But I was no dummy, eh? I went to that bear in the morning and fed him, and he soon got to like me. I even went from town to town wrestling that bear. We got to be good pals, eh? And that's how I got to be known as Bonin the bear wrestler around the NHL."

Death of a Defenceman

Ellie Goldham called me on a Friday morning in September 1991 with devastating news. Her loving husband, Bob, was dead of a stroke at age 69. Tears fell freely at both ends of the line as we

146

remembered Bob, the good times we had shared and the countless friends he had made in business, on the ice and in the broadcast booth. She asked me to prepare a eulogy for the memorial service.

Every pew was filled that day and I was amazed at how many former Red Wings had travelled to Toronto to pay their respects. It shouldn't have come as any surprise; every teammate he had ever played with had loved and respected the big defenceman.

Bob Goldham never considered himself to be anyone special, I told those assembled. Only others thought him to be a rare and special individual. There was never any danger of Bob displaying an inflated ego; in his low-key, laid-back, good-natured, humble way he was an enormous success as a man.

Right from the beginning, he wanted to be a hockey player. Perhaps his dream was born one exciting day in the early 1930s, when he rode down from Georgetown, Ontario, sitting on an apple crate in the back of a truck, to see his first NHL game at Maple Leaf Gardens. No doubt he watched in amazement as the Kid Line and King Clancy performed their heroics on the ice below. And if he happened to gaze up to the broadcast gondola that night, where Foster Hewitt sat hunched over a microphone describing the play in his inimitable fashion, it probably wouldn't have occurred to young Goldham for even a second that, many decades later, his wit and wisdom and expert analysis of hockey would become an integral part of *Hockey Night in Canada*.

Bob must have known at an early age that his hockey dreams were all but hopeless. Of the thousands of young men playing the game, only 100 or so held steady jobs in the NHL, and only 25 or 30 of those were defenceman. But young Goldham made up his mind to practice longer and harder than the other boys. He decided to make more personal sacrifices, to study the game and listen to his coaches, to focus on becoming one of the elite.

And eventually he did.

He had a memorable indoctrination into the National Hockey League, playing for Toronto against a team of hard-nosed Red Wings. Seeing action in 19 regular-season games, the 19-year-old rookie seemed destined, as most rookies are, to sit on the bench and watch his more experienced teammates battle furiously against Detroit in the 1942 Stanley Cup finals.

Goldham looked on in frustration as the Leafs lost three straight games. They were about to be swept into oblivion when Leafs coach Hap Day made some desperate moves. He benched several of his top stars and called on Bob and others to help stave off disaster.

In game four, Goldham excelled on defence and the Leafs came from behind for a 4–3 victory. The Leafs added rookie Gaye Stewart to the lineup for game five and cruised to a 9–3 win, Goldham contributing a goal and an assist. In game six, Goldham scored a key goal in a 3–0 win and the series was suddenly even. Detroit took a 1–0 lead into the third period of game seven, the crucial match for all the Stanley Cup glory, but Goldham set up another huge goal as the Leafs stormed back to 3–1, having engineered the greatest playoff comeback in NHL history. Could any rookie have asked for a more exciting debut?

Goldham barely had time to savour the moment before he was asked to switch uniforms. He moved from Maple Leaf blue to navy blue. After three years of wartime service, Bob went on to play a major role in a second Toronto Stanley Cup victory in 1947. Later that year, he was involved in one of hockey's biggest trades when he was shipped to Chicago, along with Gus Bodnar, Ernie Dickens, Gaye Stewart and Bud Poile, in return for Max Bentley, the Hawks' dipsy-doodling centreman, and journeyman Cy Thomas.

A subsequent trade brought Goldham to Detroit, where he performed with some of the greatest stars in the game — Sawchuk, Howe, Abel, Lindsay and Kelly. Goldham kept in step with all of those future Hall of Famers; by then he was a master of the blue line and a key performer in Detroit's Stanley Cup win in 1952, achieved in the minimum of eight games. He spent half of his 12-year career in a Detroit uniform and became one of the most popular Red Wings of all time. Chroniclers of the game often wonder why Goldham, with his uncanny ability to drop down and block shots, with his remarkably solid play, has not himself been inducted into the Hockey Hall of Fame.

Someday, hopefully, the oversight will be rectified. But Goldham himself would neither have suggested nor sought such recognition. Personal glory and personal rewards meant little to him. Let others take the credit; let others bask in the spotlight. He was proud to be known as a team player, satisfied to turn in a good, honest performance night after night. It was a trait inherited from his father, the popular Georgetown butcher who took pride in honest service and who never cheated a customer by pressing his thumb on the scales.

In one of Goldham's post-NHL careers, he joined us on *Hockey Night in Canada*. He was supposed to replace me — my bosses had offered Bob the job of colour commentator on Leafs telecasts — but he refused to accept until he talked with me.

He told me, "I'd never seek or take a job from another person if it would hurt them. If it turns out it's between you and me for the job, I'll simply tell them I'm not interested in the position."

As it turned out, things worked out so that there was room for both of us on the telecasts.

Adams' Teams Were Awesome

Jack Adams was one of the most successful executives in the history of the National Hockey League. After joining Detroit as coach and general manager in 1927, his teams won seven Stanley Cups and 12 league titles. From 1949 to 1955, his Detroit Red Wings finished in first place seven years in a row, a rate of success even baseball's New York Yankees couldn't claim. He often boasted that "our 1951–52 team that won the playoffs in eight straight games was the greatest hockey team ever assembled."

His greatest satisfaction came from picking a rawboned kid out of a Detroit training camp and watching him develop into the dominant player of his era. The youngster's name was Gordie Howe, who signed with Adams for a pittance — and the promise of a Red Wings hockey jacket.

For many years, the admiration between Howe and Adams was mutual. Gordie once said if he didn't have such wonderful parents back home in Saskatoon, he'd be proud to be known as a son to his manager, coach and adviser.

Despite his nickname, "Jolly Jack" could be a ruthless adversary. He shunted Ted Lindsay, his great left winger, off to Chicago when Lindsay became president of a fledgling players' association. Adams detested unions and considered Lindsay's motives treasonous. He rarely spoke to Lindsay during the last two seasons they were together.

"Hockey's the greatest game there is," Adams once said. "It has to be, to survive the number of jerks that are in it."

One night, the rotund manager jumped onto the ice during a crucial playoff game with Toronto and bulled his way into an altercation between game officials and several players. It was charged, and denied by Adams, that he threw punches at referee Mel Harwood. Some reporters and columnists wrote scathing denunciations of Adams' behaviour and called for him to be banned from hockey forever. When he threatened to sue them for libel, they hastily penned apologies.

Adams served the Wings for 35 years, leaving at the end of the 1961–62 season to become president of the Central Hockey League.

Adams died of a heart attack on May 1, 1968.

Adams Doesn't Deserve the Accolades, Lindsay Says

Over the years, Jack Adams won many accolades for his intelligent handling of the Detroit hockey club. In 1959 he was ushered into the Hockey Hall of Fame, and his long and meritorious service to hockey in the United States earned him the distinction of being the first-ever winner of the Lester Patrick Memorial Trophy in 1966. Did that make him a brilliant coach, manager and executive? Not according to another Hall of Famer, Ted Lindsay.

"I say Adams was a lousy hockey man," states Lindsay angrily. "That's my opinion. I say Adams cheated me out of at least five and maybe as many as seven or eight Stanley Cups.

"After we won two Cups in a row in 1954 and 1955, he traded nine players away from the Red Wings — nine players! Why? We could have stayed on top; instead, we went downhill from there.

"What really rankles me is the trade he didn't make. After we won in '55, the Canadiens wanted Terry Sawchuk. We could have parted with Terry, because we had a great goaltender in the wings in Glenn Hall. And we could have had defenceman Doug Harvey in return. Adams refused to make the deal, and the Habs went on to win five consecutive Stanley Cups with Harvey leading them every step of the way. He was the Bobby Orr of his era.

"Adams told somebody he wouldn't make the trade because he didn't want to make Montreal stronger [instead, he traded Sawchuk and a few others to Boston for a package of players who made little impact in Detroit]. They won the next five Cups — how much stronger could he have made them?"

Johnny Wilson Looks Back

Johnny Wilson played left wing on four Stanley Cup–winning Detroit teams between 1950 and 1955, and at one time was the NHL's all-time iron man, playing in 580 consecutive games. He recalls the aftermath of one of the Cup wins being the genesis of an ill-starred player revolt.

"In those days the players got a $3,000 bonus from the league for winning the Cup. Of that amount about $500 went to the IRS, so we wound up with about $2,500. Well, we got our bonus money one year and it amounted to only $1,900. That puzzled us, especially Ted Lindsay. So Teddy called a meeting of the players and he said, 'I want to know what happened to the other six hundred.' We all wanted to know, so Teddy said he'd try to find out. He went to Jack Adams, and you know what Adams said to him? He said, 'Look, there's more than 17 players who should get a share of this bonus money.'

"Lindsay said, 'Yeah, the trainer gets a share, the coach gets a share and the assistant trainer gets half a share. Who else should get a share?'

"Ted found out that Adams had given shares or partial shares to the box office manager, the scouts, the head electrician, the public relations director — everybody. There were 29 people in the organization who shared in the playoff money, and that wasn't right. Why should Jack Adams be giving our money to everybody in the organization?

"That's when Teddy started thinking seriously about starting a players' association. When it came to money, Jack would knock us down. I don't know why. And Ted got so mad about it he went over Jack's head one year. Signed his next contract with the Norris brothers because he felt he was worth a lot more money than Jack would pay him. And Ted was right. He was always in the running for the scoring title, on the All-Star teams, a great leader."

On a lighter note, Wilson remembers when Glenn Hall joined the Wings. He laughs and says, "We were playing in the Montreal Forum and Terry Sawchuk was hurt. So they flew Glenn Hall in from Edmonton to play in his first NHL game.

"Now, the Forum dressing room was kinda small. Everything was in one area — the showers, the john, everything. So there's not any privacy.

"Poor old Glenn is suiting up, getting ready to face the Rocket, Geoffrion, Beliveau — all those great Montreal players. And is he nervous — who wouldn't be? Now he bolts for the toilet and starts to throw up. He's barfing in there and you could hear him a mile away. We start laughing, and Gordie and the guys are yelling, 'Way to go, Glenn, get all that stuff up. We don't want you doing that out on the ice.'

"He comes out of the john and his face is as white as a sheet. And we're all thinking, 'Geez, what kind of a game is this kid going to play?' Well, if memory serves, he played a helluva game and I believe we beat the Canadiens that night."

Wilson coached the Red Wings for a couple of seasons in the early 1970s and he is asked which coach made the greatest impression on him. He says, "When I was traded to Chicago I had Dick Irvin as my coach, and he was quite a gentleman. We had training camp at the old rink in Welland one year, and Dick was disturbed when he looked over the record of the team after a couple of exhibition games. No wonder he was upset: we hadn't scored any goals and we'd given up quite a few.

"So we're in the dressing room one day when Dick drags a goal net in. In this small space the net looks as big as a soccer goal. He holds up a hockey puck and says, 'You mean you fellows can't put a tiny hockey puck into this big net? That's unbelievable!' He made it appear to be the easiest thing in the world.

"Another time he called us into the dressing room and he had the chairs lined up like in a classroom. Then he had someone pass pencils and paper all around. 'Gentlemen, today we're going to have a little quiz,' he said. 'I'd like to test your knowledge of the game of hockey. First question: How big is the puck?'

"Nobody puts his pencil to the paper. Dick waits while 20 players fidget and frown and try to peek over the shoulder of the guy ahead of him. Nobody seems to know the answer to the question, so he moves on.

" 'Question number two. What's the maximum length of a hockey stick?' Again we hem and haw and guys are just guessing at the answer.

"After a couple more questions with no better results, Dick gives it up. He says in disgust, 'You men shouldn't be playing hockey for a living. You should be back in school.' "

Johnny Wilson played a role in the trade that sent Red Kelly to Toronto. Wilson was a member of the Toronto Maple Leafs when Kelly retired rather than accept a deal that would have seen him become a New York Ranger. Wilson casually mentioned to the Leafs brass that Jack Adams loved the play of Marc Reaume, a borderline Leafs defenceman. "Offer him Marc, and I'll bet he'll give you Kelly," he suggested. Toronto manager Punch Imlach threw out the bait, and Adams went for it and reeled in Reaume, who played inconspicuously in 86 games for Detroit and collected three assists. Kelly helped lead the Leafs to four Stanley Cups.

Red Wings Developed Great Goalies

In the six-team league of the 1950s, the Detroit Red Wings displayed an uncanny ability to discover and develop star goalies, not only for themselves but for the rest of the league as well. During the decade, the Wings employed Harry Lumley, Terry Sawchuk and Glenn Hall, all three of whom are now Honoured Members of the Hockey Hall of Fame.

It always came as a surprise when Jack Adams traded one of his stellar netminders just at the point when each appeared to be in his prime. Both Lumley and Sawchuk were coming off Stanley

Cup championship seasons when they were traded. Some show of gratitude by management!

In 1950, Adams sent Lumley, along with Pete Babando (whose overtime goal had won the Stanley Cup for Detroit three months earlier), Jack Stewart, Al Dewsbury and Don Morrison to Chicago in return for goalie Jim Henry, Bob Goldham, Gaye Stewart and Metro Prystai. It was called the biggest trade in NHL history. Once he dumped Lumley, who was only 24, Adams promoted Terry Sawchuk from Indianapolis, a Red Wings farm club. Sawchuk led the NHL in shutouts in his rookie season and won the Calder Trophy as the NHL's top first-year player.

If Sawchuk felt his splendid play meant his job was secure, he was kidding himself. He should have known that Adams liked to shuffle his roster. In 1955, Adams dispatched the 25-year-old Sawchuk, who had sparkled in April when the Wings won their sixth Stanley Cup, to Boston along with Marcel Bonin, Vic Stasiuk and Lorne Davis in return for Real Chevrefils, Ed Sandford, Warren Godfrey, Gilles Boisvert and Norm Corcoran. Why trade a goalie who was already being acclaimed as one of the best ever, a man who eventually would register a record 103 shutouts? Why not? Adams had someone just as good in mind.

In the previous two seasons, young Glenn Hall had played in eight games as an emergency replacement for Sawchuk. The acrobatic Hall had won all but one of those games. Adams felt that Hall had more than enough talent to become one of the all-time goaltending greats. Perhaps Adams, a habitual cost-cutter, felt the money he saved in salary would finance other areas on the club.

Hall's days in Detroit were numbered after he told Adams, whom he did not like, where he might find a convenient body part into which to stuff a hockey puck. Hall was traded from the Wings after only two full seasons. His best years were yet to come; although he did not win a Stanley Cup with the Red Wings, he did backstop the Chicago Blackhawks to one Cup victory and assure them of two other trips to the finals.

Hall was traded because, after a brief stint with the Bruins, the temperamental Sawchuk had walked away from the club, citing emotional strain. The Boston papers chastised the goaltender until he threatened to sue. Adams decided to dump Hall and bring

Sawchuk back. He gave up Johnny Bucyk (who went on to a brilliant career as a Bruin) and cash for Sawchuk, and dealt Hall to Chicago with Ted Lindsay in return for goalie Hank Bassen, Forbes Kennedy, Bill Preston and Johnny Wilson. It was a quality for quantity exchange with Chicago getting the edge.

Adams was delighted to get rid of Lindsay because Terrible Ted had never hidden his disdain for the man holding the purse strings. The clincher was his efforts to start a players' association.

The trading of three great goalies in their prime may puzzle hockey fans in this era, but Adams — the Godfather — always loved making offers others couldn't refuse. Loyalty Street led straight to the Olympia and sentiment was for saps. "I must have done something right," he would say at the end of the decade. "My teams of the '50s were among the greatest ever assembled, with seven straight first-place finishes and three Stanley Cups."

Adams may have smirked at the time, but the Wings' good fortune in finding top-flight goaltenders didn't last. Nor did their postseason success. Over the next four decades, the Detroit Red Wings would struggle to find goalies who could approach the standards set by the three who had been cast away, Lumley, Sawchuk and Hall.

An Unusual Night for Pronovost

Special nights for hockey stars are not common occurrences in the NHL. In 1963, Red Wings defenceman Marcel Pronovost was so honoured, but what was unusual was that his night didn't take place at the Detroit Olympia. It was held in Montreal, at the Forum.

The good citizens of Beauharnois, Quebec, Pronovost's hometown, wanted to salute their native son. But they couldn't afford to travel to Detroit for the ceremony, so they asked Frank Selke, the general manager of the Montreal Canadiens, if they could honour Marcel during a Wings-Canadiens game at the Forum. "Why not?" replied Selke, even though such a thing had never been done before. "I've always liked Marcel. Most of our fans admire him and wish he was a Montreal Canadien." And a date was set.

Many of Marcel's boyhood friends, bursting with pride, were in the Forum for Marcel's night. As every hockey person knows, tradition dictates that a new car be presented to the guest of honour on such an occasion, and the citizens of Beauharnois wanted very much to carry on this custom. They presented Marcel with a lovely new car — the latest model. And they listened with pride to the huge ovation from the fans in the Forum when they turned over the keys at centre ice.

But this part of the evening turned out to be rather embarrassing to the event's organizers. Marcel's friends and neighbours had only managed to raise half the price of the car. Of course, they couldn't present Pronovost with half a car, so someone took him aside and asked if he would be willing to finance the other half. If Marcel was shocked or offended, he hid it well. And the folks back home had been his greatest supporters over the years. What else could he do?

"Sure," he said. "I'll buy half the car."

It was a wonderful night. And Mr. Selke insisted that the ceremony be televised on the CBC, even though the TV producers told him they were running short on time.

To this day, few people know that Marcel Pronovost is the only hockey player honoured with a night in another team's arena — or that he paid for half of the shiny new car he received.

I asked Marcel, "Did they ever hold a night for you in Detroit?"

"Nope."

Did you ever get Stanley Cup rings in Detroit?

"Nope. Well, one year a nice man, a Mr. Higgins, gave us what they called Stanley Cup rings. He bought us rings with a red stone, and wings on the side. And another time — it wasn't a Stanley Cup year — Mr. Norris gave us Rolex watches."

I asked what his salary was in 1952, the year the Wings won the Cup in eight straight games.

"I was making about $14,000. And I got an extra $2,700 for winning the Stanley Cup. I was shocked when I found out I was making more than Terry Sawchuk — and about the same as Gordie Howe."

More than Ted Lindsay?

"Oh, no. Ted was a good negotiator. And later on, when he

became manager, he paid his players well. He overpaid most of them."

You coached in the NHL, Marcel. Did you enjoy it?

"I liked it, but there were problems. When I coached in Buffalo, it was a hornet's nest. I had a big, tough defenceman who said he wasn't going to hit anymore — he was going to be a finesse player. Some bleepin' finesse player. He said, 'I'm not going to hit for those Frenchmen [the French Connection line of Richard Martin, Gilbert Perreault and Rene Robert] if they won't stand up for themselves.' And I had a star player who was hanging out with a drug dealer, a Mafia type. I had another player who was taking out another player's wife, while *his* wife was going out with a Buffalo Bills football player. And another player who packed a big .45. I'd never seen such things in hockey before."

You never had types like that on the old Red Wings?

"No, never... Well, we *did* have Howie Young."

Call It Twelve Foggy Years

When he wasn't sitting in the penalty box he was sitting in a bar. Or in jail. When he wasn't starting a fight, he was finishing one. Or looking for another one. When he wasn't drunk, he was about to get drunk.

In the 1960s, with his movie-star looks, he attracted women as successfully as Elvis Presley. He was Howard John "Howie" Young, a muscular defenceman who joined the Red Wings in 1960–61. His nickname should have been "Heartbreaker," for he shattered the hearts of his coaches and pals — and a thousand women who doted on him. He broke hearts like he broke hockey sticks, rules, team curfews and the law. He drove his bosses and his teammates wild with rage and frustration. "I'm through with the guy," Detroit manager Jack Adams snarled back in 1962. NHL President Clarence Campbell followed up with, "He's the greatest detriment to hockey that has ever laced on skates."

There are many lingering images of Young's outrageous behaviour, both on and off the ice. There was the time he showed up for a game wearing a Beatles wig. Then he shaved his head but for one strip down the middle. He once launched a shower of spit at Maple Leafs owner Stafford Smythe. He assaulted a cop and left him with a concussion. There were the times he was thrown in jail, and the time when he teetered drunkenly along the top of the rink boards at a Memorial Cup game, taunting coach Eddie Bush.

He was handsome, witty and charming. Women fell head over heels for him. His phone never stopped ringing.

It's amazing he played as long and as well as he did, considering the vast quantities of booze he consumed. "Twelve foggy years," he told a reporter once. "From 1960 and into the seventies. Always drunk, always hung over. At games and practices I felt awful because I was so hung over. And then there were all those guys on the ice who wanted to take my head off. Stayin' sober is no big deal; stayin' drunk is tough. That's what I worked at for a dozen years — drinkin' and playin' hockey."

Between 1960 and 1971 the tough defenceman played five seasons with Detroit, two with Chicago and a handful of games with the Vancouver Canucks. He was a Phoenix Roadrunner and a Winnipeg Jet in the WHA in 1974–75 and 1976–77. Along the way, there were several minor-league stops, including one with the New York Slapshots of the Atlantic Coast Hockey League when he was 48 years old.

At one time during the sixties he palled around with Frank Sinatra and even had a bit part in one of the crooner's movies, *None but the Brave*. There's an unconfirmed story that he gave Sinatra a friendly shove one day while partying on the singer's yacht. Sinatra's bodyguards are said to have wrestled him to the deck. Later, they dumped him off on a nearby beach to sober up.

Young was invited to Toronto a few years ago to appear at a major sports celebrity banquet. Jim McKenny, the former Leafs defenceman who was nicknamed Howie because of his resemblance to Young, took him to the old pond where they used to skate as kids. That was where both Howies had made up their minds to someday set the hockey world on fire. And both fell short of their vast potential because of the allure of alcohol.

After their hockey days, both wised up. Howie Young stayed on the wagon for the rest of his life, doing "a little cowboyin' and truck drivin', a little movie actin' and farmin'."

In Detroit he was second only to Gordie Howe in popularity, at least with the fans. He was the unpredictable kid with the crewcut, the big smile, the baby blue eyes and the willingness to mix it up with the toughest hombres in hockey. His teammates were less patient with him. One year they lobbied to keep him out of the playoffs because they felt he hurt their chances.

Near the end of his life, he said he regretted his alcoholic ways. "When I was a kid I believed that's what men did — real men: they drank. But really, I was scared to death. Scared of myself and the whole world around me. The booze made me feel good. It became more important than the hockey."

It was after Howie was released from a drunk tank in Los Angeles that he called a halt to his boozing. Enough was enough.

George Gamester of the *Toronto Star* caught up with Howie at his home in tiny Thoreau, New Mexico, where he was driving a school bus.

"It's been 33 years since I had my last drink," Howie said proudly. "I love these wide open spaces. Got my wife here and my quarter horse named Red and a coupla dogs. If I was any happier I couldn't stand it." Within a few months, Young was dead of a heart attack.

Detroit's Mr. Clean

Isn't it odd that the NHL's *Official Guide and Record Book* lists the players who take the most penalties yet completely overlooks those who draw the fewest? There's old Tiger Williams topping the career penalty list with 3,966 minutes (4,421 when playoffs are counted) and Dave "The Hammer" Schultz clinging to his record for most penalty minutes in one season: 472. That's more than seven hours in the sin bin.

One former Red Wing of the 1960s could make a claim on the title of "cleanest player" if the NHL guide listed such trivia. During one stretch in his 13-year NHL career, he played in 185 consecutive games without serving so much as a minor penalty in the box. And he later managed to compile a streak of 157 penalty-free games. Now *there's* a player who believed in obeying the rules.

His name, you may have guessed, is Val Fonteyne, a skinny little guy (five feet nine, 155 pounds), who excelled as a penalty killer in his Detroit days. He avoided the penalty box as if he suffered from claustrophobia. It appeared he would rather visit the House of Horrors than be given the gate.

In 820 regular-season games in the NHL, he served all of 28 penalty minutes. Compare that with Randy Holt of the Los Angeles Kings, who was once assessed 67 minutes in one period! Unlike Holt, Williams or Schultz, Fonteyne never got to be on a first-name basis with the NHL's penalty timekeepers. He's the only player to complete three consecutive seasons without taking a single minor, and the only one to compile five penalty-free seasons during his career. It should come as no surprise to learn that he never served a major penalty for fighting — at least, not in the NHL. He vaguely recalls getting into a fight when he first turned pro with Seattle of the Western Hockey League. That the details are so hazy suggests he is still ashamed of that incident and wants to erase the memory of it from his mind.

Fans who like to ponder records, and long to see them broken, may have to wait for decades — perhaps forever — before someone as gentlemanly as Fonteyne comes along to break fewer hockey rules.

The Goal Gadsby Can't Forget

Defenceman Bill Gadsby was one of the unluckiest guys in hockey. He played the first 15 years of his career with Chicago and New York, teams that made the playoffs a combined four times from 1946 to 1961.

Then, in June 1961, New York traded Gadbsy to Detroit (for Les Hunt, who never played an NHL game), where he experienced the joys of winning. The Red Wings breezed to the Cup finals in three of Gadsby's last five seasons. Surely now he would get to taste champagne from Lord Stanley's old basin.

But it was not to be. Toronto swept the Wings aside in five games in the 1963 finals. In 1964, the Leafs required seven games to capture their second consecutive Cup. Leafs defenceman Bobby

Baun scored in overtime in game six, a turning point. Baun was elevated to hero's status for winning the game while playing on a broken leg.

"Bah," says Gadsby. "His leg wasn't broken. He may have had a hairline fracture, but the media played it up big. I remember skating up to Baun before game seven. I said, 'Who do you think you're kidding?' He just kind of shrugged."

The following season, 1964–65, the Chicago Blackhawks ousted the Wings in seven games in the semifinals. "Bobby Hull and Glenn Hall did us in that year," recalls Gadsby. "By then I was almost 38 years old and running out of time.

"In the '66 playoffs we turned the tables on the Hawks and ousted them in seven games. That put us into the finals against Montreal. The Habs were huge favourites, mind you, because we'd finished something like 16 points in back of them during the regular season. We played the first two games at the Forum and Roger Crozier, our little goalie, just stoned them. He was sensational and we won the first two games.

"I really thought we had them. But the Habs stormed back and won the next two back on our ice. They won again in Montreal, and now we're back at home for game six. Suddenly we're hot again and we're tied with the Canadiens after regulation time.

"The overtime period was a couple of minutes under way when Henri Richard flew in on Crozier. Somehow Richard fell down and went sliding toward the goal and Crozier. Just then the puck came to him and he slid with it into the net. He shoved the damn thing in with his arm. I know he did. But the red light flashed and the Habs began jumping on the ice. I looked at the referee, John Ashley, and just stood there. He didn't wave it off. The series was over. I still can't believe it ended like it did.

"After all these years, I still say Ashley should never have allowed that goal. It was a lousy way for us to lose. I knew right then I'd probably never get another chance at the Cup."

Long after the series was over, Montreal coach Toe Blake confessed that he, too, had thought the Richard goal would be called back, so he ordered his players to leap onto the ice immediately and start celebrating. He didn't want to give the referee time to think about the legitimacy of the goal, nor time to confer with anyone else.

To the Habs, another Cup win was old hat. It was their seventh in the past 11 years. But to Gadsby, it was a tragedy, the end of a dream.

He came back for a final season with the Red Wings, but the team was in decline. After a first-place finish in 1964–65, Detroit slipped to fourth the following year, then to fifth and finally all the way into the basement in 1967–68.

It should be noted that it was not John Ashley who refereed the playoff game that Gadsby can't forget. It was Frank Udvari. Udvari once said, "Dave Balon shot the puck, it hit Henri Richard on the arm or the shoulder, and he slid into Crozier on his stomach. I called it a goal."

John Ferguson, watching from the Montreal bench, remembers it this way: "Richard kept sliding and sliding and sliding at Crozier until he slid right into the net, with the puck and Crozier. The goal judge had no choice but to hit the red light because the puck had crossed the line. Meanwhile, Toe Blake was watching the whole thing and the minute the red light flashed he yelled down the bench, 'Get out on the ice! Get out there!' So we tumbled over the boards and headed for Richard. Toe figured if we jumped on the ice and made it appear that everything about the goal was legit, maybe Udvari would swallow his whistle. And Toe was exactly right. Udvari seemed stunned and did nothing to wave off the goal. The Red Wings were in a trance as well, and by then we knew the goal was going to count and we could start whooping it up in earnest."

Adams Picks His Best

No other team, not even the Montreal dynasty of the late 1950s, has ever matched Detroit's run of seven consecutive first-place finishes in the NHL standings, which lasted from 1948–49 until 1954–55. A decade after the Wings' reign ended, and after Montreal had achieved five first-place finishes from 1957–58 to 1961–62, the architect of those Detroit teams, Jack Adams, was asked to name the players who had contributed the most at each position during the seven-year stretch.

His selections came easily; he put the famed Production Line at the top of his list. "Sure they were the best," he said. "Sid Abel at centre, Gordie Howe on right wing and Ted Lindsay on the left side. The greatest line ever, no matter what they say in Montreal. Then I'd choose Red Kelly and Bob Goldham as my defencemen from that era. And don't tell me I've overlooked two great ones in Bill Quackenbush and Jack Stewart. Each was a marvel in his time, but Quackenbush played in only one of the seasons we're talking about and Stewart played in two. Goldham contributed gilt-edged hockey for five of those years. I'm amazed they haven't put him in the Hall of Fame. In goal, who else but Terry Sawchuk?"

The Cheerleader

In the late 1960s, rugged centreman Pete Stemkowski enjoyed two good seasons in a Detroit uniform. He might have stayed around much longer if it hadn't been for his rebellious nature.

Adherence to club rules was not one of Stemmer's priorities, and when new coach Ned Harkness, a coaching legend at Cornell University, joined the club in 1970, there was an inevitable clash of personalities. Stemkowski, sometimes called the Polish Prince during his days as a Maple Leaf, was known for his relaxed, fun-loving approach to the game, while Harkness prided himself on being a stern disciplinarian.

Stemkowski recalled two incidents that he felt led to his departure from Detroit in a trade to the New York Rangers.

"You know, when Harkness came along, we had a bunch of old pros on the Red Wings, guys like Gordie and Alex Delvecchio and Gary Bergman and myself. Frankly, we didn't know what to make of Harkness. He was a rah-rah college guy, and the first thing he did was order us to wear blue blazers and gray slacks and to butt out our cigars. Geez, that last rule was a blow to Alex, because he's had a cigar in his mouth since the day he was born. So we made a few comments about the guy behind his back, and one day he was late for a morning practice. I was goofing around in the dressing room, and for some reason I stood up and played the role of a cheerleader. 'Gimme a C!' I yelled. 'Gimme an O, gimme an R, gimme an N...' But before I could spell out Cornell, I realized the guys had stopped responding. After the first couple of letters, they'd hushed up.

"I soon found out why. Ned Harkness had slipped into the room and was standing right behind me. Talk about mocking someone and being caught red-handed — that was me. I knew right then that my stay in Detroit was probably not going to be a long one."

Stemkowski moves on to the other incident. "Bobby Baun, my roomie at the time, loves to tell this story. We played an exhibition game in Port Huron one night. I was single at the time, so I invited a great-looking girl I knew to come up and see the game. It was just an exhibition game, and I didn't figure Ned would lay on a blinkin' curfew afterwards. But he did, telling us, 'One o'clock curfew, men. No ifs, ands or buts.'

"So I meet this girl after the game, and already it's about 11:30 p.m. We have a couple of drinks, and it's obvious she's a little amorous, so we take a walk on the beach. This is in September, and it's cold out. We drop down in the sand and roll around a bit, but I say, 'This won't do. This is ridiculous. Come on back to my room.'

"She says, 'What about your roommate?'

"I say, 'I'm rooming with Bobby Baun. There won't be a problem — the guy sleeps like a log. Once he hits the sack, nothing will wake him up.'

"So we hurry back to the hotel, and now I've missed curfew by about fifteen minutes. Figure I better sneak up the back stairs. I tell the girl, 'You follow along. I'll make sure the coast is clear.'

"I get up to my floor, and who the hell is standing there but Ned Harkness. His room is just a couple of doors away from mine. He says, 'Come on in for a minute.' So I say, 'Sure,' and I go into his room — what else could I do? He says, 'You've got sand on your clothes.' I look surprised and say, 'Geez, how'd that get there?'

"He says, 'Great game tonight.' I say, 'Thanks. We're coming along; we'll be all right.' He looks at his watch and says, 'You know, you've missed curfew by a few minutes.' I say, 'Did I? Geez, the guys were all getting food at the take-out counter around the corner. My food arrived a little later than the others.' I thought it was a good excuse. He didn't seem to notice that I wasn't carrying any food.

"So he smiles and says, 'That's okay. Get a good night's sleep. I'll see you tomorrow.'

"He throws open the door to let me out, and guess who's standing there, brushing sand off her skirt? She grins and says, 'Hi, Pete. Can I come in now?'

"There was no way I could talk my way out of that situation. Ned slapped me with a fine, and sure enough, it wasn't long before I got a phone call. 'You've been traded to New York.'

"At first I was disappointed, but everything turned out swell for me as a Ranger. Had half a dozen good years, met my wife there, bought a house, had some kids. Found a career in broadcasting after hockey. New York turned out to be a good move for me.

"I suppose I've got Ned Harkness to thank for that, but I'm not really sure. You see, he told me once that it wasn't his idea to trade me — that Sid Abel was the one who insisted on the deal. But years later, I ran into Abel and he looked me right in the eye and said he'd wanted to keep me with the Wings, but that Ned Harkness was adamant that I be dealt. That's hockey for you."

Smarten Up, Baun Tells Howe

Defenceman Bobby Baun had played 11 years with Toronto and one with the Oakland Seals before he joined the Detroit Red Wings for the 1968–69 season. In those days, players' salaries were seldom discussed. The teams wanted it that way, and some of the players did, too — probably because they were embarrassed to reveal how little they were earning.

Baun went against the grain. He always gave off the appearance of being well heeled, even in junior hockey when he would flash a fat roll of bills and drive a bigger, faster car than the other teenage stars.

In his second season as a Red Wing, Baun invited Gordie Howe to lunch. This was during training camp in Port Huron, Michigan. Baun came right to the point: "Gordie, you old fart, when are you going to smarten up?"

"What do you mean by that?" Gordie answered, perturbed by the question.

"Listen to me," said Baun. "I want you to know something. You've got the biggest name in hockey and I'm making twice as much money as you are. What do you think of that?"

Howe gulped. He couldn't believe it. He'd been assured many times over the years that he was the highest-paid Red Wing.

"How much are you making?" Howe asked.

"Ninety grand a year," Baun replied without missing a beat. "Double what you're getting."

Baun added to Howe's discomfort by saying with a laugh, "If that isn't hard enough to swallow, how about this: Carl Brewer is making more money than both of us."

Baun's words left Howe steaming. He knew what to do with that kind of information. The following day, he marched into the Red Wings' front office and demanded a renegotiation of his contract. Owner Bruce Norris embarrassed to have been caught deceiving the Red Wings' greatest asset, quickly agreed. Howe's salary was more than doubled. But a rift in Gordie's relationship with the owner had been created, one that would never heal.

Norris couldn't resist taking a verbal shot when Gordie left his office. "Well, I hope that'll make Colleen happy," he snorted, referring to Gordie's wife, who always took a keen interest in contract negotiations.

Playing the Pest Position

How is a forward able to play 16 seasons in the NHL with six different clubs, average just one goal per season, and still keep his job?

It's easy if your name is Bryan "Bugsy" Watson.

Watson, a Detroit favourite for most of five seasons, was hockey's premier pest, a pugnacious little guy, and a shit disturber of the first degree. He displayed an amazing ability to drive opponents to distraction with his tricky play and his in-your-face approach to the game.

"Nobody could get under your skin like that little so-and-so," Leafs manager Punch Imlach once said. "No wonder they nicknamed him Bugsy. In the '60s he drove most of the best players in the game absolutely crazy."

Bobby Hull agrees. During the 1965–66 season, Chicago's Golden Jet reached superstardom by scoring 54 goals, shattering the 21-year-old standard of 50 set by Rocket Richard. When the Blackhawks met the Red Wings in the 1966 semifinals, the Wings had to find a way to stop Hull.

"Hell, I can do that," Watson said confidently, even though Hull outweighed him by 20 pounds and was strong enough that he could have picked Watson up by the scruff of the neck and dropped him off in the penalty box — which, incidentally, was Watson's second home.

Detroit coach Sid Abel knew Bugsy was the perfect man for the job. He knew Watson would stick to Hull like gum to shoe leather.

Throughout the series, which lasted six games, Watson made Hull's hockey life miserable, following him maniacally and goading Hull into some stupid penalties. "The secret was to shadow him but not get him too mad," Watson recalled. "I didn't want him to get so angry he'd go crazy and score goals all over the place."

Sid Abel said with a grin, "It looked to me like they were chained together out there. Watson was a big reason we won the series four games to two. I thought he was going to follow Hull into the showers when it was over."

"Boy, did he bug me," snapped Hull, who'd never been so thoroughly shadowed in his career.

"That was my role in hockey," Watson said. "If I could have scored like Hull, do you think I'd have been such a pest? When you score 17 goals in 16 seasons you'd better have something else to offer. I used every trick I knew to get to the opposing team — to get their best players stirred up. I could often foul an opponent like Hull and get away with it. An elbow, a crosscheck, a sneaky little trip, interfere with the guy — if you're slick you can pull it off and not get a penalty."

Not that Watson's many sly fouls in his career went undetected. At one time he led all NHL players in penalty minutes and served over 2,000 minutes in the box. That's nearly three minutes per game.

Sometimes he would become such an irritant that opponents would lash out at him and a fight would break out. That was fine with Watson. It usually meant both he and the rival team's best player would sit out five minutes.

Watson learned how to dish it out from one of hockey's most feared competitors, Montreal Canadiens enforcer John Ferguson. Early in their careers, they were roommates with the Habs. Ferguson had quickly established a reputation as hockey's heavyweight champ, while Watson had aspirations to hold the middleweight title. They are still good friends despite the jokes they play on each other. Ferguson has been known to phone Watson, who owns a restaurant in Washington, and order 100 pizzas to go. Perhaps he's seeking revenge for the time he was riding tandem on a snowmobile with Watson. When they took a corner, Watson elbowed Fergy off the machine and raced away, leaving him to walk through the drifts back to their starting point.

Ferguson says, "That Bugsy; pound for pound he was the toughest kid in hockey. He took an awful lot of punishment from some of the biggest guys in the game. But he never quit, never backed off. Everyone in the NHL admired his tenacity."

Watson's battered mug, with its dented nose and its multitude of scars, reveals the kind of player he was. Hockey writer Frank Orr once described his face as looking like "a bagful of door-knobs."

When told of the comparison, Watson offered a loopy grin. "If you hand it out, you'd better be prepared to take it," he said. "That's the way it's always been in the NHL."

Over the years, Watson had spent a lot of time working with Special Olympics. Fans who remember him as a bundle of fury on the ice are amazed at the softer, gentler side he displays when he's among the handicapped. "His commitment to the handicapped and the less fortunate is truly amazing," said Frank Selke Jr., who was an executive with the Canadiens when Watson first broke into the NHL.

"Here's a personal anecdote," said Selke. "My son Gary was nine when he was hospitalized with rheumatic fever. I put a note on the dressing room wall asking the Montreal players, if they had time, to visit Gary. The only one who did was Bryan Watson. And he came every day to talk with Gary, to help him with his homework. And he signed countless autographs for all the other kids in the ward. Gary is in his forties now and he still thinks Bryan Watson is one of the greatest individuals he's ever met."

Ullman Sets Playoff Record

Norm Ullman played in the NHL for 20 seasons and never won a Stanley Cup, but he did set a Stanley Cup record that has never been broken — he scored two goals in five seconds, and he did it against one of the greatest netminders in history.

"We [the Red Wings] were playing Chicago in the 1965 play-offs," Ullman recalled, "and Glenn Hall was tending goal for the Blackhawks. He was always hard to beat. Late in the second period I took a shot from well out, maybe 40 to 50 feet. The puck skimmed along the ice, caught the goal post and went in. Then, right off the face-off, I intercepted a pass and took another shot. This time, [Chicago] defenceman Matt Ravlich screened Hall, and another long shot found the net. I was amazed because all of this happened in just five seconds. The goals came at 17:35 and 17:40. Only later did I learn I'd set a record for the fastest two playoff goals. I don't think Glenn saw either shot. He didn't miss very many."

Ullman was a Red Wing for over 11 seasons and led the Wings in goals three times, and twice in points. He was traded to Toronto a year after the Leafs won the '67 Stanley Cup. He scored 490 career goals and, as a Red Wing, was selected to play in eight All-Star Games. He was inducted into the Hockey Hall of Fame in 1982.

Detroit's Second Banana Is a First-Class Guy

He played in more than 1,500 NHL games, scored 456 goals and added 825 assists, all with the same team. Yet he retired as the number two performer in each category on his team's all-time list. By now, any Detroit fan of a certain age knows we're referring to Alex Delvecchio, who spent his entire career on the ice under the monstrous shadow cast by Gordie Howe.

"It never really bothered me," Delvecchio says. "Gordie was the greatest player of all time. When you played with him, and you gave him the puck, you just knew that some good things were going to happen for the Red Wings.

"As a centreman, I felt it was my job to make plays, to set up other players for the goals."

Delvecchio placed a lot of emphasis on team play and sportsmanship. During his long career, he was a three-time winner of the Lady Byng Trophy, awarded for "sportsmanship and gentlemanly conduct combined with a high standard of playing ability."

Although Delvecchio's career totals in goals, assists and points have been surpassed by Steve Yzerman, he still holds down third place across the board, 30 years after his retirement. When he hung up the skates after 24 seasons and 1,549 regular-season games, only one player in league history outshone him in those categories: again, it was Howe. (He currently sits eighth in games played, and in 2003–04 Mark Messier of the New York Rangers finished his 25th NHL season, taking sole possession of second place on the all-time list. But Alex is still Number 2 in both categories in Detroit history.) And what is truly remarkable is that, unlike most other NHLers noted for their longevity — Howe, John Bucyk, Tim Horton, Messier or Ron Francis — Delvecchio played his entire career with one club.

At one point, Alex did contemplate changing teams. A year after Gordie Howe came out of retirement to play for Houston of the World Hockey Association, Delvecchio was offered an enticing contract to jump to the Aeros. But after 24 seasons in Detroit, he decided he was "too old" to switch.

Delvecchio's career scoring stats might have been even more impressive if he hadn't encountered a bizarre slump during the

1969–70 season. He skated through the first 32 games of the schedule without scoring a goal. His scoring famine made international news, and fans sent him dozens of good luck charms to help him snap the horrendous jinx. Then Miss America came to his aid: Pamela Anne Eldred, of Birmingham, Michigan, had worn a small jeweled pin on her brassiere when she captured the Miss America crown in August 1969. She sent the pin to Delvecchio and wished him luck. Alex attached the pin to his suspenders, and eureka! On New Year's Eve, 1969, he scored his first two goals of the season in a 5–1 rout of Boston. Three nights later, with the pin firmly in place, he scored a hat trick against Philadelphia. He connected 21 times in the 41 games that followed — his most prodigious rate ever.

Later, as coach and general manager of the Red Wings in the mid '70s, Alex's easy-going style won the respect of Detroit players. His hard-nosed predecessor, Ted Garvin, had insisted on a multitude of silly rules: long hair had been banned, strict curfews were instituted along with $500 fines to those who missed them and players' children were barred from the dressing room and the ice surfaces. Delvecchio threw out those rules and quickly turned the team around, silencing the critics who said he was too nice a guy to be coach.

"He communicates," said winger Nick Libett. "Alex has class. He knows how to handle men. How could you not want to play for him?"

On his office wall, Delvecchio hung a framed poem, one he could quote from memory that sums up his philosophy:

> Sometimes when you're feeling important,
> Sometimes when your ego's in bloom,
> Sometimes when you take it for granted
> You're the best qualified in the room,
> Take a bucket and fill it with water,
> Put your hand in it up to the wrist,
> Pull it out and the hole that's remaining
> Is a measure of how much you'll be missed.

The Golden Anniversary

The game at the Olympia on the night of November 24, 1976, was special not only because of the 4–3 win over the Toronto Maple Leafs, but because it also marked the 50th anniversary of the storied Detroit franchise.

Prior to the game, Budd Lynch, for 25 years the voice of Red Wings hockey, served as master of ceremonies. Standing under the spotlight at centre ice, Lynch introduced the evening's special guests.

First, three new members were inducted into the Red Wings Hall of Fame: Tommy Ivan, coach of the team for seven years; Jimmy Skinner, a former coach and at the time the assistant general manager; and Marguerite Norris Riker, team president during the 1950s and the first woman to have her name engraved on the Stanley Cup.

Then the spotlight played over the stands, picking out people associated with those great days. The beam couldn't help but fall upon Mrs. Helen Adams, who had been married to the late Jack Adams. Then there was the widow of the former Olympia general manager, Nick Londes. One by one, the spotlight's beam fell upon a hundred more members of the Red Wings alumni, many of them members of the Hockey Hall of Fame.

Next, Lynch directed the crowd's attention to the entranceway to the ice, for a reunion of the famed Production Line. First came Ted Lindsay — what a competitor he was! And now a very successful businessman in partnership with former teammate Marty Pavelich. Those who knew Ted were aware that he was still very active with the Red Wings alumni and as coach at Hillsdale College. Then came Sid "Boot" Abel, a premier centreman in his day who later became the coach and GM of the Red Wings and the GM of the Kansas City Scouts.

Finally, there was a deafening roar of applause, as everyone in the arena rose to their feet to honour old Number 9, Gordie Howe. No need to repeat the lengthy list of accomplishments attached to his name. The greatest hockey player in the world, who had jumped to Houston of the WHA, was back on Olympia ice, and it was as if he had never left.

Among the players lined up along the blue lines, centreman Dennis Polonich couldn't keep his eyes off the Red Wings legend. "I want to meet Gordie," he told defenceman Terry Harper. "I can't wait to see him after the game. You know, shake his hand…"

"Why wait?" Harper laughed. "Go over now."

Without pausing, Polonich dashed over to where Gordie was standing and grabbed him by the hand. The crowd roared. The other players followed suit, and a long line formed behind Polonich.

Oh yes. Detroit 4, Toronto 2. A fitting result.

Rangers

Opening Night

On November 16, 1926, the New York Rangers made their Madison Square Garden debut against the swashbuckling Montreal Maroons, a big, bruising club and the defending Stanley Cup champions. Lester Patrick's hastily assembled team, initially called Tex's Rangers, was the underdog. Someone had designed a crest for the Rangers jersey — a depiction of a cowboy on a bucking bronco with the rider holding a hockey stick aloft. But the cowboy and his mount were sent out to pasture when owner Tex Rickard rejected the artwork. They were replaced by the word *Rangers* splashed diagonally across the front of the royal blue jersey.

The Rangers were a near-unanimous choice to finish last in the American Division of the 10-team NHL. They had been a sorry-looking club during training camp scrimmages held in Toronto, and manager Conn Smythe, a newcomer to professional hockey, bore the brunt of the blame for their apparent ineptitude. Smythe had been hired to assemble a competitive team, and he got off to a fine start when he signed the Cook brothers, Bill and Bun, and Frank Boucher, stars of the defunct Western Hockey League. From Minnesota, he recruited a pair of strong defencemen, Ivan "Ching" Johnson and Clarence "Taffy" Abel (the first U.S.–born player to become a regular in the National Hockey League). Both were balding belters who could heave opponents over the boards or lay them flat out on the ice. He added goaltenders Lorne Chabot and Hal Winkler, the latter of whom drew the opening game assignment even though Chabot would ultimately prove to be the better performer. Finally, Smythe added Murray Murdoch, who played the next 11 seasons without missing a game, and the smooth-skating Paul Thompson.

When hockey people were asked what they thought of Smythe's lineup, they replied, "Not much" — words that so unnerved Rangers president John Hammond that he fired Smythe during training camp and replaced him with Lester Patrick, a more experienced coach and manager. The articulate Patrick, then 42, would guide the Rangers from behind the bench for the next 13 years. When the NHL introduced All-Star Teams in 1930–31, Patrick was named top coach in seven of the first eight seasons.

In addition to Smythe's relative inexperience, his demise was speeded by a stubborn streak that infuriated Hammond. Cecil "Babe" Dye, the high-scoring winger for the Toronto St. Patricks, was on the market, and Hammond had been told that Dye would be a superstar if he played for the Rangers.

Hammond ordered Smythe to acquire him.

"I will not," barked Smythe. "Dye's a goal scorer, but he's not a good team man. I know him well and I won't have any part of him."

"I've heard that Dye's a great player and we should get him," Hammond insisted.

"You heard wrong," Smythe snorted.

Hammond sighed. "Connie," he said, "maybe you're too young and inexperienced for this job. Lester Patrick would jump at a chance to come to New York."

"Then hire Patrick," said Smythe, with a fire in his eyes. "I've put a good team together for you and there's no room on it for Babe Dye."

Hammond promptly bought Smythe out and hired Patrick. As for Dye, he never became a Ranger. He enjoyed one good season with Chicago, and then broke his leg in training camp and was never the same player again, scoring only one goal in his final 58 NHL games (compared with 200 in his first 213).

Jimmy Walker, New York's popular mayor, accepted an invitation to drop the puck for the ceremonial face-off in the opening game against the Maroons. But the mayor was still en route to Madison Square Garden when the big moment arrived. Fortunately, Lois Moran, a beautiful movie star, was introduced to the crowd that filled the Garden. Most of the gentleman fans, accustomed to Broadway openings, were attired in tuxedos, while the ladies wore fashionable evening gowns.

The applause was generous as Miss Moran minced across the ice, waving to her fans with one hand and holding a puck in the other. She dropped the disc carefully between the sticks of Nels Stewart, the hardrock centreman of the Maroons, and spindly Frank Boucher, who was about to begin a playing and coaching career with the Rangers that would last for the next 29 years.

Boucher would later recall that the opening game was "as rough as any ever played." Blood poured from cuts when high sticks connected, and the grunts from players bodied into the ice or boards could be heard 10 rows up. Referee Lou Marsh couldn't possibly see all the fouls — crosschecking, slashing, hooking and holding. Even the mild-mannered Boucher, who accumulated only 119 penalty minutes in 557 regular-season games, got into it. When challenged by Montreal tough guy Bill Phillips, Boucher threw off his gloves and laced into his opponent. Phillips knocked him flat with a punch. Boucher bounced up and knocked Phillips to the ice. Each drew a five-minute penalty; Boucher's major was one of only three he would incur in 14 seasons of NHL hockey.

Only one goal was scored, and it came late in the second period. The Cooks teamed up to beat Maroons goalie Clint Benedict, who, years later, would introduce the first facemask to the NHL. Bill Cook flipped the puck over Benedict, who, in attempting the save, struck the goalpost with his head. There was a lengthy delay while the semiconscious netminder received medical attention before propping himself back in the net.

The Garden ice, soft to begin with, was in terrible condition by the third period. There were no Zambonis in those days, so ice was not resurfaced between periods. Workmen simply used heavy scrapers to remove the snow and slush that accumulated.

The Rangers withstood every Maroons attack and emerged from the contest bruised, battered and, most importantly, triumphant. They received a prolonged ovation at the game's end, the applause from the vast audience lingering long after the players were back in their dressing room, where they pounded each other on the back, as thrilled as the spectators with the outcome.

"We beat the world champions!" someone shouted.

"Did you hear that crowd?" a player shrieked. "They love us here."

Lester Patrick shook hands all around. "Boys, you play some more games like that and this franchise will be a huge success here in New York. It's really exciting to think of what's ahead for all of us. This is just the beginning."

The Silver Fox: A Hockey Legend

Lester Patrick, the Silver Fox of hockey, reached the pinnacle in every phase of hockey, whether as a player, coach, manager or owner. He would have refereed if they'd asked him — and no doubt would have excelled. And one night in 1928, at age 44, he made history by donning the goal pads for a playoff game — and, of course, winning it in overtime.

Lester was born December 30, 1883, in Drummondville, Quebec, the first of five sons sired by Joseph Patrick, a storekeeper and lumberman. At age nine, Lester sawed off the limb of a tree and made himself a hockey stick — one good enough for shinny. He received his first pair of skates when he was 10, and three years later, by now living in Montreal, he became a stick boy for the fabled Ottawa Hockey Club (later the Silver Seven) whenever they played in Montreal.

He aspired for a time to become a cowboy, and gave it a try one summer after his freshman year at McGill University. But his true love was hockey. "I thought if I could play just one game in big-time hockey, I could die happy," he once told reporters. Tall, rawboned and powerful, with a mop of hair that was to turn silver prematurely and earn him his nickname, he broke into professional hockey in 1903 as a defenceman in Brandon, Manitoba. A part-time job in a laundry was part of the deal. At the end of his first season, his team challenged for the Stanley Cup, and Patrick wound up performing against the team he'd once guarded sticks for: the Silver Seven of Ottawa. During a long and fascinating career, he would star on defence with several teams and play on or manage 15 teams in Stanley Cup competition.

At age 22, Lester was the captain of the famed Montreal Wanderers, whom he led to a pair of Stanley Cup triumphs. Then he headed west to work with his father in the lumber business in Nelson, British Columbia. After work, he continued to play hockey in a senior league.

It was a financial proposal he couldn't refuse that brought Patrick back east. He had offered his services to Art Ross's All-Montreal club for $1,200, and Ross had expressed horror at his demand. "No player is worth that kind of dough," snorted Ross, "except possibly myself." But Ottawa and the little town of Renfrew, Ontario, also wanted Patrick. He told Ottawa he'd consider $1,500 and wired Renfrew that his price was $3,000. "Renfrew's just a dot on the map," he told his brother Frank. "They'll never cough up $3,000, which is fine with me because I don't think I want to play there, anyway."

To his amazement, Lester received a wire back from Renfrew: "Proceed here at once. Will pay you $3,000." Still uncertain about moving to the remote northern Ontario town, he sent another wire: "I'll report if you'll sign my brother Frank — at $2,000." Renfrew replied immediately: "Bring your brother. It's a deal."

Renfrew imported other top stars, and even offered Hay Millar, an Edmonton player, a thousand dollars to play a single game when Frank Patrick was injured.

The Patrick brothers were pioneers, among the first to realize that hockey was more than a winter pastime: it was big business. In the summer of 1911, the Patricks decided to introduce professional hockey to the Pacific coast. On his honeymoon that year in the east, Patrick investigated the artificial ice rinks that were cropping up along the eastern seaboard of the United States. He returned to the coast, and with the backing of his wealthy father, he built, in partnership with his brother Frank, Canada's first artificial rinks in Vancouver and Victoria, B.C.

The Patricks launched the Pacific Coast Hockey Association, a circuit that lasted for 13 seasons before merging with the Western Canada Hockey League. They raided eastern teams for talented players and revolutionized the game with their innovations. They brought in the blue lines and the forward pass that made the game lightning-fast. They added numbers to players' uniforms — a first in team sports. They devised the playoff system, now in universal use in hockey and other sports.

In 1925, Lester Patrick's Victoria Cougars stunned the Montreal Canadiens and won the Stanley Cup largely because he tried something new: using two forward lines. Until then, most players were 60-minute men.

In the summer of 1926, the Patricks sold all the players from the Western league to the NHL. Weeks later, Lester signed with an NHL expansion team, the New York Rangers — replacing Conn Smythe, a young manager from Toronto who was fired before the team had played a single game.

"That was embarrassing," Patrick once said. "I did know Connie Smythe. Then I had to go to Toronto, where the Rangers were training, and take over his job. In spite of this, Smythe was always one of my biggest boosters."

Patrick inherited a number of tough and talented players from Smythe — men like Taffy Abel, Ivan "Ching" Johnson, and the Cook brothers, Bill and Bun. As a result, the Rangers, in their premiere season, captured first place in their division. Bill Cook scored 33 goals in 44 games and won the scoring title. Patrick himself suited up for one game to display his defensive skills, and the following spring, he made another, much more stunning one-game comeback — as a goaltender — to help his Rangers win their first Stanley Cup.

With New York, Lester Patrick devised plays and passing patterns that made the modern game a thing of beauty. It started with his number one line — the Cook brothers, centred by Frank Boucher — and reached its ultimate in finesse and combination play when the Colville brothers, Neil and Mac, teamed with Alex Shibicky in the 1930s.

Shibicky once said, "Lester was more than a hockey great. He was a man who lived by a high moral code. He had a tremendous amount of personal feeling towards his players. He was an educated man in a tough sport. He would conduct classes in the Ranger dressing room, asking the capital city of nations and the names of rivers."

Patrick was brilliant and charming and had a gift for language. He was renowned as a raconteur. His best tales were told with a

French-Canadian dialect he had acquired in his youth in Drummondville. He was not without warts: he could be arrogant and short-tempered. Frank Boucher once said of him, "Lester could, in turn, be pleasant, excitable, kind, sarcastic, pompous, headstrong, understanding, gentle, callous and contrite, depending on the circumstances."

Many of his rivals resented the adulation Patrick received from the New York media. They conceded that Lester had made huge contributions to the game of hockey, but they felt that Lester had convinced the New York writers that he had *invented* the game.

He coached the Rangers for 13 seasons and, after the NHL began selecting All-Star teams in 1930–31, he was named coach of the First Team in seven of eight years.

On February 22, 1946, Patrick resigned as general manager of the Rangers. He was succeeded by the popular Boucher, an original Ranger, marking the beginning of the end of the friendship between the two men. Patrick agreed to stay on with the team in an advisory capacity, but during Boucher's first training camp in Winnipeg, Patrick complained loudly that Boucher neither sought nor wanted his advice. They seldom spoke to each other after that.

Patrick retired to Victoria, where he ran a minor-league hockey team. In his seventies, he fought his final battle — against cancer. The Silver Fox succumbed to the disease on June 1, 1960, at age 76.

Tributes poured in from all over North America. Perhaps the old-time hockey great Newsy Lalonde said it best: "Whenever I look back on my career I always think of Lester, because he represented to me all the finest things about the game. He was a tremendous skater and stickhandler, he always played hard — a real never-say-die type — and he was a fine gentleman on and off the ice."

Was Cook the Greatest Right Winger?

When Bill Cook died in Kingston, Ontario, in the summer of 1986, he was hailed as the greatest right winger ever to play for the New York Rangers. From the Rangers' very first game, he played alongside brother Bun and Frank Boucher on a line that performed brilliantly for many seasons.

Cook was 30 — "a seasoned pro," the writers called him — when he joined the Rangers for their inaugural season in 1926. He'd been through the First World War, having enlisted at age 17, and had survived battles at Ypres, Vimy Ridge, the Somme and Flanders. Cook was described by a fellow soldier as "one of the bravest men I have ever seen." After the war, he took advantage of a Canadian government program for land grants in Saskatchewan. He took a half-section (a 320-acre plot) that adjoined his brother Bun's property.

Bill and Bun starred for Saskatoon in the Western league, and when the Rangers began recruiting players for an NHL expansion team, Bill Cook was happy to turn in his bib overalls for a Ranger uniform. He was the first player signed.

With Bun in tow, he arrived in New York and immediately became a team leader. He would be responsible for many "firsts" while clad in Rangers livery. He became the club's first captain, and in the team's first game, Bill scored the first goal in Rangers history. It came on a pass from Bun, who earned his nickname after a Manhattan reporter wrote that he was "quick as a bunny." The marker was also the first game-winner in the team's brief existence.

On the strength of his 33 goals and four assists for 37 points during his first season, he became the first Ranger to win the Art Ross Trophy as the NHL scoring champ. A year later, he captured the award again and helped lead the Rangers to their first Stanley Cup.

When he retired at age 40, Cook had accumulated 228 NHL goals and had been the Rangers' leader in goals during six of his 11 seasons.

Frank Boucher, who spent 29 years in New York as a player, coach and manager of the Rangers, once said, "Bill was the finest all-round player in Ranger history. And he's my choice as the best right winger hockey ever knew, despite the fact that others disagree and give their votes to Rocket Richard or Gordie Howe. I say Cook topped them both."

After his playing days, Cook made a triumphant return to Madison Square Garden. In 1968, he helped close out the old

Garden and usher in the new. "They brought me back because I scored the first goal [for the Rangers] in the old Madison Square Garden," he told reporters. "Then they gave me a puck and sent me out on the ice to put one in the net to christen the new Garden. Now that was quite an honour."

Winning in Wartime

When Canada declared war on Germany in September 1939, thus joining the Second World War, the NHL was only a few days away from opening its 48-game schedule. There were indications that the booming guns in Europe would soon interrupt brilliant careers.

Seven teams would compete for league honours in 1939–40, with the Boston Bruins showing the most clout, finishing atop the standings with 67 points, three more than the second-place Rangers. The Bruins' Kraut Line of Milt Schmidt, Bobby Bauer and Woody Dumart made history by copping the top three positions in the individual scoring race. The Rangers' Bryan Hextall led all players in goals scored, with 24.

Prior to the season, Lester Patrick stepped down as coach of the Rangers, to be replaced by Frank Boucher. Boucher was delighted with the play of his main line of Neil Colville, Alex Shibicky and Mac Colville, and equally impressed with the performance of the combination of Hextall, Phil Watson and Lynn Patrick. By mid January, the Rangers had lost only three games and had gone a record 19 games without a defeat. After dropping a 2–1 decision to Chicago, they ran off another five wins before losing again. The streak of 25 games with only one loss was simply incredible, and Dave Kerr, the Rangers' goalie since 1934, was largely responsible. He had the agility of a gymnast and a tongue that never stopped flapping. He'd shout instructions at his team-mates, exhorting them to make the proper plays. Kerr fashioned a 1.60 goals-against average to go with his eight shutouts. Both stats were league highs. He won his only Vezina Trophy that season.

The Rangers and Bruins played a pair of games late in the schedule. One ended in a scoreless tie, while the other was a 2–1 victory for Boston. For the third season in a row, the Bruins had compiled the best record in the NHL.

The playoff system was quirky and generous in those days. Every team but one, the last-place Montreal Canadiens, qualified. In the first round, the second-place Rangers faced the defending champion Bruins, which might have made sense in that era but would be incomprehensible today. Dave Kerr, with a shutout, was the opening-game hero at Madison Square Garden, as the Rangers dropped a 4–0 goose egg on the visitors.

The Bruins roared back with a pair of victories, 4–2 and 4–3. Then it was Kerr's turn to shine again. Before the largest crowd of the season in New York, 16,504, he registered his second shutout, chalking up a 1–0 victory. Two nights later he did it again, back-stopping the Rangers to another 1–0 win and picking up his third shutout of the series. New Yorkers had never seen such shot blocking. The Rangers ousted the Bruins from the Stanley Cup hunt with a 4–1 triumph in game five. The victory earned them a bye into the finals.

Toronto survived by eliminating Chicago and Detroit, only to face off against the Rangers for the Cup. The first two games were slated for New York on April 2 and 3.

In the opener, Rangers defenceman Alf Pike scored the winner in overtime, while Bryan Hextall was the star of game two, which New York won 6–2. Hextall, who had been held scoreless for seven games, suddenly exploded for three goals and was virtually unstoppable. After the game, his performance was still being cheered, even as the boards were being removed to make way for the incoming circus that traditionally occupied the Garden in April.

Back in Toronto, the Leafs rebounded with a 2–1 victory. With seven minutes to play, Hank Goldup beat Kerr for the game winner.

In game four, the Rangers missed Alex Shibicky, who was out with a sprained ankle, and were shut out by Turk Broda and the Leafs, 3–0. Shibicky was back for game five, but his tender ankle gave out and he was unable to finish the match. Murray "Muzz" Patrick won the game for New York, 2–1, in the second overtime period with a shot that eluded Broda's grasp.

Facing elimination, the desperate Leafs jumped to a 2–0 lead in game six. In the third period, the Rangers rallied. Neil Colville and Alf Pike scored to tie the game and Bryan Hextall potted the winner at 2:07 of overtime, after taking a pass from Phil Watson.

Manager Lester Patrick proudly posed for a photographer alongside his sons Murray and Lynn. For the first time, the Stanley Cup would display the names of four members of one family: Lester and Frank Patrick, and Lester's sons Murray and Lynn. More than half a century later, another Patrick name would be added to the famous trophy after Lynn's son Craig managed the Pittsburgh Penguins to a Cup triumph over Chicago.

After winning the Cup in 1940, the Rangers celebrated back at their hotel — the Royal York. They drank some beer from Lord Stanley's big basin and smoked cigars. The next day, half the team boarded a train for New York while others headed off to western Canada. New Yorkers were pleased with the triumph, but there was no big celebration. Nobody considered holding a victory parade or ordering championship rings. The players were given gold watches worth about $30.

The rings would come 50 years later. In 1990, Rangers general manager Neil Smith decided that the seven surviving members of the 1940 championship squad had waited long enough. He presented each of them with an expensive Stanley Cup ring to mark the golden anniversary of a memorable moment in Rangers history.

To show his appreciation, Clint Smith dug out his old Rangers jersey, embroidered with the number 10, and presented it to Neil Smith. "Maybe it'll bring you luck," the old-timer said. The Rangers manager had the jersey framed and placed on a wall in his office. Within four seasons, his team broke a 54-year drought to capture the Stanley Cup.

Rangers' Streak Ends on a Sour Note

Frank Boucher was a huge success in 1939–40, his first season as coach of the Rangers. His team lost a mere 11 games out of 48 and his goaltender, Dave Kerr, was phenomenal, allowing only 77 goals — 21 fewer than the runner-up, Boston ace Frank Brimsek — for a goals-against average of 1.60 and a Vezina Trophy win.

That was the season the Rangers embarked on an undefeated streak that stretched to 10, then 15, then 19 games. The 19th game in the Rangers' streak was played in Toronto on January 13 — a 4–1 New York victory. The next night at Chicago Stadium, after a long train ride, Kerr and his mates suited up to play the Blackhawks, a team that was getting splendid goaltending from rookie Paul Goodman, who played in 31 of his 52 career games that season.

Prior to the game, Boucher took Kerr aside and gave him explicit instructions: "If the Rangers happen to be trailing by a goal late in the game, watch for my signal. I may pull you from the net even though the play is in progress. Got it?"

"Got it, coach," was Kerr's reply.

Up until that time, a goalie had never been pulled from the net for another attacker unless there was a face-off. But there was no rule stating he couldn't be pulled on the fly, and Boucher was determined to try it. The move might surprise and confuse the Hawks and lead to a game-tying goal.

Sure enough, the Rangers fell behind Chicago, 2–1. They outshot and outskated the Hawks, but couldn't put the puck past Goodman.

With less than two minutes to play, and with the puck in the Chicago zone, Boucher signalled Kerr, who made a beeline for the bench. Ott Heller replaced him on the ice and hustled after the puck.

While this was happening, Lester Patrick, the Rangers' general manager, was standing between the players' benches. He didn't notice, nor did he anticipate, that Kerr might leave his net. But he *did* see Heller, the extra man, leap into the action.

"Too many men!" he shouted at Boucher. "Frank, you've got too many men on the ice."

Paul Thompson, the Chicago coach, heard Lester's warning cry and began to shout at the referee. "Too many men on the ice!" he screamed over and over.

The referee took a quick head count and blew his whistle. "Penalty to New York," he announced.

Boucher threw his hands in the air in frustration, and then pointed at the empty net. "I pulled my goalie, you dummies," he muttered, shaking his head in anguish.

The referee waved off the penalty, Patrick came over to apologize to Boucher for ruining a unique bit of strategy and Paul Thompson sighed with relief, as the Ranger pressure in the Chicago zone had been intense.

The Hawks held on to win the game by a 2–1 score. The longest undefeated streak in Rangers history was over.

Blueshirts Were First on TV

Here's one for trivia fans. Name the year in which television first covered a hockey game; and, for bonus points, name the two teams involved.

Just to be sporting, I'll make the first part of the question multiple-choice. Take a guess: was it 1960, 1950 or 1940?

You'll find the answer somewhere in this account of a game played between the Montreal Canadiens and the New York Rangers. The game was played at Madison Square Garden on February 25, 1940. That night, fans who couldn't attend the game were able to watch it at home, thanks to a miraculous new invention called television. Of course, not many New Yorkers would have taken advantage, since there were only 300 TV sets scattered throughout the city, and their screens were a minuscule seven inches wide.

At Madison Square Garden, a single cameraman followed the play, and the announcer who called the play was Skip Walz, although he often used the name Bill Allen. The game went out over W2XBS, an experimental station set up by the NBC network that broadcast on — believe it or not — Channel 1. The previous summer, the station had transmitted the first-ever baseball telecast, a Brooklyn-Cincinnati tilt at Ebbets Field.

Rangers fans remember the 1939–40 season not for television but for their team's marvellous accomplishments on the ice. It was one of New York's finest seasons. The Rangers played a record 19 games without defeat. In the playoffs, they ousted Toronto, four games to two in the finals, capturing the Stanley Cup on April 13 at Maple Leaf Gardens.

Many years would pass before NHL officials welcomed TV cameras to hockey games. When the CBC began televising games from Montreal and Toronto during the 1952–53 season, NHL President Clarence Campbell called television "the greatest menace in the entertainment world."

The Rangers figured prominently in U.S. network television's second foray into hockey in the 1950s. New York hosted the first CBS telecast on January 5, 1957, and defeated Chicago 4–1. The Rangers were involved in four of the nine games telecast by CBS that season and won three of them. The following year, CBS produced an *NHL Game of the Week* with Bud Palmer and Fred Cusick in the broadcast booth. In 1960, with Palmer at the Olympics, your author joined play-by-play man Cusick as colour commentator. Prior to each intermission, I would leave my perch in the broadcast booth, hustle down a back stairwell to rinkside, throw on a pair of skates and interview players on the ice. These segments often included demonstrations of hockey's fundamentals by the stars of that era.

Buzinski Was a Beautiful Bust

The Rangers have employed some of hockey's best goaltenders over the years — Dave Kerr, Terry Sawchuk, Eddie Giacomin and Mike Richter — but they've also been stuck with two of the all-time worst.

The record books show that Steve Buzinski, a little man who weighed only 140 pounds, served a nine-game stint with Frank Boucher's Rangers during the 1942–43 season, when wartime duties had robbed the NHL of much of its top talent.

"I thought I'd seen some lousy goaltending during my career in hockey," Boucher once recalled, "but all of the sieves I'd seen were aces compared to Buzinski. One night in Detroit, the Red Wings plastered nine goals past him in the first two periods. In the third period, Buzinski rushed from his net, caught the puck in his glove, and tumbled in an awkward heap on the ice. Ott Heller

187

went over to help him up and heard Buzinski say, 'Just like pickin' cherries, Ott.' "

Lynn Patrick topped Boucher's story with one of his own.

"We were playing Toronto one night, and when the Leafs scored an easy goal, Buzinski swooned to the ice as he did on an average of once every period. He lay there, apparently unconscious, while blood trickled from a tiny cut on his cheek. We turned to the referee and argued that a Leaf player was in the crease and he'd been hit by that Leaf's stick and the goal shouldn't count. The Leafs argued that it was a puck that did the damage.

"Suddenly, Buzinski sat bolt upright. 'It was a stick, dammit!' he shouted, and fell back unconscious again."

"All the players on the ice stopped arguing and started laughing," Patrick continued. "We even went over to the benches to tell the rest of the guys what had happened. Buzinski gave us enough funny moments to make up for all the pain he caused us. Well, almost…

"How did he fare in those nine games he played for us? Well, he gave up about six goals a game [posting a goals-against average of 5.89], which must be one of the highest in history."

In 1984, Buzinski was interviewed about his NHL career and admitted he'd made the remark about "pickin' cherries."

"But I have no recollection of that other incident where I suddenly woke up and claimed it was a stick that hit me. But it sounds like something I would do," he laughs. "In wartime hockey, you had to keep your sense of humour."

"Steve was a beautiful little guy," said Boucher. "He was earnest and sincere and we all liked him tremendously. There was just one little problem. He couldn't stop a puck worth a damn."

No wonder he became known as Steve "The Puck Goes Inski" Buzinski.

"The next season we had a goaltender who was just as bad: Ken McAuley from Edmonton," Boucher said. "He played in all 50 games, including a 15–0 shellacking we took from Detroit — and finished with a goals-against average of 6.24."

The NHL record book reveals that McAuley and the Rangers won a mere six games in 1943–44 and allowed 310 goals, the most to be scored against an NHL team to that point in history.

The record stood until 1970–71, when the California Golden Seals gave up 320 goals, and by that time the schedule was 78 games, more than half again as long as in 1943–44.

McAuley got off to the poorest start of any NHL goalie. Fifteen seconds into his second game, Gus Bodnar of the Toronto Maple Leafs raced in and scored on him. It was both the fastest first goal to be scored by a rookie, and the fastest first goal to be given up by a rookie netminder.

The One that Got Away

Think of it: the Rangers had Gordie Howe in camp for almost a week, and let him get away. How many Stanley Cups did that mistake cost them?

Growing up in Saskatoon, young Howe began his career as a goaltender. In 1942, his first year of minor hockey, he was converted to defence and became the outstanding player on the King George Athletic Club team.

He moved on to bantam and midget hockey, and by the time he was 15 years old, he was heavily muscled, fast on his feet and an accomplished stickhandler and shooter. He looked right at home whenever he played against older, tougher, more experienced players.

A Rangers scout spotted him in a game one day. "He's young, but you've got to take a look at this kid," he told Frank Boucher, his general manager. "Why not invite him to training camp in Winnipeg?"

Howe was thrilled to receive the invitation, but was thoroughly intimidated by the grown men with whom he shared ice time and dressing-room space.

The Rangers players, fighting for positions and contracts, paid little attention to him. They kidded him some. "First time away from home, kid? Got your homework with you?" And "Comin' to the bar with us tonight, Gord? Maybe we can buy you a milkshake." In the mess hall, one joker stole the food off his plate when he wasn't looking. The players suited up for a scrimmage, and Gordie watched their every move. Some of the equipment he'd been handed was new to him; he'd never worn a jock before, and watched curiously as the others pulled theirs on. Years later, at banquets, he would tell his audience that he almost put that jock on over his head.

In Winnipeg, Howe was homesick and terribly lonely. He missed his mother's home cooking and his friends. The Rangers suggested he try for a scholarship at Notre Dame College in Wilcox, Saskatchewan, a school with a fine hockey program. All Gordie wanted to do was go home.

The Rangers gave him train fare back to Saskatoon and wished him well. He'd been in Winnipeg less than a week.

Years later, when Howe was billed as the greatest player in the game and guiding Detroit to Stanley Cups, a Rangers scout would say, "It's too bad we didn't take a little more time with him in Winnipeg that fall. Why, he didn't even have a buddy from Saskatoon to room with, hardly a soul to talk to. Detroit manager Jack Adams learned a lesson from that. He took Gordie to Detroit's camp a year later and made sure four or five young kids from Saskatoon accompanied him. Not long after that, when Howe scored a couple of goals in an exhibition game, Adams signed him for $2,700 and the promise of a Red Wing jacket. And to think we could have had him…"

Buddy's Big Bonus

Gnat-sized Buddy O'Connor was feeling blue when the 1947–48 NHL season ended and who could blame him? The diminutive Ranger centre had led the league in scoring through most of the campaign, but in the final weekend he was nosed out for the Art Ross Trophy by a single point. And it was a former teammate, Elmer Lach of the Canadiens, who stole the title away from him, 61 points to 60.

O'Connor found consolation of a sort when he was named winner of both the Hart Trophy (MVP) and the Lady Byng Trophy (gentlemanly play). And he was overwhelmed when he added up his bonus money — a small fortune at the time. The post-season payoff came in the following manner:

$500 from the NHL for finishing second in the scoring race;

$500 from the Rangers as runner-up scorer;

$1,000 for winning the Hart Trophy (ahead of Frank Brimsek);

$1,000 for winning the Lady Byng Trophy (ahead of Syl Apps);

$500 for making the Second All-Star Team;

$500 from the NHL, his share of the Rangers' playoff money.

Hockey's horn of plenty spilled the loot into O'Connor's lap after his seventh NHL season and his first as a Ranger. For half a dozen years, the 140-pounder had skated for the Canadiens, always in the shadow of first-line centre Elmer Lach. He had burst on the scene as the pivot on the Habs' Razzle Dazzle Line with linemates Gerry Heffernan and Pete Morin. The trio had been so hot in the amateur ranks that the Canadiens signed them as a unit in 1941.

O'Connor was the only one who clicked in the NHL but it took a trade to New York in 1947 to ease him out of Elmer Lach's big shadow.

There was a note of irony in the deal. A few weeks before the trade was completed, the Habs and the Rangers engaged in a wild brawl. All of the players threw punches, but it was O'Connor who suffered the most. The Rangers' Bryan Hextall threw a right that caught him in the face and broke his jaw. Guess what happened? When O'Connor joined the Rangers his roommate turned out to be — Bryan Hextall.

The Ranger Who Outplayed the Rocket

Every hockey fan knows the name Rocket Richard, the dynamic Montreal Canadien who once held the NHL record for career goals with 544. But how many fans recall a Ranger winger named Pentti Lund, who finished his career with 500 fewer goals than Richard?

And yet, on at least one occasion, it was Lund who stole the NHL limelight from Richard. It happened in the 1950 playoffs, during Lund's second season in the NHL.

Lund was the first Finnish-born player to make his mark in the NHL. His family had emigrated to Thunder Bay, Ontario, and it was there that six-year-old Pentti first donned skates. In 1948–49, he clicked with the Rangers and captured the Calder Trophy as the NHL's top rookie after a 14-goal season. He improved to 18 goals in 1949–50 while Richard was netting a league-leading 43 for Montreal. When the Rangers met the Habs in the 1950 semifinals, it was Lund's job to shadow the Rocket, who was the most explosive scorer in playoff history.

Richard was accustomed to being shadowed, of course. Some checkers stuck to him like barnacles on a ship. But Lund took a different approach.

"I gave him a lot of room," he recalled. "But I always made sure I was there to cut him off every time he charged across the blue line. It seemed to work, because he scored only one goal in the series, which the Rangers won in five games. And the goal he scored was on a Montreal power play — when I was on the bench."

Lund's outstanding work against the Rocket earned him much praise from Ranger management. He was told he could count on a long career with the Blueshirts. But when his goal production fell to four the following season, New York traded him to Boston.

Dr. Tracy Casts His Spell

Early in the 1950–51 NHL season, the Rangers could have used someone like Dick Tracy to detect the reason for their 12-game winless streak. Instead, they got Dr. David Tracy, a hypnotist who claimed he could instill much-needed confidence in the players while they were in a trance-like state.

"Let's try it," said coach Frank Boucher. "Some of my boys are playing like they're already half asleep."

Prior to a game with Boston on November 15, the doctor stood in the centre of the Rangers' dressing room and soon had several players under his spell. One of the deepest sleepers was forward Tony Leswick. The good doctor delivered words of inspiration and encouragement and then snapped them awake.

When they charged out the door, eager to face the Bruins, one of the players asked Leswick, "What did you think of all that?"

"Not much," said Leswick. "The guy didn't have any effect on me."

The Rangers performed well that night. They showed plenty of confidence and were tied 3–3 with the Bruins until the final minute. Then Boston scored a late goal to win the game.

Dr. Tracy was crushed. He said, "Next time I'll concentrate more on the Ranger goaltender, Charlie Rayner."

But he never got the chance. He was never invited back.

The Bentleys' Last Hurrah

It was past midseason in 1954 when the Rangers issued a call for help. Would Doug Bentley, brother to the Rangers' Max, come down from Saskatoon, where he was playing for the minor-league Quakers, and help the club mount a long-shot playoff bid? Doug would and did. He arrived in New York in time for a game with Boston. Despite the fact that he'd been away from the NHL for two seasons, he scored a goal and added three assists in his first game. Brother Max chipped in two goals and two assists. At 38 — four years older than Max — Doug played in 20 games to finish out the season. The Bentley brothers failed, by four points, to push the Rangers into the '54 playoffs. Both brothers retired from the NHL after that campaign, with one slim point separating their career totals: Max had racked up 544, while Doug retired with 543.

Gadsby Survives Tragedy at Sea

The steamship *Athenia* was off the Irish coast, bound for Canada, when the German torpedo struck with devastating force. It was September 3, 1939, the same day that Britain declared war on Germany, and the Nazi submarine *U-30* was waiting for the ship — the last passenger liner to leave the English port of Southampton.

193

Twelve-year-old Bill Gadsby, travelling with his mother, was knocked out of his bunk by the explosion, which ripped a huge hole in the hull and quickly sent the liner to the bottom of the sea. The Gadsbys, and about 50 other passengers, found themselves jammed into a single lifeboat. Bill remembers it being pitch dark and very cold. "I was too young to realize how serious the situation was," he says. "But I saw men and women going crazy with panic. I saw up close the horror, the terrible things I can never forget."

Within hours, a rescue ship spotted the lifeboat and the survivors returned to Southampton. The Gadsbys finally arrived home, via New York, on the *Mauretania*. When the ship docked, Gadsby no doubt stared goggle-eyed at the towering skyscrapers of Manhattan, never dreaming that he would one day return to New York, walk amongst the tall buildings, and play hockey at Madison Square Garden.

Bill was 18 when he signed his first pro contract with the Chicago Blackhawks, having completed two seasons of junior hockey in Edmonton. After 12 games as a left winger with Kansas City in 1946–47, he was called up to the Hawks, was shifted to defence and never played forward again. In 1952, he contracted polio and was placed in isolation for 10 days. In that era, before Dr. Jonas Salk invented his miraculous vaccine, polio crippled thousands of young people. Gadsby was fortunate; his symptoms gradually disappeared. He was with Chicago until the 1954–55 season, when he was traded to the Rangers with Pete Conacher in return for Nick Mickoski and Allan Stanley.

The reason behind Gadsby's departure from Chicago is a simple one. During the previous season, Chicago had played Detroit in Omaha, Nebraska. Attendance at the Blackhawks' home games had been pitiful, so playing in Omaha seemed like a good idea at the time. Gadsby got into a shouting match with Detroit coach Tommy Ivan during the game, calling the dapper Ivan every name in the book. That summer, Ivan was hired as general manager of the Hawks, and Gadsby knew he was toast.

He was reluctant at first to join the Rangers, but Frank Boucher urged him to give New York a chance. He did, and quickly became a fan favourite with his reckless, fearless style of play. He blossomed with the Rangers, making the First All-Star

Team three times, in 1956, '58 and '59. He set a record for defencemen with 46 assists in 1958–59, breaking Doug Harvey's mark of 44 established two years earlier.

In 1960, Gadsby and Eddie Shack were traded to Detroit in exchange for Red Kelly and Billy McNeill. The Rangers happened to be in Detroit when the trade was announced, and Shack was overjoyed. "What a relief to get away from the Rangers," he announced. Gadsby, wisely, said nothing. Within hours, the trade was cancelled: Red Kelly had refused to report to New York and announced his retirement. (Later, he would be shipped to Toronto, where he was to lead the Leafs to four Stanley Cups.) Shack and Gadsby remained with the Rangers, Shack no doubt saying, "What a relief it is to be back."

Gadsby was traded to Detroit the following season, and wound up playing 20 years in the NHL, but never on a Stanley Cup winner.

His penchant for getting in the path of a puck or stick was a costly one. His nose was broken seven times; his face bears the scars of over 400 stitches; his left leg was broken twice, and both of his big toes and thumbs have been fractured.

After his playing days, he turned to coaching. His stint behind the Red Wings bench was remarkably brief. He survived one season (1968–69) with a poor club, and won his first two games the following year. Team owner Bruce Norris congratulated him after the second victory. The very next afternoon, Norris fired him. "I decided to make a change," Norris explained.

Gadsby took his hurts, his firing and all of his disappointments in stride. He had survived two decades at the top of his profession, and in 1970 he became an Honoured Member of the Hockey Hall of Fame. Not bad for a kid who might have been crippled by polio or drowned in the sinking of the *Athenia*.

Ivan the Terrible

Every Sunday morning, when a few old crocks get together for a hockey game in Pickering, Ontario, the play of defenceman Ivan Irwin, a 76-year-old former Ranger, draws a lot of comment.

"I can't get around the old bird," said Bobby Lalonde, the Theo Fleury–sized centre who played in the NHL for 10 seasons. "And if I pass the puck into the slot, it always seems to hit one of his big boots."

"And he's always laughing out there, always happy to see one of us mess up," said Pete Conacher, another former pro.

Irwin, nicknamed Ivan the Terrible when he played for the Rangers in the early 1950s, hasn't lost his knack for playing positional hockey. "When you have one of the weakest shots in the NHL and you can't skate, you have to know how to play positionally," he once told a reporter.

When asked about his offensive play as a Ranger, his booming laugh preceded his answer. "I scored just two goals in my NHL career, and wouldn't you know, when they held a surprise 65th birthday party for me, someone found a film of one of them. That must have been like looking for a needle in a haystack."

Ivan Irwin is remembered for two reasons — no, not his pair of goals. He was the first NHLer to cut the palms out of his gloves, which made it easier for him to grab an opponent by the shirt and escape a penalty because the referee couldn't detect the grab.

"He's also remembered," said former referee Red Storey, "because he was the best fighter I ever saw in hockey. I never saw him lose a fight in the NHL or any other league. He has the biggest hands I've ever seen."

Storey recalled a fight between Irwin and a player named Dean McBride that erupted during a minor-league game played in Quebec City about 50 years ago. When McBride swung his stick at Irwin, cutting his lip clean through, the gloves came off. The two players slammed into each other and exchanged sledgehammer blows. The battle raged on and on — five minutes, six, then 10, and still they slugged it out. Finally, McBride went down and couldn't get up. Irwin fell on top him. Both men were totally exhausted. McBride's face was a mass of welts, cuts and bruises while Irwin bled from a torn lip and a gashed ear.

Irwin said recently, "I've been in a few scraps in my career but I'll never forget that battle with McBride. When it was over, we were both so tired and beat up we could hardly skate to the penalty box."

Irwin picks a former Ranger among the three most impressive players he ever saw. After Gordie Howe and Rocket Richard, he says Camille Henry, the pint-sized power-play specialist with New York in the 1950s, was a bona fide marvel. "He had a better scoring average than the Rocket, incredible for a kid who wasn't much bigger than a jockey."

Watson's Postgame Punishment

A coach couldn't get away with it today. The NHL Players' Association wouldn't allow it. But back in the 1950s, coach Phil Watson ruled the Rangers roost. When he barked, "Jump!" his players almost banged their heads on the ceiling. One night he ordered them onto the ice for a full-scale practice immediately after a game. It was an NHL first.

On a February night in 1959, Ranger goalie Gump Worsley was en route to a shutout victory over the best team in hockey, the Montreal Canadiens. Midway through the third period the Rangers were leading, 1–0. Then the Habs, winners of four straight Stanley Cups and waltzing toward their fifth, suddenly exploded for five straight goals. Three of them came in four minutes as they scuttled New York 5–1.

The shell-shocked Rangers stumbled into their dressing room after the shellacking and began hurling gloves, sticks and jerseys against the walls. They were stunned when a red-faced Watson stormed into their ranks and screamed like a drill sergeant, "You're all going to pay for this. Put that equipment back on!"

He ordered his sullen players back on the ice for a gruelling practice. The players weren't the only ones in shock. Their wives phoned their babysitters to say, "We're going to be a lot later than we expected."

Gump Worsley was the only Ranger to be excused from the midnight workout, which he remembers well.

"When Watson said that I was excused, I got dressed as fast as I could and took off. But I didn't go home. I sat far up in the seats out of Watson's sight. I watched him put my teammates through drill after drill for at least an hour. What a bastard! It was painful to watch, punishment like I'd never seen before — a terrible thing."

Leapin' Lou Doesn't Dwell on the Past

Rugged defenceman Lou Fontinato — "Leapin Lou" to a few million fans — was one of the most colourful Rangers ever. His Madison Square Garden supporters admired his bashing style, his fearless, rhino-like charges that stunned opponents large and small. Fans hated him everywhere else around the league.

Today he lives alone on his cattle farm near Guelph, Ontario. He'll gladly talk about tractors and cattle and mending fences. A typical farmer, he goes to bed at sundown and rises before dawn. He seldom talks hockey, doesn't dwell on the headlines he helped create during his turbulent stay in the NHL — first as a Ranger, then as a Canadien. It doesn't matter to him if fans have forgotten he started his career as a replacement for Allan Stanley and that he ended it with a near-fatal injury.

If he's remembered at all after more than 40 years away from the NHL stage, it's mainly for a few seconds of devil-may-care behaviour when he duked it out with Gordie Howe and led with his nose. When the brief battle ended, a reporter would describe Fontinato's battered beak as "an afterthought, like it was stuck on his weather-beaten face by a careless sculptor."

The battle began during a 1959 game at the Garden when Eddie Shack, a Rangers teammate, went after Howe, nipping at his heels like a yapping dog, tormenting Mr. Hockey until his blood began to boil. The gloves flew off behind the Rangers' net, where Howe planned to administer a solid punch to Shack's prominent nose. But it was Fontinato's face that was to absorb the full force of the blow.

Leapin' Lou raced to the scene, pushed Shack aside and threw himself at Howe. Howe stepped away from a Fontinato haymaker before returning fire with a flurry of punches so hard that one of Howe's fingers popped out of its joint.

"I threw everything at him," Fontinato would later recall, "and nothin' happened. The best punch I ever threw didn't even faze the guy. He didn't seem to notice it. 'Geez,' I said to myself, 'why doesn't the guy go down?' Then *pow!* Gordie hit me with a dandy punch. Just a short one, mind you — but it caught me right in the nose and spread it all over my face. Broke all the blood vessels and everything."

An alert photographer captured the damage on film and photos of Fontinato's shattered proboscis appeared in papers from coast to coast.

The referee was Art Skov, who said, "I grabbed Fontinato and he had his head down. Then he looked up. There was blood everywhere and it looked like his nose was gone. Then, when Fontinato was leaving the ice, Ranger coach Phil Watson grabbed him by the arm and lifted it up. Like he'd *won* the fight!"

Did Gordie feel any remorse? "No, none at all," he stated "Louie had been after me for years. He had it coming." Fontinato, incidentally, was later traded to Montreal where he slammed into the boards one night in 1963, suffering a career-ending injury that might have killed a lesser man.

Today, Fontinato would rather talk about a new calf, the cost of feed or the weather than about his ten-year career in the NHL, which ended abruptly when he suffered a broken neck in that 1963 game at the Montreal Forum.

As for the Howe incident, there's not much he has to say about that either. "It doesn't interest me," Fontinato states with a shrug. "But other people always want to hear about it."

Belisle Was Just Following Orders

Danny Belisle never took himself — or the game of hockey — too seriously.

In 1960, Danny received the greatest Christmas gift he would ever get: a chance to play for the New York Rangers on Christmas Day. His NHL debut would be against the Montreal Canadiens, who were seeking their sixth consecutive Stanley Cup title.

The Rangers, deep in the league basement, had lost some key players to injuries — Dean Prentice and Camille Henry, to name a couple — and Belisle was called up from Vancouver to replace

Henry in the lineup. The rookie responded with a goal in his first NHL game and scored another in the three games that followed. Not bad, he thought to himself, beginning to think he might stick around a while.

In the Rangers' dressing room before the next game, Belisle was putting the last of his equipment in place when coach Alf Pike stuck his head in the door and said, "Hey, kid, not so fast. Camille Henry may be fit enough to play tonight. Take your gear off."

Belisle shrugged and started to strip off his equipment. Two minutes later, Pike was back with further instructions. "Hey, kid, you better suit up. Henry probably can't play, after all." So Belisle started to haul his equipment back on.

Moments later, Pike made a third appearance. "Hey, kid, Henry's still a question mark, but he's feeling better. Tell you what: get half-dressed."

By this time, Belisle had had enough. But in those days, rookies didn't dare voice an opinion. Dutifully, he pulled on his shin pads and socks and stepped into his hockey pants. Then he put on his street shoes and laced them up. He donned his shirt and knotted his tie. He was half-dressed. Then he sat back and waited.

The other Rangers, when they looked at him, started to break up. Belisle began to chuckle, too. Soon, howls of laughter filled the dressing room.

Outside the door, Pike heard the commotion and stuck his head in the door.

"What the hell is going on in here?" he barked. Then he saw Belisle. "Christ!" he exclaimed. "Take your goddamn gear off, Belisle, and turn it in. Henry will play tonight if it kills him."

"And that was my last game in the NHL," laughs Belisle. "I did exactly what the coach ordered — I got half-dressed. But putting on that shirt and tie pissed him off so much I was back in the minors the following day."

Belisle went on to enjoy an outstanding coaching career, earning coach of the year honours in the minor leagues on four occasions. He also coached the Washington Capitals for a season and, until his recent retirement, spent more than two decades with the Detroit Red Wings as an assistant coach and top scout.

Bathgate's Ross Trophy Chances Scuttled in '62

From the mid 1950s through the mid 1960s, Andy Bathgate was one of the NHL's most prolific scorers. Yet he never captured the Art Ross Trophy as the league's individual scoring leader. He did come close, finishing fourth on four occasions, third twice and capturing the runner-up slot three times.

His best chance to win the scoring honours came in 1962, when he led Chicago's Bobby Hull by a single point after 69 games. The final game in New York pitted the Rangers against the Blackhawks, Bathgate against Hull.

Hull was not only striving to overtake Bathgate in the scoring race, but he was hoping to score 50 goals in a season for the first time in his career. He scored the landmark goal early in the game, joining Rocket Richard and Boom Boom Geoffrion as hockey's only 50-goal men to that date. He also logged more than 30 minutes of ice time in his attempt to get 51 and set a new league record.

With less than a minute to play and the Rangers trailing by three goals, Bathgate and Hull each had 84 points. But Hull had 50 goals to Bathgate's 28, and it was common knowledge that, in the event of a tie, the Ross trophy would go to the player with the most goals.

Bathgate skated out, determined to get a point, or at least hoping for one final shot on net. The Hawks were equally determined to keep him off the score sheet.

On the Chicago bench, Bobby Hull turned to coach Rudy Pilous. "Let me go out and check him."

"Siddown," growled Pilous. "Reggie Fleming's the perfect guy for that job."

Fleming, one of the toughest, crudest men in hockey, hopped the boards and lined up opposite Bathgate. The puck was dropped; Bathgate lunged for it, while Fleming lunged for *him*. Fleming grabbed Bathgate's stick and jumped on his back. Bathgate fell to his knees as another Ranger scooted away with the puck. The referee's arm shot up to signal a delayed penalty.

Meanwhile, the Rangers moved the puck from man to man, waiting for Bathgate to get up. The seconds ticked away. The

referee's arm stayed up — he would blow his whistle only when the Blackhawks touched the puck. In front of him, Fleming continued to wrestle with Bathgate, clutching, holding, punching and pushing.

The Rangers wanted a whistle. One of them shovelled the puck toward a Blackhawk, who shrewdly jumped aside and refused to touch it. Still no whistle. More seconds ticked off the clock. The crowd was in an uproar. Bathgate continued to struggle under the weight of Fleming.

The second hand reached the top of the dial and the game was over. The howls from the crowd reflected their indignation.

On the ice, a weary Bathgate struggled to his feet, his chance to be scoring champ lost forever. He would never again come so close.

On the Chicago bench, players pounded a grinning Hull on the back. Then they embraced Fleming, congratulating him on his masterful display of wrestling, one that went unpunished — and one that assured a teammate of a scoring crown.

Leaving Rangers Was Gump's Big Break

For 10 NHL seasons, Lorne "Gump" Worsley was the netminder for various Rangers lineups that were often dreadfully inept. Gump and his teammates seldom made the playoffs, and when they did, they were tossed aside like yesterday's newspaper. A regular night's work for Gump would see him face about 50 shots. A renowned quipster, Gump was asked one day to name the team that gave him the most trouble. Without hesitating, he replied, "The Rangers." It made all the papers.

After the 1963 season, on the eve of the annual draft meetings, Gump was barhopping with his boss, Rangers general manager Muzz Patrick. Gump had heard some disturbing rumours about his future, so he bluntly asked, "Muzz, you gonna trade me?"

"Of course not," was the answer. "How would we ever replace you in New York?"

"If you do trade me," Gump continued, "deal me to Montreal. This would be hockey heaven for a guy like me."

"We're not gonna trade you, Gump."

The next day, Muzz Patrick traded Worsley to Montreal, and it turned his career around. He played most of six seasons for the Habs, no longer peppered by 50 or more shots per game. He went from obscurity to stardom, and backstopped his team to four Stanley Cups.

Asked to comment on the difference between playing for the two teams, Gump said, "In New York, we wanted to win the games. In Montreal, we *had to* win the games. Simple as that."

Gump was particularly motivated to do his best as a Hab because the legendary goalie Jacques Plante went to the Rangers in the trade.

"I had to prove to the Montreal fans that I was just as good as Plante, didn't I? And I think I did that before very long."

Gump has encountered plenty of heroes and villains in his time. He talked about some of his good — and bad — times on the eve of his induction into the Hockey Hall of Fame in 1980.

"I was with the Rangers, playing against Gordie Howe one night. In a goalmouth scramble, I fell on my back while the puck popped high in the air. It came down and landed squarely on my face. And who do I see lookin' down at me, his stick poised for a rebound? Yeah, big Gordie Howe."

"He could have torn my kisser apart if he'd shot," said Gump. "I closed my eyes and gritted my teeth. When I looked up again, he'd eased the puck off my face and tucked it underneath me while the ref blew the play dead. Funny how you don't forget things like that."

And the bad?

"Guys like Reggie Jackson, the ballplayer. My son Dean asked him for an autograph once in a restaurant. Jackson wasn't eating or anything, and the kid was polite. Said 'Excuse me' and 'Please.' Jackson said no and turned away. Just like that. 'No.'

"I guess I had it all wrong when I played. I always thought that signing autographs, especially when a kid asked politely, was part of the job."

Any other unpleasant memories?

"Yeah, my fear of flying. I hated planes. I was on a flight once when there was so much turbulence, the meals jumped off the trays and stained our clothes. A flight attendant came by and promised that the airline would pay for the cleaning of all jackets and slacks. I said, 'That's great. What about my shorts?' "

By the time he turned 40, Gump had pretty well decided he had had enough hockey. Besides, with Rogie Vachon, Phil Myre and a tall kid named Dryden, the Habs seemed hip-deep in young goaltending talent. But the Minnesota North Stars came calling, offered Sam Pollock some money for Gump's services, then offered Gump a lot more money than he ever thought he'd make in hockey. So he stayed in the league another four years, his career spanning 21 seasons in all.

Tears Flow as Old Garden Closes

Sixty-two of the greatest players in NHL history were on hand to help close the doors of Madison Square Garden on Sunday, February 11, 1968. In ceremonies that preceded the final game between the Rangers and the Red Wings, the old-timers skated around the rink while the organist played "Auld Lang Syne." The capacity crowd stood and applauded. Some had tears in their eyes.

Before the opening ceremonies, souvenir hunters began tearing loose signs that pointed to rest rooms, exit markers — anything they could get their hands on. At the finish, some tried to rip the seats from their moorings and had to be chased by Garden police.

Rocket Richard was there, reminiscing in the dressing room about a four-goal night he once enjoyed at the expense of the Rangers.

Former Ranger Wally Stanowski wagered 10 bucks that he'd get a bigger cheer than the Rocket during the player introductions — and he did. When Stanowski was introduced, he raced onto the ice and did a couple of lovely figure eights and a pirouette, earning the ovation he needed to surpass the Rocket's.

Goalie Jacques Plante, who played for Montreal and the Rangers, recalled November 2, 1959, and the game in which he made the face mask a permanent part of hockey.

"My nose had been ripped open by one of Andy Bathgate's hard shots. I told Toe Blake, my coach, that I wouldn't go back in the game without the mask I'd been using in practices. Toe didn't like the mask but his only other choice was to use Joe Shaeffer as my replacement. Joe was the standby goalie for the Rangers, and Toe had heard that he was a very poor goaltender. So he let me wear the mask. After that, I never took it off [except for one game later that season]. When I came on the ice that night, a Ranger fan yelled, 'Hey, Plante, Halloween is over.' "

Every living member of the NHL's first All-Star team was invited to the closing, as well as players who took part in the first game at the arena on November 16, 1926. Ranger heroes like Lynn and Muzz Patrick, Ching Johnson, Davey Kerr, Bill Cook and Frank Boucher were there. When Johnson struggled into his rusty old skates he wrapped them in hockey tape to cover the holes. "These are the skates I took from the team when I left," he said, chuckling.

In the NHL game that followed, the Rangers came from behind to tie the Red Wings 3–3. It seemed fitting that two of the Rangers' finest, Rod Gilbert and Jean Ratelle, as they had done so many times in the past, teamed up for the tying goal early in the third period. Ratelle converted Gilbert's pass at the 45-second mark and the red light flashed for the final time in the old building.

Gilbert Died and Came Back to Life

Around Manhattan, even today at age 63, Rod Gilbert is still a high-profile hockey celebrity. Kids seek his autograph and old-timers recall when he was the number one star of the New York Rangers.

When he reflects on his 16 high-scoring seasons (406 goals in 1,065 regular-season games), Gilbert surely must thank his lucky stars for being able to make a name for himself in hockey. There was a time when he would have been happy even to get in a season or two. Back then, he never once thought he'd someday be summoned to the Hockey Hall of Fame.

That's because he's a survivor of two delicate back operations, as well as a blood clot that might have cost him his life. During the second operation, he claims he died on the operating table and endured a mystical out-of-body experience.

In 1960, Gilbert was a teenager, playing junior hockey for the Rangers' affiliate, the Guelph Royals. One night, a brain-dead fan casually tossed an ice cream wrapper onto the ice during a game. Gilbert, skating at full speed, stepped on the wrapper with his skate, crashed into the end boards and lay writhing on the ice. The result was a back injury that would torment him for the next several years.

During the off-season, he underwent major spinal fusion surgery that kept him off skates for several months. After the operation, he was told that a blood clot had developed in his leg. Gilbert had read about blood clots. Sometimes they were fatal. The surgeons conferred and debated whether or not to amputate the leg. "I was scared to death," Gilbert recalls. "Not only was my hockey career in doubt, but there was a chance I might leave the hospital with one leg missing — if I left at all."

Fortunately, the medics were able to dissolve the blood clot, and within days, Gilbert was able to start his rehab. During the spring of 1962, apparently fully recovered, he was back on skates, playing for the Kitchener-Waterloo Beavers of the Eastern Pro League.

In April, the Rangers, down two games to nil in a semifinal playoff series with Toronto, called on Gilbert, hoping his fresh legs and booming shot would get them back in the series. It was a tall order for a nervous rookie playing before the howling mob at Madison Square Garden, the largest crowd he had ever seen.

Game three, won 5–4 by New York, was a confidence builder. In game four, Gilbert exploded for a pair of goals and assisted on the winner. His splurge against Johnny Bower of the Leafs, even though the Rangers ultimately lost the series four games to two, left New Yorkers rejoicing. They took the good-looking rookie with the dazzling smile and the French-Canadian accent to their hearts.

But NHL stardom is never assured, no matter how dazzling the debut. Gilbert recorded 31, 64 and 61 points in his first three seasons on Broadway. Then his wonky back began to trouble him again, and the medical verdict was grim: he would have to undergo a second spinal fusion. No way, he said. He challenged the diagnosis and persuaded the doctors to let him play with his back trussed up in a steel brace. After half a season, and with 10 goals to his credit, he limped into general manager Emile Francis' office and said, "It's no use. I need the surgery. Let's do it right away so that I'll have time to heal and be ready for next season."

"Good idea," said Francis.

Gilbert went under the knife for the second time on February 1, 1966. And he almost didn't survive.

"I died on the operating table that day," he confided to me recently. "I was gone for maybe three or four minutes, and I left my body. It was an amazing experience. I looked down from above the table and I saw them working on me, trying to restore my heartbeat. Emile Francis was there, and when the nurse said, 'I think we've lost him,' Emile jumped up and shouted, 'You can't lose him. He's my best right winger. Bring him back!' And somehow, they brought me back."

For the next two weeks, Gilbert lay immobilized, suffering intense pain. Finally, he was discharged and allowed to fly home to Montreal to recover and prepare his body for another season of hockey.

In his prime, Gilbert was often called "the Joe Namath of hockey." Like the matinee idol who played quarterback for the New York Jets, Gilbert was forced to stickhandle his way through hordes of female groupies after games. In the nightclubs he frequented, a steady stream of gorgeous women would stop by to say hello, wish him luck or make an X-rated suggestion that would have made Madonna blush.

"Namath's women couldn't compete with Rod's," Brad Park once said. "Rod's were always classy, as bright as they were beautiful. One night after a game, Rod was showered and shaved and all spruced up. I remember he had a fantastic-looking suit on, and I said to him, 'You got a big date tonight?'

"'Yeah,' he said, 'a great date. We're going out galvanizing.'

"I said, 'Galvanizing? You sure you don't mean *gallivanting*?'

"He shrugged and said, 'Don't forget: French was my first language.'"

During that era, a magazine conducted a poll and Gilbert was named one of the sexiest men in sports.

"Women are the best things in life," he once told the journalist Alan Ebert. "I only wish I knew a way to be with *one* women — devote the time necessary to be with her — and still play hockey."

Eventually, Rod did, marrying the Coppertone girl — a dazzling blonde flight attendant who was seen on billboards across North America promoting Coppertone suntan products. The marriage failed, but a second has been "the best thing that ever happened to me," he says.

At the 1996 Hall of Fame induction ceremonies in Toronto, I asked Rod Gilbert if he would mind my using a quote about him from one of his former girlfriends.

"What's the quote?" he asked.

"Well, it's the one an actress friend made many years ago, about you being the most fantastic lover she's ever had."

Rod's eyes lit up and he laughed. "Geez, use it!" he said. "Be sure and use it. It's a great quote. Hell, that's a lot better than being called a great hockey player."

Espo Learned to Love New York

It all began in the fall of 1975 when Boston superstar Bobby Orr hurt his knee. Bruins general manager Harry Sinden began looking around for another top defenceman to replace Orr. When he asked around and discovered that Rangers GM Emile Francis would give up Brad Park in exchange for an aging but still productive Phil Esposito, it wasn't long before a major trade was completed. Francis shipped Park, popular centreman Jean Ratelle and minor leaguer Joe Zanussi to the Bruins in return for Esposito and defenceman Carol Vadnais.

Esposito and Vadnais were both jolted by the deal — Espo because he thought Sinden had promised him he wouldn't be traded and because he hated New York, and Vadnais because he had a no-trade clause in his Bruins contract. A furious Esposito told Sinden, "Harry, you make me puke." In Vadnais's case, the

Rangers hurriedly found some cash to persuade him to waive the no-trade clause.

Esposito left Boston with regrets. He told a reporter, "I regret not signing with Vancouver of the WHA. I would have had the same kind of deal Bobby Hull got in Winnipeg. A million bucks in the bank and a five-year contract at $300,000 per. Then another five years at $250,000. And I turned it down for Boston. A month later, Harry Sinden says I'm gone, traded."

Esposito admits it took more than a year to adjust to life with the Rangers. "But when I did," he says, "I really got to love the place and the good things it had to offer."

Esposito showed only flashes of his old-time form with the Rangers. His best moments came in the 1978–79 season, when he led the Rangers to the Stanley Cup finals against the Montreal Canadiens. The Rangers lost in five games.

At age 38, Esposito felt he was slipping a notch and the big thrills were behind him — the huge victory for Team Canada over the Soviets in 1972, when he had supplied the leadership the team needed; the two Cup wins in Boston in 1970 and '72; and the Rangers' dash to the finals in 1979.

Then, midway through the 1980–81 season, Espo was gone. He played his final game at the Garden against the Buffalo Sabres, and when he was introduced to a sold-out crowd of 17,500, the fans chanted his name for more than four minutes. He fought back tears as he told the crowd, "I've had a wonderful career and I'm sorry it has to end. When I was a kid growing up with my brother Tony in Sault Ste. Marie, I never dreamed I would make it to the NHL. I never thought I would do the things I've done. Now that I've done them, I'm proud of them."

Teammate Walt Tkaczuk took the microphone and drew a laugh when he said, "Phil, I want to thank you for the nine miserable years you gave us while you were in Boston and the five wonderful years you've given us as a Ranger in New York."

Gordie Howe stepped to centre ice and said, "Phil, you are such a class guy. We're really going to miss you."

In a press release, the NHL noted that Esposito was the first player to crack the 100-point barrier (in 1968–69). He totalled at least 55 goals in five consecutive seasons and he enjoyed his greatest season in 1970–71 when he scored 76 goals and 152 points — records later erased by Wayne Gretzky. He retired with 717 career goals and 873 assists.

After his retirement, Espo remained in New York and became an analyst on Rangers telecasts. Later he became coach and general manager.

When John Ferguson was GM of the Rangers he had mixed emotions about Esposito. Fergie could never forget how Espo had led Team Canada to a stunning victory over the Soviets in 1972. On the other hand, he blamed Espo for persuading him to trade with Boston to get Ken Hodge, an Esposito crony and former line-mate in Boston. Ferguson gave up Rick Middleton for Hodge in what he calls "the worst deal in hockey history." He also blamed Esposito and Rod Gilbert for the friction that was so often evident in the Rangers dressing room. Ferguson called them "clubhouse lawyers," and maintained they were always fighting among themselves, with half the team siding with Gilbert and the other half supporting Espo.

Ratelle Never Fought, Never Swore

On May 28, 1981, Jean Ratelle retired from hockey after a 20-year career, during which he excelled for two NHL clubs, the New York Rangers and Boston Bruins. When he left the game at age 40, Ratelle was the league's sixth-leading scorer with 491 goals and 776 assists for 1,267 points.

Ratelle spent 14 of his 20 seasons (plus part of a 15th) with the Rangers, many of them centreing the high-scoring "GAG Line" — the letters stood for "Goal a Game" — with Rod Gilbert and Vic Hadfield. At his peak, he meant as much to the Rangers as Jean Beliveau did to Montreal, as Bobby Clarke did to Philadelphia or as Gilbert Perreault meant to Buffalo.

"My friend Jean was every bit as good as anyone I ever saw or played against," said Rod Gilbert. "He was one of those classic players, a real artist on the ice. He could do it all; in fact, he would have been successful at anything he decided to do."

Gilbert knew Ratelle better than anyone in the game. They started playing together as lads in Quebec, and were teammates for almost 30 years. In all that time, Gilbert says he never once saw Ratelle in a fight — on or off the ice — and never heard him swear.

The soft-spoken, devoted family man could have taught a course to other players and called it Consistency on Ice. Emile Francis coached Ratelle for a dozen years, beginning in junior hockey in Guelph. "He was really unbelievable," Francis says. "I can't remember him ever having a bad practice, let alone a bad game. He was the most consistent player I've ever seen."

Ratelle was a key player in one of hockey's most shocking and spectacular trades. In November 1975, he was shipped to Boston, along with Brad Park and Joe Zanussi, in return for Phil Esposito and Carol Vadnais. He hated to leave New York. "It was a huge jolt at first," he recalls. "I'd lived in New York all those years, and I'd never been with any other organization. I always considered the Rangers to be my team."

Five years later, he would say, "Getting traded was the biggest break of my life. If I had stayed with the Rangers I would be out of hockey by now. I got a whole new lease on life with the Bruins, and I really enjoyed playing for coach Don Cherry."

Bruins tough guy Wayne Cashman said Ratelle brought a measure of dignity to the game, a quality perhaps absent from his own slam-bang approach to the game. "He's the man we'd all like to be," Cashman told the sportswriter Frank Orr. "The man has such peace in his life. He's never wasted as much as 15 seconds being petty or small."

Incredibly, Ratelle never took a major penalty in two decades of NHL play, and twice won the Lady Byng Trophy for gentlemanly play. His biggest regret? Never having played on a Stanley Cup–winning team.

Rangers' Rejection Leaves Giacomin Stunned

It was a bombshell. That's the word Eddie Giacomin used to describe his sudden rejection by the Rangers after 10 seasons of loyal service. He was a beloved Ranger, the team's heart and soul, an extraordinary goaltender who had been a five-time All-Star and a Vezina Trophy winner. His daring, roving style — he darted swiftly from his net to snare loose pucks and lash them up ice to teammates — combined with his acrobatic saves to make him the darling of the Garden faithful from 1966 through the mid 1970s.

"I was amazed, disappointed, shocked, all of those things," he said of the cruel trick played on him on Halloween night 1975.

Emile Francis, under pressure from team owners to make some changes, placed Giacomin on waivers, and the Detroit Red Wings snapped him up. Giacomin was flabbergasted at the news. He recalls shaking Francis's hand, but being unable to speak a single word. It was as though Francis had grabbed him by the throat, not the hand.

As fate would have it, the Red Wings were to face the Rangers at the Garden two nights later. Coach Doug Barkley had originally planned to use Jim Rutherford in goal, but he wisely switched to Giacomin at the last minute, knowing that the Rangers players would have had trouble firing their best shots at their longtime friend.

When Giacomin skated out for the warmup, the fans went wild. The gray-haired goalie could barely see for the tears that filled his eyes. His gaunt body trembled with emotion. Chants of "Ed-die, Ed-die" drowned out the anthem and rained down on him after every save, easy or hard.

The Red Wings leaped to a 4–0 lead as the Rangers floundered. Rookie Wayne Dillon scored the first goal on Giacomin, and the crowd groaned — many booed. Dillon was so upset that he skated over and apologized to his former teammate.

Brad Park said: "If you ever saw a team intentionally lay down for a game, that was it. We felt so strongly about Eddie. That was a game that we did not want to play. We did not want to shoot on him. And it's true that guys like Dillon and Steve Vickers apologized to Eddie when they put the puck past him."

The Red Wings won the game, 6–4. Giacomin left the ice completely drained. A standing ovation ushered him to the visitor's dressing room. When he stepped onto the scale there, he found he'd lost 13 pounds during the contest.

Reporters, some as visibly upset as the fans, wrote about his amazing career as a Ranger and the bizarre path he took to the NHL. Ironically, he might have been a Red Wing from the beginning if he hadn't been such an unlikely prospect. As a teenager, Giacomin was cut by a Red Wing–sponsored team in Hamilton. He returned to his hometown of Sudbury, Ontario, and played with the Bell Telephone club in the city league. Two weeks before the season ended, his brother Rollie, five years older and also a goalie, received a call from the Washington Presidents of the old Eastern Hockey League. Could he come down and fill in for a netminder who had been injured?

"Not me. Not interested," said Rollie. "Why not give my kid brother Ed a shot? You won't regret it."

"Well, okay," was the answer. "Send him down — we'll take anybody. We've only five games left to play and we're out of the playoffs."

Giacomin headed for Washington, won all five games, and the next season was invited to try out with Providence of the American Hockey League. During the off-season, however, he suffered severe burns in a house fire and was advised by doctors to forget about hockey — permanently. The advice fell on deaf ears. Giacomin had once promised a schoolteacher that he would play goal in the NHL one day, and he intended to keep that promise.

He played in the minors with the Clinton Comets and New York Rovers before clicking with Providence, where he starred for five seasons.

Meanwhile, in New York, Emile Francis faced a dilemma. He could no longer rely on the temperamental Jacques Plante as his goalie, and Marcel Paille wasn't the answer, either. He decided to gamble on Giacomin and delivered a bag of bodies to Providence — three players and Paille — to land him.

Eddie's promise had finally been kept, his boyhood dream realized. He had made it, all the way from the midnight league in Sudbury to the National Hockey League.

His rookie season as a Ranger was horrendous, and Francis began to wonder if he'd made a huge mistake. Giacomin won eight games while losing 19, and his goals-against average was a disappointing 3.66. Francis dispatched him to Baltimore, where he began to show his old form.

In 1966–67, he was back, and he won the starting job in training camp. But Cesare Maniago, a proven veteran, battled him for the position, and it was only when Maniago was injured one night and refused to go back into the game that Giacomin became the number one goaltender. He won 30 games that season — tops in the league.

During his decade in New York, Giacomin won more games (226) and rang up more shutouts (49) than any other netminder in Rangers history.

Despite his successful start as a Red Wing, he was unhappy with Detroit, a team that was going through a state of upheaval. In January of 1978, Wings GM Ted Lindsay told him he'd been placed on waivers — and this time, there were no takers.

A year earlier, Rangers president Bill Jennings had promised him the head coaching job in New York, but he was overruled by owner Sonny Werblin, who selected Fred Shero instead.

But Phil Esposito didn't forget his old friend and teammate. One of Phil's first moves as general manager of the Rangers was to sign Giacomin as his goaltending coach in July of 1986.

After an 11-year exile, Eddie was back where he belonged, where he would hear the roar of the Garden crowd once again. First, there was a rousing welcome-home salute on opening night of the 1986–87 season, when he was asked to drop the first puck of the new season. Then there was an even greater ovation on Eddie Giacomin Night, when his jersey number, 1, was retired and hoisted to the rafters alongside Rod Gilbert's 7. After the season, another honour awaited Eddie, this time in Toronto, where he was inducted into the Hockey Hall of Fame.

Three years later, when Neil Smith replaced Esposito as GM, he allowed the new coach, Roger Neilson, to choose his own assistants. Neilson asked Wayne Cashman to stay on, but Ed Giacomin's contract was not renewed.

Blackhawks

Birth of the Blackhawks

Most of the 5,000 sports fans who attended the Chicago Blackhawks' on-ice debut on November 17, 1926, had never seen a hockey game before. Many of the attendees held high social positions in the city — the department store king Marshall Field, for example — and they were there for two reasons: they had heard the game was fast, rough and exciting, and they were willing supporters of the various charities that would share in the gate receipts.

Earlier in the day, the city's elite had attended a luncheon of the Union League Club, where they greeted a famous visitor to Chicago, Queen Marie of Romania. Major Frederic McLaughlin, the owner of the Blackhawks, was hopeful that she would make an appearance at the game that night — imagine having a queen drop the puck for the first-ever face-off in Blackhawks history! — but Her Majesty was a no-show.

Major McLaughlin had made his fortune in the coffee business; McLaughlin's Manor House Coffee was a favourite with housewives across America. He was also a sportsman, said to be one of the most skillful polo players in North America. Among his friends was the noted sports entrepreneur from New York, Tex Rickard, who a few months earlier had established an NHL team of his own, the New York Rangers. It was Rickard who suggested that McLaughlin consider buying a franchise for Chicago. "Think of the great rivalry we can develop," Rickard told McLaughlin.

McLaughlin liked the speed and harsh body contact the game featured and thought the franchise fee of $12,000 was a bargain. He quickly formed a syndicate of more than a hundred friends, wrote out a check, and almost overnight became the owner of one of the 10 teams that then comprised the NHL. He counted himself lucky to be welcomed into the lodge because two other parties had shown interest in landing the Chicago franchise.

Imagine the Major's delight when his Hawks, playing before a full house of shrieking fans, many of whom would become life-long addicts of the game, defeated the visiting Toronto St. Patricks in the first game by a 4–1 score.

A newspaper account of that opening was, by today's standards, overly wordy, a puzzle to read and leisurely in reporting the final score. The opening paragraph read as follows:

> Professional hockey under league auspices was ushered in here under most propitious circumstances last night, the Coliseum being crowded to capacity by a cheering throng who went away supremely happy because the Chicago Black Hawks made good their first time of asking at the expense of the Toronto St. Pats. The Rosebuds transplanted from Portland proved anything but bloomers, taking kindly to their new surroundings and winning handily from the speedy Toronto team by 4–1. The victors had a nice margin on the play throughout, no doubt due to the fact that they have had the benefit of several tidy tilts of an exhibition nature while the Queen City crowd were making their first appearance with colours up for the coming season.

McLaughlin had promised the Windy City fans he would cough up a large part of his fortune to buy players for his club. The demise of the Western Hockey League at the end of the 1925–26 season had all the NHL franchises, new and old, scrambling to sign players who were anxious to continue playing big-league hockey. McLaughlin boldly purchased the entire roster of the Portland Rosebuds from Frank and Lester Patrick for $150,000.

The prize in the package was forward Dick Irvin, a future Hall of Famer who had scored 31 goals in 30 games to tie Bill Cook for Western league scoring honours in 1925–26. Irvin would be named the first captain of the Blackhawks and would finish second in league scoring with 18 goals and 18 assists. When a skull fracture ended his playing career in 1929, he turned to coaching, and at the helm of the Blackhawks, Toronto Maple Leafs and Montreal Canadiens he would set a long-lasting NHL record for coaching wins.

Dick Irvin Jr., the noted Canadian hockey broadcaster, tells an amusing story about his father's coaching renown. Some time ago, a Chicago journalist called the Irvin home in Montreal.

"Mr. Irvin," said the voice on the phone, "I wonder if you could tell me what it was like for you to coach the Chicago Blackhawks in the late 1920s?"

Irvin Jr. laughed and responded, "The man who could tell you, if he were still around, would be about 110 years old now."

Prior to the 1926–27 season, the NHL governors decided to align the teams into two divisions, the Canadian and the American. The former included the Montreal Canadiens and Maroons, the Toronto St. Pats (who were rechristened the Maple Leafs in February 1927), the Ottawa Senators and, oddly enough, the New York Americans. The American Division consisted of the Blackhawks, Boston Bruins, Detroit Cougars (later the Falcons and finally the Red Wings), New York Rangers and Pittsburgh Pirates. The Bruins had been around for a couple of seasons, and Pittsburgh had one NHL campaign under its belt. The other three teams were all newcomers.

After much deliberation, McLaughlin chose the name Blackhawks for his team. Some say the unit he had commanded during World War I inspired the name. His 333rd Machine Gun Battalion was part of the 86th Infantry Division, also known as the Blackhawk Division. The division's insignia, a black hawk on a red shield, honoured Black Hawk, a famous Sauk chief who fought alongside the British in the War of 1812, but who, after his death, came to be respected by American Midwesterners for his courage. Others say McLaughlin named his team after a Chicago nightclub he owned, called the Blackhawk. There is probably some truth in both stories.

It has long been reported that the Major's unit was part of the 85th Division, but a bit of delving into military history sets the record straight — it was in fact the 86th. It's interesting to note that the 85th Division was known as the Custer Division. Given the woeful caliber of Chicago's teams throughout the 1940s and '50s, maybe the Chicago Custers would have been an apt nickname.

Oddly, until 1986, the team name was always written as two words: Black Hawks. That year, owner Bill Wirtz decided to change the spelling to conform to Chicago's original NHL charter of 1926. For six decades, the name had been misspelled on thousands of pieces of correspondence, team score sheets and publicity handouts.

When it came time to design the team's uniforms, the Major's wife volunteered to help out. She was the former Irene Castle, a famous dancer and actress, and McLaughlin was quick to say "Yes, dear" when she suggested a colourful depiction of an Indian chief for the front of the new sweaters.

The Blackhawks' first home was the 5,000-seat Chicago Coliseum, a building on South Wabash Street that was often used for cattle shows. Wealthy Chicagoans, many of them friends of McLaughlin's, attended those early games. Out of respect for the Major, few of them ever dared suggest that the lingering odour of the building might have been caused by the performance of the home team, struggling through another game on the ice.

Muldoon's Irish Curse

In 1926, Pete Muldoon became the first of many coaches Frederic McLaughlin would hire to run his Blackhawks over the years. Muldoon guided his new team to a third-place finish in the American Division and thought he had done a commendable job with the talent placed at his disposal. He was proud of the fact that his Hawks had scored 115 goals, more than any other NHL club.

If he expected a pat on the back from the Major, he didn't get it. The impatient owner told Muldoon the Hawks should easily have finished in first place. Muldoon was fired on the spot and replaced by Barney Stanley.

"You SOB," Muldoon is reported to have said. "Why, I'll place an Irish curse on your club that'll keep them out of first place forever! You just wait and see."

The Major just laughed.

A decade went by, then another. And a third and a fourth. The Hawks suffered through many bad seasons and celebrated a few good ones. They won Stanley Cups in 1934, 1938 and 1961, but 40 years later they still hadn't found their way to the top of the league standings.

From time to time, journalists and broadcasters would bring up Muldoon's "hex," which certainly seemed to be working. In 1963 and '64 the Hawks came close, finishing just one point out of first each year. It wasn't until 1966–67 that Bobby Hull, Stan Mikita and company led Chicago to the top spot in the NHL. That season, they compiled 94 points, well ahead of second-place Montreal's 77. Major McLaughlin, who died in 1944, wasn't there to see the "curse" lifted.

But was there really a curse? In conversation with the noted Canadian sports columnist Jim Coleman one day, I found the answer.

"Years ago, I had a daily column to write," he told me. "I was a drinking man in those days, and meeting a deadline was sometimes a bit of a problem."

An impish smile crossed his face. "With the blank page in the typewriter staring back at me, and my deadline looming, I concocted the story of Pete Muldoon and the strange curse he once placed on the Blackhawks. It was pure fiction and it filled a column. I figured it would be forgotten in a day or two, but years later, people kept referring to the famous Muldoon Curse as if it was fact. Especially when the Hawks appeared destined never to finish ahead of the pack.

"Maybe I should have had old Pete condemn the Hawks to last-place finishes. They managed to do that often enough — at least 14 times."

The Stingy Scot

Although he was born in Edinburgh, Scotland, Charlie Gardiner — one of Chicago's, and for that matter hockey's, greatest goaltenders — learned the fundamentals of hockey on the frosty plains of Winnipeg, Manitoba. Even though his team only won seven games in each of his first two seasons in the league, and he finished with a losing record of 112 wins, 152 losses and 52 ties, he was regarded as a superb goalkeeper who was gifted with incredible skill. In seven seasons, he won the Vezina Trophy twice and was named to the First All-Star Team three times.

Year after year, Charlie was the lone bright spot on a porous Chicago team. And although he had led the Hawks to the Stanley Cup finals in 1931, by the time the 1933–34 season rolled around he had almost given up his dream of winning it. The Chicago scorers were pitiful that season, tallying only 88 goals, the poorest offensive output in the NHL. But Gardiner had allowed only 83, ringing up a league-leading 10 shutouts and compiling a goals-against average of 1.63 (second best in the NHL).

The Blackhawks nosed their way into the playoffs, and for the next month Gardiner played the best hockey of his life. His back-stopping brilliance led the Hawks to playoff victories over the Montreal Canadiens and then the Maroons.

That left only one team standing between Gardiner and the Cup: the Detroit Red Wings. Most hockey people didn't give the Hawks much of a chance against the powerful Wings, and for good reason: they hadn't won a game in Detroit in four years.

Even Roger Jenkins, one of Gardiner's teammates, down-graded his team's chances. He bet Charlie that not even he could stop the Wings. "If you do, I'll wheel you around the Loop in a wheelbarrow."

In the opener of the best-of-five series against the Wings, Gardiner turned in an outstanding performance, and the Hawks won, 2–1. Two nights later, he was just as good in a 4–1 Chicago win. The Red Wings came to life in game three, firing five pucks past a dazed Gardiner en route to a 5–2 thrashing. The fourth game was scoreless at the close of regulation time, and required more than 30 minutes of overtime before Chicago's Mush March scored the Stanley Cup–winning goal. Gardiner's effort remains the only double-overtime shutout in the history of the Stanley Cup finals.

Gardiner's season couldn't have come to a more fitting end. He had lost only one of eight playoff games and compiled a goals-against average of 1.33. He had captured his second Vezina

Trophy and been named to the First All-Star Team. And Jenkins made good on his promise, treating Gardiner to a bumpy ride through Chicago's downtown streets in a wheelbarrow.

What no one could have foreseen was that Charlie Gardiner's greatest performance would be his last in the NHL. Two months later, he died of a brain hemorrhage in Winnipeg. He was only 29 years old.

A Dummy in Goal

Hockey people, including those players who choose the position, will tell you a fellow has to be a real dummy to play in goal. But once in the long history of the Blackhawks, a bona fide dummy actually stood between the pipes.

In the early 1930s, Chicago's eccentric owner, Major Frederic McLaughlin, decided his team needed a second goaltender for practice sessions — one who had no fear of shooting drills, never complained when high shots whistled past his head and, best of all, never asked to be paid. Miraculously, he found one, inventing hockey's first goaltending dummy.

McLaughlin had a member of his staff stuff bags filled with straw into a scarecrow-shaped figure that roughly resembled a goalie. After the dummy was thoroughly stuffed, it was hauled across the ice and strung up in the centre of the net. During practice, while All-Star netminder Charlie Gardiner tended goal at one end of the ice, the dummy defended the opposite goal. Chicago players blistered their hardest shots at the chunky figure, hoping to knock the stuffing out of their stoic new teammate, but nothing rattled the "rookie."

Meanwhile, Gardiner had to endure the snide remarks of his mates. "That dummy's lookin' better every day. He never yaps at us for not clearing the puck. He deserves a start, don't you think? In fact, I hear the owner's signed the dummy to a long-term deal and wants to send our other guy to the minors."

Gardiner soon grew weary of these jibes. After scrimmage one day, he ripped the dummy from the net, dragged him into the dressing room and flopped him on the massage table. "Give this poor kid a rubdown," he told the trainer. "He's falling to pieces out there. Then find some clothes for him, give him a few bucks for a beer and a sandwich, and get him the hell out of here."

A Magic Moment for Alfie Moore

Nursing a cold beer, minor-league goaltender Alfie Moore sat slumped on a stool in a Toronto tavern on the afternoon of April 5, 1938. Moore had given up all hope of getting a ticket to the first game of the Stanley Cup finals, between the Chicago Blackhawks and Toronto Maple Leafs, that night at Maple Leaf Gardens. Then Alfie got the surprise of his life. Two Blackhawks stars, Johnny Gottselig and Paul Thompson, barged into the tavern and began looking around.

Alfie jumped to his feet and called out, "You guys got an extra ticket for the game tonight?" The Chicago players rushed over and shook Alfie's hand. One of them called for his tab, while the other helped him into his topcoat. "Come along with us, Alfie. We're taking you to the game, and you won't need a ticket. You'll be standing, not sitting."

"What are you guys talking about?"

Gottselig grinned. "Alfie, you're going to be the Chicago goalie tonight. And we expect you to play the game of your life against Toronto."

Backed by the stellar goaltending of Mike Karakas, the pride of Aurora, Minnesota, the Chicago Blackhawks had stunned the Montreal Canadiens and New York Americans in a pair of best-of-three series in the 1938 playoffs.

But in the finals, it looked as if their Cinderella ride was about to come to an end, not only because the Leafs had outpointed Chicago 57–37 during regular-season action, but because Karakas couldn't play! A broken toe suffered in the final match of the preceding series was so badly swollen that his foot wouldn't squeeze into the boot of his skate.

Bill Stewart, the Hawks coach, pleaded with Leafs owner Conn Smythe to let him employ Davey Kerr, a Rangers regular, as a substitute. But Smythe was no fool. "Forget about Kerr," he snarled. "He's one of the best around. But I'll let you use a minor-leaguer — a fellow named Alfie Moore. That is, if you can find him."

The two men argued until they almost came to blows. Then Stewart threw his arms up in the air and turned to Gottselig and Thompson. "Go find Moore," he commanded.

The search party tracked down Moore, who had plied his trade with the Pittsburgh Hornets that year, hauled him from the tavern and hustled him to the Gardens, where they witnessed another hot debate between Stewart and Smythe, one that ended in a flurry of fisticuffs. It was obvious that Stewart didn't have much faith in Moore's ability, especially when he found out where the goalie had spent most of the afternoon.

Moore threw on his goaltending gear and heard a buzz from the fans when he was introduced as the goaltender. He stopped a few pucks in the pregame warmup, then pronounced himself ready.

In the famous gondola high over the Gardens ice surface, broadcaster Foster Hewitt commented on Moore's shaky play in the opening minutes of the game. "He appears to be very nervous, as who wouldn't be in his position," observed Hewitt. "And it showed a moment ago when Gordie Drillon scored on the first Toronto shot of the game."

However, if Hewitt and the Leafs' fans expected Moore to cave in under a barrage of shots, they would be disappointed. Moore pulled himself together and managed to put his anxiety aside. He was the picture of composure as he blanked the Leafs the rest of the way. The Hawks won the game, 3–1, with Gottselig scoring twice for the victors. The Hawks pounded Moore on the back and pumped his hand. As he skated off the ice, the grinning goaltender couldn't resist thumbing his nose at Conn Smythe.

Perhaps it was the thumb that did it. Smythe was outraged with the outcome of the game, and Moore's unexpected stellar performance, and he refused to allow the Hawks to use Moore in game two of the series. Paul Goodman, a Hawks farmhand, was recalled in time for the match, and Toronto won, 5–1. Karakas declared himself fit for game three, at Chicago Stadium, during which he wore a special boot to protect his toe. He played brilliantly, backing the Hawks to 2–1 and 4–1 wins, and the Cinderella Blackhawks had captured the Stanley Cup.

Asked what he thought his contribution to the championship was worth, Alfie Moore said, "How about $150?" The grateful Hawks paid him double that amount and threw in a gold watch, a memento he treasured long after his lengthy minor-league career and his one-shot Stanley Cup heroics were history. "I also treasured all the praise I got from the Chicago players, the management, the city and newspapers nationwide," he said. "As it turned out, I played in only 21 regular-season games in my entire NHL career, none of them with Chicago; and yet, in the only game I played as a Hawk, and thanks to Mike Karakas's sore toe, I got my name engraved on the Stanley Cup. Who'd have believed that would ever happen?"

Sad End to a Great Career

It was a sad ending for a player who had a great career. Earl Seibert died in the small community of Agawam, Massachusetts, on April 12, 1990, at the age of 78. Seibert was one of the greatest defencemen ever to play for the Chicago Blackhawks and was an NHL All-Star for 10 consecutive seasons. He was a cornerstone of the Hawks' 1938 Stanley Cup–winning team, averaging 55 minutes a game. He and his father Oliver were both inducted into the Hockey Hall of Fame. Yet, sadly, no representative of the NHL attended his funeral, no league official sent a wreath or even a card of condolence. "It was so, so sad," murmured Sam Pompei, one of the pallbearers. "A big, big man like him…"

Perhaps it was because he walked away from hockey after he retired in 1946. "He vanished from the face of the earth when he got out of the game," said Art Coulter, once traded straight up for Seibert. "He had all the skills of Eddie Shore." What set them apart, perhaps, was flair, colour and controversy.

Seibert's story was tragic because of an incident that ended the career of Montreal Canadiens star Howie Morenz. One night in 1937, Earl checked Morenz into the Forum boards. Trying to get away from the tight check, Morenz caught his skate blade in a rut in the ice and fell awkwardly, breaking his leg in many places. Six weeks later, Morenz died in a Montreal hospital.

Seibert, until his dying day, felt responsible for the death of Morenz. But he should be remembered as an outstanding defenceman, not as the man who contributed to the demise of Howie Morenz.

Sam Was a Survivor

Sam LoPresti was not the reincarnation of Georges Vezina. He was a wartime goalie from the hockey hotbed of Eveleth, Minnesota, who played two seasons with the Blackhawks after joining the club in 1940. In his NHL career, he won 30 games and lost 38.

If Sam is remembered at all, it's for a game he played against Boston on March 4, 1941. In 60 minutes, he made 80 saves in a 3–2 Bruins win. LoPresti saved the match from becoming a rout. The number of saves he made that night remains an NHL record.

It's one thing to stop pucks; it's another to find yourself facing a German torpedo.

LoPresti joined the U.S. navy after his second (and final) NHL season, and in February 1943 was aboard the merchant ship *Roger B. Taney* in the South Atlantic when the German U-boat *U-160* spotted the American vessel and blew it apart with two well-aimed torpedoes. Within minutes, the *Taney* had plunged to the bottom of the ocean.

LoPresti scrambled into a life jacket and was later hauled aboard a lifeboat, where a couple dozen of his dazed shipmates were huddled. The survivors were a few hundred miles off the coast of Africa, but strong winds swept them into the middle of the Atlantic. They had little food, and water was rationed to an ounce per day per man. Sharks circled their small craft, and they drifted for a month before a steady rain provided fresh water for drinking. On the 42nd day, LoPresti, who was on watch, spotted land. It was the coast of Brazil.

The survivors were picked up by a Brazilian ship and taken to port, and then to hospital. LoPresti had lost 74 pounds during his ordeal. The navy had reported him missing in action and his family had given him up for dead.

When he regained his weight and his health, LoPresti returned to active duty. He survived the war and went back to Eveleth when it was over.

"Facing 83 shots in a hockey game was child's play compared to facing those torpedoes in the South Atlantic," he once told a reporter.

If LoPresti was proud to be a Blackhawk, he was even prouder to see his son Pete, also a goalie, make the NHL in the 1970s. Pete played six seasons with Minnesota and Edmonton, finishing with a 43–102–20 record.

Conacher Lashes Out

Big Charlie Conacher enjoyed phenomenal success on the ice as a player. As a coach it was a different story. In close to three years behind the Chicago bench, from mid 1947–48 through 1949–50, his teams never made the playoffs, finishing last in two of the seasons and second last in the other.

Little wonder, then, that Conacher was seething with frustration and anger during a game at the Detroit Olympia on February 9, 1950. His Hawks were being pummelled by Howe, Lindsay, Abel and Company — 9–2 was the final score — and one of his best players was crumpled on the ice, looking like he might never see the sun rise in the morning.

"Doug Bentley was charged by the Wings' George Gee and lay there, his legs quivering. I thought he was dead," Conacher told reporters afterward. "And that bleepin' referee, Bill Chadwick, didn't even call a penalty. He always favours the front-runners, anyway. To hell with the guys on the bottom.

"Then he wouldn't come to the bench to talk to me. I told one of my players to tell him the game wouldn't start again until he did. Well, he came over and told me he didn't see it and neither did the linesmen. Hell, it happened in front of everybody and they didn't see it."

Witnesses claim Conacher reached out and grabbed Chadwick by his jersey and the referee had to wrestle his way into the clear. "If Conacher had put his big mitts around Chadwick's neck, it might have been curtains," one bystander stated.

In the Chicago dressing room after the game, the irate coach reached for another victim, this time a reporter for a Detroit paper.

"I have no use whatsoever for Lew Walter of the Detroit *Times*. The bleeper called me a bleepety-bleep and I don't have to take that from anyone."

Walter had recently written that a new coach for Chicago might not be a bad idea.

"How many times did you hit him?" Conacher was asked.

"It was only necessary for me to hit him once," replied Charlie. In his playing days, once was often more than enough to do away with an adversary.

Walter's account was quite different. "I was talking things over with Charlie when he blew up and criticized some of the stories I'd written about Chicago in the past couple of seasons. The next thing I knew I was on the floor with Conacher on top of me and with his hands around my throat. We wrestled around for a minute or two and then Charlie got up and ordered me out of the room. I stayed right there until Doug Bentley, a friend of mine, came over and suggested it would be better if I left. So I did."

The following day, Walter filed assault-and-battery charges against Conacher. When Conacher called to apologize, he withdrew the charges.

Conacher resigned as Chicago coach at the end of the season, saying, "Three years of this kind of life is more than enough."

Mosienko Sinks Three Fastest

Wayne Gretzky had 50 hat tricks in his illustrious career, but he never scored three goals in 21 seconds. That remarkable record, which has stood for more than half a century, is held by Bill Mosienko, who toiled for the Blackhawks from 1941–42 until 1954–55.

Mosienko was a winner on a team that seldom strayed out of last place. He played in five All-Star Games and won the Lady Byng Trophy in 1945. But, during his 14-year career, Chicago finished last or second-last in the NHL standings 10 times!

Of Mosienko's 258 career goals, three would always be close to his heart and easily recalled, not only by him but also by everyone who knew him.

On March 23, 1952, the Blackhawks journeyed to New York to close out their regular season against the Rangers. The Hawks had won only 16 games that season and were destined to finish in last place for the third year in a row. If they lost their match at the Garden, Chicago would finish a distant 20 points behind the fifth-place Rangers.

Earlier in the season, Mosienko had mentioned to a teammate, "You know, it doesn't look like I'll ever get to play on a Stanley Cup winner, but I'd sure like to do something in hockey that I'll be remembered for."

He was to get his wish — in spades.

Fewer than 2,500 fans witnessed Mosienko's shining moment. The Garden was almost deserted, and no wonder. Who wanted to pay good money to see a meaningless game between the NHL's doormats?

What's more, popular Rangers goalie Chuck Rayner had been injured a few days earlier. In his place was a rookie, 20-year-old Lorne Anderson, playing in only his third NHL game.

A few years ago, in Winnipeg, I encountered Bill Mosienko and asked him what he remembered of that game.

"How could I ever forget it?" he said, his eyes glistening. "I scored three goals in record time, and I almost scored a fourth. Gus Bodnar was my centreman, you know, and he set a record, too — for the three fastest assists. We won the game 7–6 after trailing 6–2. But let me tell you about my goals.

"When Gus passed me the puck off the face-off, I was already in motion. I cut around the opposing winger and went around defenceman Hy Buller, who was playing on a bad ankle, and cut in on goal. Now, this kid Anderson had already beat me three times, and I thought to myself, 'He's not going to touch this one.' I slid the puck along the ice on his right side and the light went on. Never thought much about it, except it was my 29th goal of the year. But for some reason I hauled the puck out of the net to keep it as a souvenir. Remember, in those days a 30-goal season was a tremendous feat. I gave the puck to our coach, Ebbie Goodfellow, and told him to keep it for me.

"So now we go back for the face-off, and Bodnar gets the puck over to me again. I whip around my winger and whip around the same defenceman and cut in on goal again. And I put the puck in the net exactly the same way as I did it before. I scrambled into the net to dig the puck out, thinking, 'Heck, I don't want the 29th goal puck, I want the 30th.' And I gave that puck to Ebbie Goodfellow.

"Now we come back to centre ice and face off again. This time, Bodnar sends the puck over to our left winger, George Gee, and he raced up with it. He threw it over to me — a perfect pass — and I sailed around Buller, the same defenceman I'd just beaten twice, and I cut in on goal for a third time. But this time I'm thinking, 'This Anderson kid is no dummy; he's going to figure me for the same shot.' Only this time, I pulled him out and threw it high into the corner of the net. I'd scored three times, just like that.

"That's when Jimmy Peters, my teammate, yelled at me from the bench, 'Mosie! Mosie! Grab that puck. It's a record!'

"Heck, I didn't know anything about a record. But I grabbed the puck and took it to Ebbie. I said, 'Ebbie, hold on to this for me.' That's how Ebbie managed to collect all three pucks, and they took a photo of me holding them up after the game."

Recollections differ as to what happened next. Gus Bodnar says that Goodfellow changed lines at that point, to the chagrin of the players on the ice.

"He yanked us off," Bodnar recalls. "Said we were tired. Hell, we hadn't done anything but help Mosie celebrate his goals. Mosie might have had a couple more goals in his stick if he'd left us out there."

Mosienko doesn't recall a line change. He remembers staying out and almost adding to his goal total.

"What is seldom mentioned, is that I almost scored a fourth goal on the same shift. We faced off and I'd say within 45 seconds

I had the goalie at my mercy. I pulled him out and fired the puck along the ice behind him. It went right across the crease and missed the far goal post by a couple of inches. That's when I went to the bench for a change and Goodfellow yelled at me, 'What's the matter, Mosie? You slowing down?'

"When I think back to those days, and how I wanted to leave some sort of a mark in hockey, I never dreamed it would be by scoring the three fastest goals. It seems everybody remembers me for that. Hardly a day goes by without somebody wanting me to talk about it. And I'm sorry I helped end the career of the kid goalie, Anderson. He never played another game."

Mosienko was the right winger on Chicago's famed Pony Line with brothers Max and Doug Bentley. On July 8, 1994, he died in Winnipeg of cancer.

Jack Fitzsimmons, the secretary of the Blackhawks' alumni association, once paid a glowing tribute to Mosienko: "Mosie always displayed class and dignity on and off the ice. I dare anyone to find one disparaging word ever written or said about him during his career."

Rollins Was the Best, but Not an All Star

Goalie Al Rollins had a terrific season for the Chicago Blackhawks in 1953–54. Even though he won only 12 games (Terry Sawchuk of Detroit racked up 35 victories) and his team finished dead last in the standings, at season's end Rollins was a surprise winner of the Hart Trophy as the NHL's most valuable player.

Amazingly, the All-Star voters overlooked Rollins that season. They placed Toronto's Harry Lumley on the First Team and Terry Sawchuk on the Second. Which raises the question: How can a player be the best in the entire league and not be an All-Star at his position? But Rollins was accustomed to being snubbed by hockey's awards voters. In 1951, he captured the Vezina Trophy as top NHL goaltender. He was passed over in the All-Star balloting that season, too. Detroit's Sawchuk was voted number one, while Chuck Rayner of New York was the Second Team choice.

A Habs Fan Steals the Cup

On the night of April 1, 1962, Ken Kilander, a 25-year-old Montrealer, carved out a few moments of hockey notoriety for himself with a brazen act of theft, one that saw his name and photograph splashed across the sports pages everywhere.

It happened at the Chicago Stadium, late in a playoff game between the Canadiens and the Blackhawks. But wait; let's hear how Kilander described what happened.

"In the '60s I used to follow the Habs around all the time. I'd finance my trips on the road by playing piano in bars in most of the [Original Six] cities. I'd wear my Canadiens jacket and lots of times I'd travel on the same train as the players. Everybody knew me 'cause I'd been following the Canadiens for years, at home and on the road.

"I was in the cocktail lounge of the LaSalle Hotel in Chicago that day and I was talking to some reporters who were covering the series. They were talking about the Stanley Cup, and one of them said that Chicago was likely to knock Montreal out of the playoffs. Naturally, I got upset and told them that the Cup belongs in Montreal, nowhere else.

"At that moment I knew where the Cup was — locked up in a showcase in the lobby of the Chicago Stadium. So I said to these guys, just kidding, of course, 'What would you fellows do if I went and got the Cup and brought it here to give to the Canadiens?'

"They all laughed, and one of them said, 'Well, it is April Fools' Day. If you go and steal the Cup I guarantee I'll take your picture and put your name in the paper.' Another said, 'What a story that would be. And what an uproar that would cause here in Chicago.'

"Nothing much more was said, but when I went to the game that night I walked by the Cup on display in the Chicago Stadium. I could tell right away that the lock on the glass case was a flimsy thing and easily broken.

"I took my seat in the stands and watched the first two periods of play. My Habs were getting clobbered, and halfway through the third period the Hawks led 4–1. I couldn't take any more of that.

"I jumped out of my seat and ran down into the lobby to take another look at the Stanley Cup. There was nobody around, so I pushed in on the glass and the lock gave way. I couldn't resist reaching in and taking the Cup in my arms. The Hawks were about to win [the semifinals] and who knew when I'd ever see it again. The Cup meant everything to me.

"I started carrying it across the lobby when an usher spotted me. He asked me what the hell I was doing and I said, 'I'm taking the Cup back to Montreal where it belongs.'

"He did a fancy double take and then started yelling at the top of his lungs. 'Stop him! Help! Some guy's stealing the Cup!' If he hadn't spotted me I might have got away with it. But his screams brought some policemen running and they grabbed me and arrested me before I could get very far. It's hard to run very fast when you're lugging the Stanley Cup.

"The next morning, I had to appear before a judge who looked very stern. He said to me, 'You can go back to the Stadium tomorrow night and cheer all you want for your Canadiens. But the Cup stays here unless the Blackhawks lose, which I doubt very much they will.' Then he smiled at me and let me go."

Fleming Comes Through

A huge Stanley Cup goal scored by Reggie Fleming? You've got to be kidding.

No, sir, we're not. And the Hawks haven't won a Stanley Cup since that long-ago evening.

It happened on the night of April 16, 1961, at the Olympia in Detroit.

Muscular Reggie Fleming, a part-time player often ridiculed for his lack of skill, sent the Stanley Cup to Chicago for the first time in 23 years with a goal that lit a fire under the Hawks and turned the tide in the sixth game of the Stanley Cup finals.

"A lot of people laughed when we picked up Fleming from the Habs," said Chicago manager Tommy Ivan. "I wonder how many of them are laughing now."

In game five of the series, Hawks right winger Murray Balfour shattered his forearm. In the next game, Fleming was moved up to the top line, where he shared the ice with Bobby Hull and Bill Hay.

The Hawks were trailing the Red Wings 1–0 in the second period when Chicago's Wayne Hicks was whistled off for hooking. Moments later, Len Lunde lost the puck to penalty killer Fleming, who barrelled down the ice seeking a shorthanded goal. Vic Stasiuk knocked him off the puck, but he regained it when Stasiuk made a sloppy pass.

"I saw my chance and threw it in the short side," Fleming explained. "Hank Bassen, the Detroit goalie, just stood there and watched it go in."

Fleming's goal brought the Hawks to life, and they scored four more times to win in a 5–1 romp.

After the game, Fleming spotted Frank Selke Jr., the Canadiens' public relation director, in the crowd and shouted, "I told you guys I'd play for a winner when you let me go, and all of you just laughed."

Fleming would score only three playoff goals in his 12-year career, and his first was always his favourite.

Mahovlich for Sale — Or Is He?

In *The Globe and Mail*, the respected Canadian columnist Scott Young called it H-O-K-U-M. He also called it bunkum, nonsense, guile, delusion, gullery, bluff, hanky panky, sham, make-believe, spoof, hoax, bamboozle, gerrymandering and humbug.

What was he talking about? If you guessed the great million-dollar non-deal involving Frank Mahovlich, you can go straight to the head of the hockey class.

Friday, October 5, 1962, was the eve of the annual All-Star Game that kicked off each new season. Harold Ballard, Stafford Smythe and John Bassett had just taken over the Toronto Maple Leafs, and Ballard was downing drinks with the owner of the Blackhawks, Big Jim Norris, in a Toronto hotel room. When midnight rolled around, Norris made Ballard an offer.

"I hear you fellows are having trouble signing the big kid Mahovlich," he began. "I'd pay a lot of money to have that kind of a problem."

"How much money?" Ballard asked.

"I'd give you a million dollars for him," Norris countered.

Ballard almost dropped his drink. "A million? For a hockey player? Jim, for a million, you've got him. He's yours."

The two men shook hands on a deal that took them mere seconds to consummate. Norris stood up and peeled ten $100 bills from a roll in his pocket and handed them to Ballard.

"A down payment," he said. "I'll get the rest of the money to you tomorrow morning."

Ballard wrote out a note: "We except [sic] on behalf of the Toronto Maple Leafs." He signed the scrap of paper and handed it to Jack Amell, a Maple Leaf Gardens executive, who also signed the paper. Norris then told Tommy Ivan, his general manager, to get on the phone to Chicago and tell the team's publicity director to release the news to the media immediately. Bulletins were flashed by the major news agencies into newsrooms and radio stations from coast to coast. The sale of Mahovlich for $1 million was electrifying news.

Meanwhile, back in Room 11-268 of the Royal York Hotel, Stafford Smythe had made an appearance. "This will put the World Series off the sports pages tomorrow," he crowed, treating the matter as a joke. Not once did he say, "Guys, we're all just kidding, right?"

Toronto coach and GM Punch Imlach didn't think there was anything funny about it. He refused to shake hands with Norris to help cement the deal, choosing instead to go home, disturbed and disgusted with what he had seen and heard.

The next morning, Tommy Ivan appeared at the Gardens with a big grin on his face and a cheque for a million dollars in his pocket. He was wondering how he was going to fit both Mahovlich and Bobby Hull, the game's top two left wingers, into his lineup. "I might have to bench Hull once in a while," he kidded a friend.

Ushered into a meeting room, Ivan tried to hand the cheque, signed by Norris, to the Leafs' triumvirate of Ballard, Smythe and Bassett. None of them would take it. By this time, former Leafs owner Conn Smythe had thrown his two cents' worth into the mix. He'd blistered his son and the others, saying that they were making fools of themselves if they agreed to sell Mahovlich.

The Leafs brass politely told Ivan to take his boss's money and leave. "We've decided that Mahovlich is not for sale," they said. "Not even for a million dollars."

Meanwhile, Frank Mahovlich was waiting in a nearby room to talk contract with Imlach. When asked about the deal, he said, "It sure sounds like a lot of guff to me."

But it was no guff to Jim Norris. "It was a straight deal and the Leafs welshed on it," he said. "Simple as that."

Scott Young's take on the shenanigans, in which he mocked the actions of the Leafs brain trust, cost him dearly. At the time, he held a second job on *Hockey Night in Canada*. Shortly after his column was published, he was told he was no longer welcome in that capacity. Seems the Leafs had the final say on who could work on the telecasts.

Young ended his column in a typically humourous vein. He wrote:

On the day that the Leafs sell Mahovlich (now 24), when he is worth a million dollars to any hockey man who has it to spare:
- the sun will rise in the west;
- Eddie Shack will be named Miss Body Beautiful of the half-century;
- Sonny Liston will read the lesson at Timothy Eaton Memorial Church;
- Punch Imlach [who was bald] will appear in a television commercial plugging that greasy kids' stuff.

Scorer's Mistake Cost Hull the Record

With 35 goals in the final 31 games of the 1961–62 season, Bobby Hull had accomplished what only two other men had done in the past: score 50 goals in an NHL season. Two Montreal Canadiens, Rocket Richard and Boom-Boom Geoffrion, were the only other two players to hit the mark. And all three had hit the target on the nose, with exactly 50.

The Golden Jet's second-half surge also vaulted him into a tie with the Rangers' Andy Bathgate for the individual scoring title and the Art Ross Trophy. Both men finished with 84 points, but Hull was awarded the Art Ross Trophy because he had scored more goals (50 to 28).

But did you know that Hull actually scored 51 times over that 70-game campaign? All but forgotten is a goal he scored early in the season, one that would have given him a new NHL record, as well as the undisputed scoring crown.

A few weeks into the season, in a game against Detroit, Hull ripped a slap shot at Red Wing goalie Terry Sawchuk. The puck clearly hit a stick in front of Sawchuk and deflected into the back of the net. The goal was awarded to Hull's linemate, Ab McDonald.

After the game, McDonald told the referee that the puck had never touched his stick on its way to the net. It had been deflected by a Red Wings defenceman and Hull should have received credit for the goal. The referee told McDonald that he had waited too long to point out the mistake. The official game report had been filed with the league office and nothing could be done.

Hull paid little mind to the scorer's error until he was reminded of it on the final day of the season. In typical Hull fashion, he shrugged and said, "That's hockey."

When Espo Met Mr. Hockey

Phil Esposito, who joined the Blackhawks in 1963, has a vivid memory of the first time he played against the great Gordie Howe.

"It was my first game in the NHL. Well, my second one, actually, because I sat on the bench throughout my first game, which was against Montreal at the Forum. I almost got to play in that game. With two minutes to play we were losing 7–2. Coach Billy Reay looked down the bench and yelled, 'Esposito, get out there!' Well, I was disappointed I hadn't taken a single shift, so I yelled back, 'Okay, coach, do you want me to win it or tie it?' He yelled back, 'You can sit back down, you smart-ass.'

"Two nights later, we were in Detroit, and who did I find myself standing next to when I got on the ice but Gordie Howe.

Geez, he was my boyhood hero. I'm lookin' at Gordie and I'm saying to myself, 'Damn, that's the great Gordie Howe. What am I doin' out here?'

"Bobby Hull cautioned me before the puck was dropped. He yelled at me, 'Watch that old son of a bitch!' nodding at Howe. With that, Gordie blinked once or twice and got a little grin on his face, and that's when the puck was dropped. I'm still lookin' at him, thinkin' this is unbelievable, when *bam!* — he gave me an elbow in the mouth. I staggered back and I said, 'Why, you old fart, you!' and I speared him a good one and we both got penalties.

"In those days, in the penalty box, the players sat close together with a cop or an usher or somebody in between them. So I'm sittin' there holdin' a towel to my split lip and I'm real upset with big Howe. So I leaned across the guy between us and I said to him, 'To think you *used* to be my bleepin' idol.'

"He snarled back, 'What did you say, rookie?'

"I'll never forget that look. I said, 'Nothing, Mr. Howe, not a word.' "

Who Bashed Balfour?

During the 1960s, a fierce physical rivalry developed between the Blackhawks and the Toronto Maple Leafs. Each season, the 14 meetings between these two teams could be counted on to deliver more than their share of bitter physical battles. And many of the games were back-to-back weekend encounters, so a grudge triggered on a Saturday night at Maple Leaf Gardens was often renewed 24 hours later at Chicago Stadium.

Two wild donnybrooks — both of them resulting in nasty bench-clearing brawls — stand out. The first was in March 1961 and the second in December 1963.

The earlier episode broke out in the third period of a game at the Gardens. Defenceman Pierre Pilote, embarking on one of his patented end-to-end rushes, was speared by the Leafs' hard-checking winger, Eddie "The Entertainer" Shack. Pilote responded by swinging his stick in the direction of Shack's bulbous nose, a rather inviting target. Shack's linemate Bert Olmstead immediately challenged Pilote and the battle was on.

While Pilote and Olmstead squared off, the Hawks' skating fire hydrant, Reggie Fleming, grappled with Leafs defenceman Larry Hillman. Shack, after satisfying himself that any wounds he had suffered were not life-threatening, began to pick on Hawks centreman Stan Mikita. The players on the Chicago bench, seeing this mismatch, threw their sticks at the flailing Shack. Then, led by Bill Hay, they leaped onto the ice, followed immediately by the Leafs' reserves.

Fans at the arena, as well as those watching on national TV, chuckled as several of Toronto's finest slipped and slid around the ice in an effort to bring an end to the bitter brawl. It was a rare sight to see police intervene in an on-ice dispute. Later, the NHL fined the combatants for their indiscretions.

In December 1963, the Hawks again paid a visit to Maple Leaf Gardens, bringing more than Christmas greetings. By this time, Fleming and Shack were involved in a long-running personal feud, and they were bent on inflicting as much pain on each other as possible.

In a radio interview before the game, Shack said, "Fleming is only dangerous when he's in behind a player — face to face, he's a little cat who will run away." That set the stage for the evening's program.

The Leafs were leading 3–0 in the third period when Shack caught up to Fleming, planted his stick around the Hawks enforcer's thick neck and quite rudely hauled him down. Fleming waited until his next shift to get even, using his stick to impale Shack, leaving the Entertainer in pain and gasping for air.

"Gotcha!" laughed Fleming as he skated directly to the penalty box to serve a five-minute sentence. That's when Bobby Baun, the Leafs' rugged defenceman, after seeing his fallen teammate in distress, tried to slug Fleming in the penalty box. Referee Frank Udvari ordered Fleming to the Chicago dressing room for his own safety.

Not a good idea, Frank.

To get there, Fleming had to cross the ice and skate past the Leafs' bench. Udvari might as well have asked him to skate through a swamp full of alligators. Leafs leaped at him from all directions. He was challenged by Baun, by Larry Hillman and by Dick Duff. The benches cleared. Even Eddie Shack, who had seemed near death moments earlier, made a miraculous recovery and dashed around, hoping to deliver a knuckle sandwich to some unsuspecting Hawk. He caught up to Stan Mikita and hammered him. "Eddie popped me once and that's all it took. I was out like a light," Mikita recalls. Thirty minutes and 16 penalties later, rugged Reggie Fleming finally staggered through the Hawks' dressing-room door.

During the melee, Carl Brewer of the Leafs and Chicago's Murray Balfour found themselves battling in open ice. As they punched and clawed at each other, they moved toward the boards. Suddenly the gate at the Leafs bench flew open and they tumbled through it with Balfour on top. Moments later, Balfour suffered a nasty gash to his forehead, inflicted by a mysterious blow.

Hawks coach Billy Reay was livid; he accused Leafs trainer Bob Haggert of hitting Balfour. Haggert pleaded innocence. He said there were others close by, any one of whom might have clobbered Balfour.

Balfour himself said, "It wasn't Brewer that hit me. It was either Haggert or Imlach."

"I didn't hit the so-and-so," protested Leafs coach Punch Imlach.

No one ever confessed to throwing the punch that cut Murray Balfour. Haggert maintained that a spectator had caused the damage, and although he recognized the individual, he had no intention of naming him.

Years later, over lunch with the late Carl Brewer, the subject was discussed. He chuckled and said, "It wasn't me. I had my head under the bench and couldn't get at him. Besides, I was recovering from a broken arm and was worried about throwing punches with it. It was Dick Shatto, the Toronto Argonauts football star, who jumped in and punched him."

Why would he do that?

"Why? Because I was his son's favourite hockey player and he thought I was getting the worst of it."

Hall's Incredible Streak

In modern-day hockey it is customary for a team to employ two, three and sometimes as many as half a dozen goaltenders over the course of a gruelling NHL season. But as recently as 40 years ago, teams relied solely on one man to play between the pipes. And no team relied more heavily on its goaltender than the Chicago Blackhawks of the late 1950s and early '60s. During those years, Glenn Hall was a durable superstar for the Hawks who was always ready and willing to play.

Hall strapped on the pads game after game despite numerous aches and pains. Back in 1955, the Detroit Red Wings had tapped Hall as an eventual replacement for Terry Sawchuk. Hall played every game in 1955–56, and had not yet sought a day of rest when he was traded to the Hawks in 1957. The games piled up and the records began to fall: 300 consecutive games, then 400 and even 500. Hall couldn't be stopped. What's more, he played without a mask, risking cuts and concussions with every start.

On the night of November 7, 1962, Chicago played host to the Boston Bruins. On this night, Hall scrapped his customary routine, an energetic wrestling match with the team trainer to settle pregame jitters. He was suffering from excruciating back pain and could barely bend over. A lesser athlete would have begged for relief, but when the Hawks took the ice that night, Hall was standing calmly in his crease.

In the opening minutes of play, Boston's Murray Oliver shot the puck at Hall and it flew right between his legs. It was obvious that his back was in such poor shape that he simply could not move to stop the shot. He skated slowly to the Chicago bench, whispered a few words to coach Rudy Pilous, and headed for the dressing room. His departure, in his 503rd consecutive game, brought to an end a string of more than 33,000 uninterrupted minutes of goaltending. Hall's incredible iron man streak was over.

Today's most reliable workhorse, Martin Brodeur of New Jersey, appeared in at least 70 games each season between 1997–98 and 2003–04, but even he took a brief rest now and then. Hall's is one hockey record that will likely never be broken.

Creating Curved Blades

Bobby Hull's slap shot was devastating. And it became even more deadly in the 1960s, when he began using a stick with a curved blade. Sometimes the shot would dip in mid-flight, causing the goalie facing the missile to panic and fan on the shot.

Historians say that others before Hull — Andy Bathgate, for one — used a gently curved blade. And they may be right. But Hull credits his teammate Stan Mikita with the invention.

"Like many great discoveries, it happened by accident," Mikita says. "We were at the end of a practice one day at the Chicago Stadium and my stick cracked in the blade. I noticed it now had a little curve in the blade where it had cracked. I hadn't brought a spare stick from the dressing room, which was downstairs at the Stadium. I was too tired to go fetch another stick so I used the broken one. I took a couple of shots at the boards and noticed that the puck made an unusual sound when it hit, not like the sound of a normal shot. That made me inquisitive. Why did the puck sound different? And why did the puck feel like it was moving a little faster off the blade?"

After practice, Mikita and Hull took some sticks from the team's stick rack, heated the blades and placed them under a radiator. They applied enough force to bend the blades into a banana shape and then experimented with them on the ice. They were amazed at the results. Not only did pucks fly with more velocity, but also passing the puck with the banana blade resulted in quicker, more accurate passes.

Some players of that era pooh-poohed the innovation. Dave Keon and others tried the curved blade and tossed it aside. But most others jumped on the bandwagon, from players in old-timers' leagues to small fry and even goaltenders. Within months, it was hard to find a straight-bladed stick in any sporting goods store.

Hawks Haunted by '67 Failure

Many of the Hawks' alumni, men like Hull, Mikita, Hall and Esposito, still shake their heads in disbelief when they are reminded of a fateful afternoon at the Chicago Stadium nearly 40 years ago.

It was the turning point in a semifinal series between the Hawks and the Maple Leafs, a moment when the hockey fates and the underdogs from Toronto combined to rob the Hawks and their fans of a Stanley Cup.

"There's no doubt that Toronto stole the Cup from us that year," declared club president Bill Wirtz. "We had the best team in hockey, but they got the Cup."

You can't argue with Wirtz. Chicago finished the regular season 17 points ahead of runner-up Montreal and 19 points ahead of Toronto, their opponents in the first playoff round. Stan Mikita and Bobby Hull were one-two in the individual scoring race, Ken Wharram was fourth, Phil Esposito seventh and Doug Mohns ninth. Dennis Hull, with 25 goals, outscored everyone on the Leafs — and he finished in 24th place.

Bob Pulford, now a Chicago front-office institution, was a member of the blue-and-white brigade that season. He remembers a performance by Leafs goalie Terry Sawchuk in game five at the Stadium as "the greatest display of goaltending I ever saw. No one could have been better than Sawchuk was in that game against the Hawks."

Toronto was completely outplayed — except in goal — and outshot 49–31. Sawchuk didn't even enter the game until the second period. By then, starter Johnny Bower confessed he was "a little shaky" and coach Punch Imlach took him out.

Sawchuk, a gaunt, emotionally troubled athlete, stood in goal and faced the hard-shooting Hawks. Bobby Hull knocked him flat with his first shot, a rising slapper that practically tore Sawchuk's shoulder from his body. From the broadcast booth, we waited and watched and talked, wondering if Imlach would be forced to send Bower back into the shooting gallery. Several more minutes passed before the veteran could stagger to his feet, gingerly flexing his arm and shoulder.

He told Imlach he wanted to carry on. Then he went back to work and challenged the Hawks to knock him down again. They couldn't.

When the Leafs skated off with a 4–2 victory that afternoon, it was apparent the series was all but over. A home-ice victory in game six sent Imlach and the Leafs to the finals, where they battled Montreal for the Cup.

In the finals, Bower and Sawchuk were fabulous in goal. Pulford played a major role, too, sending the Leafs in front two games to one by scoring a dramatic goal in the second overtime period of game three. The Leafs captured the Cup in six games — a Cup that, say many, rightfully belonged to the Blackhawks.

Any old-time Chicago fan will tell you that.

The Goalie Who Did Everything Wrong

"He looks like hell in goal. The guy does everything wrong. He gives us shooters all kinds of openings and he doesn't play the angles very well. Heck, he doesn't even keep his legs together, giving you big holes to shoot at. But when you shoot at them, they're gone. He closes them up. He's amazingly quick. And the thing is, he gets the job done."

That's Bobby Orr, talking about Chicago goaltender Tony Esposito.

Even though he led his Michigan Tech Spartans to the national collegiate championship in 1965, Esposito was considered a long shot to make a career for himself as a pro. Especially since, after earning his degree, the 24-year-old signed with the Montreal Canadiens, a team with an abundance of goalies in its organization. In 1967–68, Esposito played a season for the Vancouver Canucks of the Western Hockey League, after which he was transferred to Houston of the Central league. He was called up to the Canadiens for the second half of 1968–69 and played in 13 games (five wins, four losses and four ties), collecting a pair of shutouts. But the Habs' coaching staff gave no indication that they liked him or approved of his unorthodox style between the pipes.

"The coach, Claude Ruel, was always barking at me if I let in a bad goal. I didn't need that, I needed support and encouragement," Esposito recalls. "I was glad when Montreal let me go."

The Habs did not protect Espo in the 1969 intra-league draft, and the Blackhawks snapped him up. At the time, general manager Tommy Ivan and coach Billy Reay thought he would make an ideal backup to Denis DeJordy. But from the very beginning, Esposito played so well that they decided to trade DeJordy to Los Angeles and make the rookie their number one netminder.

"We thought Tony might be pretty good someday," Reay said. "But he fooled us all. It turned out he was already one of the best in the game."

Tony made a spectacular NHL debut, setting a modern-day record with 15 shutouts in 63 games. His goals-against average was 2.17 and he skated off with two major awards at season's end: the Vezina for best goaltender and the Calder for rookie of the year.

Esposito was a Chicago star until 1983–84, when he retired. His 423 career victories trailed only Terry Sawchuk's 447 and Jacques Plante's 434, and his 76 shutouts ranked seventh in NHL history.

Esposito was inducted into the Hockey Hall of Fame in 1988. The Hawks also honoured him by retiring his number, 35.

The Wildest Game in Chicago History

On the final day of the 1969–70 season, the Chicago Blackhawks faced the Montreal Canadiens at Chicago Stadium in a match that has often been called the wildest in NHL history.

Can you believe the Canadiens considered starting the game without a goaltender? It's true — but I'm getting ahead of the story.

Going into the final day's action, Chicago and Boston were tied for first place in the East Division with 97 points. The Hawks had 44 wins to the Bruins' 39, so if the teams finished the schedule tied in points, first place would go to Chicago. Detroit, with 95 points, could only finish third. The battle for fourth spot, and the division's final playoff berth, was also down to the wire; Montreal held a two-point advantage (92–90) over the New York Rangers.

The Hawks badly wanted to finish first, because they had finished in the East Division basement the year before. Not since 1936 had a team roared from last place one season to first place the next. During their game with the Habs, the Hawks would keep a watchful eye on the out-of-town scoreboard. Boston was playing Toronto, and a Bruins victory would put Chicago into a must-win situation.

As the game began, the Habs already knew they were in desperate straits. The Rangers had played that afternoon, walloping Detroit 9–5, and earning the two points they needed to tie them with Montreal. The clubs were also now tied in wins, with 38 apiece. The Habs needed a win or a tie to be sure of securing fourth place. But if they lost to Chicago, there was still a chance, albeit a slim one, of making the playoffs.

Under league rules, fourth place would go to the team that had scored the most goals. The Rangers' outburst against the Wings had given them an edge in that category, 246–242. So, if the Canadiens lost, they could still make the playoffs, as long as they scored five or more goals against Chicago. I know, I know — it's mind-boggling.

That's why Montreal coach Claude Ruel gave serious thought to starting the game at the Stadium with six skaters and no netminder. The way he saw it, the Hawks would open up a big lead shooting into the empty net, then their top players would be given a rest and Ruel's Habs might score the five goals they needed against rookie goalie Tony Esposito.

As game time neared, Ruel decided against the unorthodox move. He realized he would be handing first place to the Hawks, which would be most unfair to Boston.

For Ruel to ask his players to score five times against Tony Esposito was a tall order, but the margin might have been even greater. In the afternoon contest, the Rangers had pulled *their* goalie, Ed Giacomin, late in the game in an effort to pad their 9–3 lead. The Red Wings had then responded with a pair of empty-net goals.

As the Chicago-Montreal game got under way, it quickly became apparent that Boston would win its game against the Maple Leafs. The Hawks knew the onus was on them to win. They took a 3–2 lead into the third period on goals by Jim Pappin, Pit Martin and Bobby Hull. Suddenly, Martin scored two more goals, putting the game virtually out of Montreal's reach.

Behind the Habs bench, Ruel's priority became goals, not points. He needed three more, and in a hurry. With nine minutes left on the clock, Ruel stunned the Stadium crowd by yanking goalie Rogie Vachon and putting out an extra attacker. He was conceding first place to the Hawks, and he no longer cared how many goals the Hawks scored. He only knew that his players must score three.

Under extreme pressure to score, the Habs faltered badly, failing to get one decent shot on Esposito in almost half a period of hockey. The Hawks, meanwhile, calmly potted goal after goal into the gaping net. The fans whooped it up as Eric Nesterenko, Cliff Koroll, Bobby Hull, Dennis Hull and Gerry Pinder all found the inviting target. At the final buzzer, the score was 10–2. The Canadiens skated off in a daze, their playoff hopes dashed.

Such a strange ending to the season can never happen again. The rules were changed shortly thereafter to make goals scored a virtually irrelevant factor to the order of finish in the NHL standings.

The game was memorable for several reasons: the incredible Chicago spree of five empty-net goals in a nine-minute span; their amazing recovery from worst to first in the space of one season; and the fact that, for the first time ever, there was no Canadian team in the Stanley Cup playoffs.

You may wonder how the Blackhawks, with 99 points, fared in the 1970 playoffs. In the first round, they ousted Detroit in four straight games — and by the same 4–2 score in each game. But they ran into real grief against the Bruins, who swept them in the semifinals. The Bruins went on to meet St. Louis in the finals and eliminated the expansion challengers in four straight. The Bruins of Orr, Esposito and Cheevers had captured the Stanley Cup in a mere 14 playoff games.

One of the Greatest Games Ever Played

John Ferguson, Montreal's long-retired tough guy, calls his final game in the NHL "one of the greatest games ever played." He's talking about May 18, 1971, the seventh game of the Stanley Cup finals between the Canadiens and Blackhawks, played in a steamy Chicago Stadium.

That season, the Canadiens, who had missed the playoffs the year before, had a rookie coach (Al MacNeil), a rookie goalie (Ken Dryden) and a couple of players — Jean Beliveau and Frank Mahovlich — who were said to be over the hill. But Dryden's play — especially in the first round against the Boston Bruins — had been sensational. Then the Habs ousted the Minnesota North Stars in a surprisingly tough series, four games to two. The only roadblock left standing in their way to a 17th Stanley Cup was Billy Reay's Chicago Blackhawks.

The Hawks had steamrolled through their first season in the West Division, placing nine players on the West's All-Star team. They had finished 20 points ahead of runner-up St. Louis and they were the only team in the division to top 100 points, finishing with 107 — ten more than Montreal, who had placed third in the East.

Bobby Hull had finished fifth amongst the league's scorers, and best among those who didn't play for Boston, with 44 goals and 96 points. His brother Dennis had potted 40 goals while Stan Mikita, Pit Martin, Cliff Koroll and Jim Pappin had been major contributors to the team's devastating attack.

In the playoffs, Bobby Hull banged in six goals in the opening round, almost single-handedly tossing the Philadelphia Flyers aside in four games. Hull and the Hawks followed up with a seven-game elimination of the New York Rangers. A victory in the final series against the Canadiens would bring the Stanley Cup back to Chicago for the first time since 1961.

The Habs' John Ferguson, who played that spring despite broken ribs suffered in an early playoff game, recalls the unhappiness, the turmoil, and the dissension in the Montreal camp as his team prepared for the final series.

"Despite all the friction, and the fact I was hurting like a son of a bitch, I figured another classic was in the works," he said.

Al MacNeil's coaching style had been severely criticized in the media, by the players (Ferguson included) and by the fans. In one game during the season, MacNeil had thrown out 23 different line combinations, causing uncertainty and anger among his troops. The French media lashed out at MacNeil for another reason — he had never learned the French language.

Despite Ferguson's prediction, the series didn't start out like a classic. Jim Pappin's goal gave the Hawks a 2–1 opening game victory at the Stadium, and they came right back with a 5–3 victory in game two. In game three at the Montreal Forum, the Hawks jumped into a 2–0 lead, but Tony Esposito gave up goals to Peter and Frank Mahovlich and the score was tied. Yvan Cournoyer snapped a shot past Esposito early in the third and Frank Mahovlich scored his second of the game to give Montreal a 4–2 win.

John Ferguson set the tone with some big hits in game four, despite playing with a torn hip muscle that required freezing three times during the game. The Habs tied the series with a 5–2 triumph.

On home ice, the Hawks closed ranks and shut down the Habs 2–0 in game five. Henri Richard was in the penalty box when Dennis Hull slipped away for what proved to be the winning goal. Richard was used sparingly after that. He and the other veterans on the team fumed over MacNeil's dizzying array of line combinations, and Richard blistered his coach after the match, telling newsmen, "I've never played for a worse coach." He would later mumble an apology.

If the Hawks thought the name-calling in the Montreal dressing room would be to their advantage in game six, they were wrong. They were leading 3–2 on Jim Pappin's go-ahead goal when the Big M struck early in the third, raising the Forum roof with the tying score. Minutes later, his brother Pete beat Esposito, and the Habs nursed their 4–3 lead to the finish. Series tied at three games apiece.

CBS Television was at Chicago Stadium to bring the deciding game into millions of American homes. The ice was slow and slushy. The Hawks started fast, with Mikita, Nesterenko and Keith Magnusson throwing hot shots at Ken Dryden, who stopped them all. Late in the period, with Rejean Houle in the penalty box, Pappin was stopped close in. So was Bobby Hull. Finally, at 19:12, Dennis Hull blasted the puck in off Dryden's shoulder to give Chicago a 1–0 lead.

The Hawks went up 2–0 at 7:33 of the second period when Danny O'Shea fired a 25-footer past Dryden. Then Montreal got a break. Jacques Lemaire fired a long shot from outside the Chicago blue line — and Esposito missed it. Fans howled in disbelief when the red light flashed. Late in the period, Lemaire centred it to Henri Richard and the 35-year-old pivot whipped the puck past Esposito. Game tied, 2–2.

Richard dashed around Magnuson inside the blue line, skated in on Esposito and faked him to the ice. Then he flipped the puck into the upper corner of the net to give Montreal a 3–2 lead.

Magnuson suffered from the humiliation of that moment for months. "I cried over it," he said. "I wanted to quit hockey, to quit everything. I wanted to move far away from Chicago, all because of Richard beating me. At least I should have tripped the guy as he went by."

The Hawks almost tied the score. With half a period to play, Jim Pappin got the puck on the lip of the crease with a gaping net in front of him. He shot and raised his arms to celebrate the goal. But Dryden's right leg shot out and deflected the puck. Nobody in the building that night, or watching on TV, could believe he made that save.

It was the Hawks' last chance. Montreal won 3–2 and left town that night with the Cup on the plane with them. And John Ferguson, who'd been on five Cup winners in eight years, was telling his mates, "That's it for me, boys. I'm through with hockey. But of all my Cups, this one over Chicago was the most satisfying."

Hull Joins the WHA

On June 27, 1972, Bobby Hull found himself riding in a Roll Royce through the streets of St. Paul, Minnesota. He was there to sign a much-publicized contract with the fledgling World Hockey Association and accept a cheque for $1 million for his signature.

For tax purposes, St. Paul was selected as the site where the Golden Jet would sign for his million-dollar bonus. After that, the Rolls sped to the airport, where a chartered plane whisked Hull, his family and a number of WHA owners and officials across the Canadian border into Manitoba. A second signing, one that bound Hull to the Winnipeg Jets for the next five years, took place at the corner of Portage and Main, Winnipeg's busiest intersection.

Hull signed with a flourish as thousands of fans cheered, and then he flashed his famous grin. Afterward, he spoke into a hundred microphones and tape recorders and honoured a thousand requests for his autograph.

"Our league gained instant respect that day," said one of the WHA owners. "If the Blackhawks and the NHL had enticed Hull back into the fold, as a league we were doomed. We might as well have cut our throats. Hull gave us the credibility we needed desperately to be successful."

The new league's seduction of Hull had begun months earlier, in Vancouver. Learning that Hull's contract with the NHL Blackhawks was up for renewal, the WHA owners threw his name into a hat. The lucky owner who drew it from the chapeau was Ben Hatskin of the Winnipeg Jets. Hatskin met with Hull in Vancouver and offered him a million dollars for five years to switch leagues.

Hull's agent, Harvey Wineberg, said, "Not enough, Ben. Come back with your very best offer." By February, 1972, after his fellow owners had pledged to chip in a hundred grand each to sweeten the pot, Hatskin had raised the offer to $2.75 million spread over ten years.

"Now you're talking, Ben," said Wineberg. "And Bobby's listening."

Arthur and Bill Wirtz, the Blackhawks bosses, watched from the sidelines. They did little to disrupt the pending nuptials between the Golden Jet and the upstart league. Like NHL President Clarence Campbell, they foresaw an early demise for the WHA. And the Wirtzes claimed they had made a generous offer to Hull — early in the 1971–72 season. Hadn't they made reference to a million-dollar pact for their star player, over five years? So what if they hadn't shown him the money — what's the hurry?

When the 1971–72 season ended, the Hawks front office remained strangely silent. Finally, the Hawks unveiled their aforementioned proposal. "But we can't match the Winnipeg offer," Bill Wirtz cautioned. By then, Hull was enamored of the WHA and the Jets' pitch. In Winnipeg, he could just play, or he could add coaching duties to his portfolio if he wished, and at the end of five years he had the option to stay on as a team executive at $100,000 per annum. In effect, the Chicago bid came far too late and was for much too little. What's more, Hull was stung by the Blackhawks' attitude toward him. They didn't seem to care!

"Chicago must have thought I was bluffing about leaving," Hull said on that June day in Winnipeg. "I probably would have stayed in Chicago if the Wirtz family had made me a decent offer. And come up with it earlier. I mean, I told them I didn't want to leave. Who in his right mind wants to pick up and move his family to a new city and a new league after 15 years in the NHL? But they didn't appear to even want to sit down and talk with me."

The Golden Jet shook his head and added, "You can say that I have no regrets about leaving Chicago. None at all."

Don Cherry didn't believe him. Cherry said, "I know Bobby and if you could crawl in his heart, I'm sure he'd say 'I should never have left Chicago.' He was the most popular guy in the entire city. If he'd stayed, he would have played a lot longer and he would have been a lot happier."

Dennis Hull says, "Bobby left, and that was devastating to the rest of the team. In fact, Jim Pappin talked to the players and convinced us we should offer to give up some of our salaries if it meant we could keep Bobby. We were naive to think the Hawks didn't have enough money to satisfy Bobby. So we agreed to Pappin's proposal. But it was too late."

Stapleton's Got the Puck

September 28, 1972, has been called the most memorable date in hockey history. That was the day that Team Canada conquered the Soviet squad in the now-famous eight-game Summit Series, with minister-to-be Paul Henderson slapping his own rebound past Vladislav Tretiak — who, years later, would accept a job tutoring the Blackhawks' young netminders.

Many assume that Henderson is the one who scooped up the precious memento of his game-winning goal, scored with 34 seconds to play in the final game.

"I wish I had," he says. "But it never occurred to me to pick it up. I was so ecstatic about scoring that goal and helping my team take the series that the puck seemed unimportant."

When the red light flashed behind Tretiak, the Canadian player closest to Henderson was Yvan Cournoyer. Perhaps he snared the puck? "No, no, I didn't get it," the Roadrunner says. "I didn't have a chance because Paul jumped into my arms."

Nobody is absolutely certain who collared one of the game's most priceless artifacts. But a former Chicago Blackhawk, Pat Stapleton, claims with a sly grin that he owns the game-winning puck and has it "tucked away somewhere" in his farmhouse. Stapleton says that while all of the Team Canada players were deliriously celebrating the victory, he calmly skated over and picked up the puck. And he has no plans to sell it, trade it or let the kids in the neighbourhood play a game of hockey with it.

Anyone doubting the veracity of Stapleton's claim might speak with Bill White. "I was there. I saw him pick it up," White says. "There's no doubt he has it. Collecting memorabilia runs in his family. His father collected a lot of baseball stuff over the years. It must be in Patty's genes."

Despite White's testimony, Stapleton's story must be taken with a grain of salt, since he was one of hockey's greatest pranksters and practical jokers. And White was often a willing accomplice.

During at least one Team Canada practice session in Moscow, Stapleton recruited White to help him dazzle Soviet observers with a number of bizarre gyrations they called the "I Formation." The two Hawks would line up one behind the other on face-offs, and when the puck was dropped they would twist, turn and dart in different directions. None of it made any sense, but Stapleton, with a perfectly straight face, called it the I Formation, or sometimes the Mohawk Formation, while the Russian observers scribbled notes furiously.

He also conned some of his teammates into getting on the tour bus for a special outing. "I've made arrangements for you guys to have golf privileges at the Moscow Golf and Country Club," he announced. "There'll be golf clubs for everybody and we'll start at the four-tiered driving range overlooking Gorky Boulevard." Two nights later, he conned them again, convincing them he had reservations for his mates and their wives at Moscow's best Chinese restaurant. In 1972, how many foreigners could have known that golf and Chinese food were nonexistent in the Soviet Union?

While Team Canada's players may remember Stapleton as the best practical joker they had ever met, Chicago fans knew him for his solid defensive work on the Chicago blue line during the 1960s and '70s. Although small in stature, he, like fellow Hawk Pierre Pilote, was one of the best.

Fans may not recall that Stapleton was once team president, part owner, coach and player in Chicago. But not with the Hawks: "Whitey" held the various positions with the Chicago Cougars of the World Hockey Association.

"I loved playing for the Blackhawks and I loved the city of Chicago. But money talks, and the WHA was offering more of it. Then there was the challenge of trying to make the new league a success. And frankly, I was concerned the Hawks were thinking of trading me. So I signed with the Cougars; I figured it would give me and my family a few more seasons in Chicago.

"Then, in my second season as a Cougar, the guys who owned the team simply walked away from hockey. So three of us — Ralph Backstrom, Dave Dryden and I — decided to buy the club. I wound up as part owner, club president, player and coach. That lasted less than one full season. After the team folded, I played a couple more years with Indianapolis and a final season with Cincinnati."

Any regrets about your career, Patty?

"No. I had a lot of thrills, even though I never played on a Stanley Cup team. There was the Team Canada series in '72, winning in Moscow. And I was there again in '74, when the WHA lost to the Soviets. With the Hawks, we came close to the Stanley Cup a couple of times. It just wasn't in the cards. But that's life, isn't it?"

The Atomic Redhead

At 32 years of age, his body bruised and battered, his right knee having been opened three times by a surgeon's scalpel, the Atomic Redhead was forced to retire. The player who went by that nickname, team captain Keith Magnuson, was one of the most popular of all the Blackhawks.

Chicago hockey writer Bob Verdi gave Magnuson his colourful sobriquet and wrote fondly of him in *The Hockey News* when Maggie quit the game in November 1979.

Verdi wrote:

From the first time he came bursting through the chute in 1969, one of several rookies who would lead the Blackhawks from last place to first, the Atomic Redhead never stopped trying.

"I wasn't helping anymore," Maggie said. "I knew I couldn't play every game because the knee wasn't getting any better.

"I didn't have much ability to begin with. I couldn't skate that well, or shoot that well or pass the puck that well. I always had to labour, even when everything was going all right. So when it wasn't going all right..."

Someone once said that if Magnuson's body were a bank account, it long ago would have been overdrawn. He broke so many bones for the Blackhawks, and sipped so many portions of liquid slop through fractured jaws, and tiptoed through so many summers with casts and canes and assorted pains. He said he would break his neck for his team, and a couple of times he even came close to doing that.

Numbers will not send him to the Hall of Fame. He collected 17 goals in 657 regular season and playoff games. He was quite capable defensively, and quite beatable in pugilistic encounters. For every Earl Heiskala or Gene Carr who was his victim, Magnuson was on the canvas tenfold. But he just kept on truckin' because it only hurt for a little while.

"His value never showed up in the stats," said Eddie Johnston, the Blackhawks' vibrant new coach whom Magnuson will now assist. "He had heart. When he played, when he practiced, he always had spirit. I wish I could spread it around to some of these other guys."

Magnuson amassed a remarkable number of penalty minutes — 1,606 — but he always dropped his stick and hit you from up front.

Magnuson's fatal flaw was that he tried to shovel 25 hours of doing things into a 24-hour day. Some of the things he did, he didn't have to do. A guy who plays hockey all winter is entitled to play golf in the summer. He hit the little white ball, but he also visited a lot of youngsters in hospitals while other athletes were hiding behind the veranda when charitable causes came knocking.

His charisma and personality and care for fellow man will take him far. If Magnuson were a baseball or football player he might have been on more magazine covers and reaped more endorsements. But because hockey in general, and the Blackhawks in particular, are either unwilling or unable to portray their athletes — the best, as a group, in professional sports — as people, Magnuson and his ilk exist in relative obscurity.

But that doesn't bother him. What bothers him is that he didn't trip Henri Richard before the Pocket Rocket scored the winning goal in game seven of a palpitating Stanley Cup 1971 final. What Magnuson should realize is that when Richard started his engines, there was no stopping him.

However, Magnuson need not apologize for ever going to the pay window. He didn't have much talent, true. Then again, maybe the greatest talent of all is the talent to work.

Author's note: The Atomic Redhead's life ended on December 15, 2003. The former Chicago captain and coach was killed instantly in a car crash in Toronto while travelling back from the funeral of former NHL player Keith McCreary, who had succumbed to cancer a few days earlier. Rob Ramage, another former NHL star, was driving the vehicle in which Magnuson was a passenger. Magnuson was 56.